STRATEGIC BALANCE AND CONFIDENCE BUILDING MEASURES IN THE AMERICAS

STRATEGIC BALANCE AND CONFIDENCE BUILDING MEASURES IN THE AMERICAS

EDITED BY

JOSEPH S. TULCHIN

AND

FRANCISCO ROJAS ARAVENA

WITH RALPH H. ESPACH

THE WOODROW WILSON CENTER PRESS
WASHINGTON, D.C.

STANFORD UNIVERSITY PRESS
STANFORD, CALIFORNIA

EDITORIAL OFFICES:

The Woodrow Wilson Center Press
One Woodrow Wilson Plaza
1300 Pennsylvania Avenue, N.W.
Washington, D.C. 20523
Telephone 202-691-4029
wwics.si.edu

ORDER FROM:

Stanford University Press
CUP Distribution Center
110 Midland Avenue
Port Chester, N.Y. 10573-4930
Telephone 1-800-872-7423

2 4 6 8 9 7 5 3 1

Library of Congress Cataloging-in-Publication Data

Strategic balance and confidence building measures in the Americas / edited by Joseph S. Tulchin
and Francisco Rojas Aravena.
    p.   cm.
    Includes bibliographical references and index.
    ISBN 0-8047-3607-3 (cloth : alk. paper)
    ISBN 0-8047-3608-1 (pbk. : alk. paper)
    1. National security—Latin America.   2. Latin America—Defenses.   3. Confidence and secu-
rity building measures (International relations)—Latin America.   4. Latin America—Strategic
aspects. 5. World politics—1989–   I. Tulchin, Joseph S., 1939–   II. Rojas Aravena, Francisco.
    UA602.3 .S77   1998
    355'.03308—ddc21

                            98-37286
                               CIP

TABLE OF CONTENTS

PREFACE

This book presents the principal theoretical concepts and practical applications regarding confidence building measures in the Americas. The preliminary versions of the papers collected in this book were presented at an international seminar held in Mexico City in the fall of 1995. The seminar was organized by Peace and Security in the Americas, a project jointly coordinated by the Latin American Program of the Woodrow Wilson International Center for Scholars and the Facultad Latinoaméricana de Ciencias Sociales (FLACSO) in Santiago, Chile. Support for the seminar also came from the Matías Romero Institute of the Mexican Foreign Ministry, the United States Arms Control and Disarmament Agency (ACDA), and the Canadian Foundation for the Americas. A Spanish version of the volume was published by FLACSO in 1996.

The book is arranged in ten chapters. To introduce the background of confidence building in the hemisphere and the purpose of the volume, the first part of the volume provides the opening presentations from the seminar by distinguished practitioners and policymakers. The second part introduces regional perspectives on the issues and applications of confidence building measures, and lessons from the historical application of strategic balance principles. As well as learning about specific challenges and arrangements in each subregion or country, the reader gains an understanding of the range of strategic issues and challenges to stability across Latin America. The appendixes examine these issues at a hemispheric level, and from the perspectives of multinational institutions involved with military balance and security. As a whole, the volume provides a comprehensive examination of strategic balance and confidence building measures, both conceptually and empirically and at the hemispheric and subregional levels.

The editors would like to thank all of those who participated in the preparation of the volume. Ralph Espach, program associate of the Latin American Program of the Woodrow Wilson Center, spearheaded these efforts with the valuable assistance of interns Heather Quinter, Amelia Brown, and Jacquie Lynch. Leah Florence and Gary Bland performed inspired, even miraculous copyediting, and Patricia Scott worked as a sleuth and in some cases a mindreader to translate the papers originally written in Spanish.

Peace and Security in the Americas is made possible by the generous support of the John D. and Catherine T. MacArthur Foundation, as well as with the collaboration of various private and governmental institutions across the Americas.

INTRODUCTION

JOSEPH S. TULCHIN
AND FRANCISCO ROJAS ARAVENA

The end of the Cold War has dramatically changed the nature of international relations in Latin America. The political and security relationships that were imposed upon the region by East-West tensions have disappeared, presenting new challenges and opportunities. Authoritarian rule has given way to democratic governance, and warring parties influenced by Cold War ideological dichotomies, especially in Central America and the Caribbean region, have forgone the use of arms for voting booths and the formation of political parties. The overwhelming acceptance of democratic rule and neo-liberal economics has opened the doors for international cooperation in the areas of economics—demonstrated most dramatically by the formation of the Common Market of the South (MERCOSUR) and Mexico's membership in the North American Free Trade Agreement (NAFTA)—and, to a lesser extent, security.

Throughout the Americas, countries face security threats of a different order. The preoccupation of many military and security officials has shifted from the traditional threats of military invasion or border conflicts to that of more ambiguous and multinational dangers such as armed drug cartels, terrorism, environmental destruction, and political crises. This new security agenda often does not involve conflicts between countries as much as the vulnerability of certain countries to threats generated by transnational organizations, or the inability of a country to maintain sovereign control over its entire national territory and resources. These threats are expanded and made more insidious by increasing international factors such as rapid advances in communication technologies and the globalization of economic systems, both legal and illegal. Because these threats are nonstate in nature and usually involve and affect many countries at once, individual nations do not have the capacity or resources to address them effectively. The new regional security agenda, therefore, requires international cooperation.

The advancement of cooperative international security initiatives is widely supported, as demonstrated recently at the Defense Ministerial meeting in Williamsburg, Virginia, in March 1995; the Deputy-Ministerial meeting in Santiago, Chile, in November 1996; and in the resolutions of the Organization of American States (OAS) Commission on Hemispheric Security. In each instance the need for associative security strategies was stressed, and confidence building measures were highlighted as important steps toward that goal. Still, in the case of many countries, tension and distrust linger on from past border disputes and conflicts and threaten to undermine regional security, as demonstrated most recently by the flare-up between Peru and Ecuador at the Alto Cénepa. As the authors stress in this volume, these fears and nationalist frictions, often the legacies of colonial disputes hundreds of years old, must be respected and carefully handled in order to establish the framework of stability and mutual confidence necessary to address the new regional-security agenda.

A window of opportunity exists today for Latin American countries to define and develop their own security agendas with relatively little interference from extraregional influences. The United States' post–Cold War security agenda is still largely undefined and the attention of its current administration is focused elsewhere; consequently, this regional superpower is more receptive than ever to multinational initiatives emerging from Latin America. At present there is room for Latin American countries to influence the design and course of action of the emerging international security system. Security must be reconceptualized, both in Latin America and across the world, to include issues that were previously not considered items of security concern, such as economics, environmental protection, human rights, international crime, disaster relief, political instability, and other such threats. Linkages among these items must be acknowledged and addressed. Economic problems, for instance, are often connected to crime and drug trafficking, and misconceived development strategies can exacerbate poverty, invite political instability, and reduce national resources through environmental destruction.

This window of opportunity for Latin American countries to have greater influence over the emerging international security system will not exist indefinitely. Latin American countries must seize the moment to define a collective security agenda that addresses regionwide interests, to promote that agenda and those interests in Washington, and to act towards definitive resolutions of border demarcation disputes.

The Peace and Security in the Americas (P&SA) program is a hemisphere-wide collaborative project of academic research and public-policy initiatives coordinated jointly by the Latin American Social Science Faculty (Facultad Latinoaméricana de Ciencias Sociales, or FLACSO) in Santiago, Chile, and the Woodrow Wilson International Center for Scholars, in Washington, D.C., with the objective of understanding the proper framework for cooperative policies toward regional security and of facilitating their formulation. With generous support from the John D. and Catherine T. MacArthur Foundation, the program has organized a series of meetings that serve as forums for dialogue and the exchange of ideas among government and military officials, members of the academic community, and international experts from across the region, with the aim of identifying possible areas of cooperation and creating alternatives in order to prevent conflict. The immediate agenda of the program is the formulation of confidence building measures (CBM) on a subregional level—specific collaborative projects that could serve to build confidence among neighbors and lay the groundwork for a wider cooperative security system.

In order to increase our understanding and explore possibilities for CBMs in the region, Peace and Security in the Americas held the Regional Conference on Confidence and Security Building Measures in Santiago in November 1995. The ideas generated from this conference are collected in this volume. In 1996, the program focused on the identification and promotion of CBMs that address the specific issues of the different subregions of Latin America. The agenda and policy recommendations suggested by the P&SA program helped shape the discussions at the Defense Ministerial meetings in Williamsburg in 1995 and in Bariloche, Argentina, in 1996.

This volume presents a variety of perspectives and insights regarding the nature and importance of CBMs and strategic balance to the security of the Americas. It offers differing analyses of the nature and significance of strategic balance and confidence building measures within the context of a rapidly changing global environment. When the perspectives at a regional or subregional level are contrasted with those of hemispheric or global interests, which this volume allows us to do, the difficult task of implementing cooperative security measures—the challenge that faces us in the years ahead—immediately becomes clear.

Part I addresses the security perspectives of several major countries or groups of countries in the hemisphere. The Andean subregion; the countries of the Southern Cone (Argentina, Chile, Uruguay, Paraguay), Chile in particular; and the Caribbean basin are among the areas receiving close attention. The United States and Brazil receive specialized treatment, owing to the exceptional role each plays within the region's economic, political, and strategic affairs. The second part of the volume, which includes the final four chapters, examines the broader theoretical and policy issues involved in regional security. We conclude the second section with an attempt to sum up the main themes and arguments presented in the various papers, and to place the volume's message within the context of current hemispheric activities and developments. Finally, in three special appendixes we present the viewpoints of three key officials involved in hemispheric security negotiations, for whom dialogue and debate such as that presented in this volume are critical tools for success.

In the first chapter, Fernando Bustamante describes the differences between the European mutual security experience during the Cold War and the security issues faced by the countries of the Andean subregion. Those differences are substantial, Bustamante contends, and they carry important implications for the Andean nations in their efforts to generate confidence building measures today. Chile's historical role in the South American security system is the subject of chapter 2, in which Miguel Navarro Meza traces the strategy Chile followed throughout the development of South America's power structure, from the colonial era to the present day. The current prospects for a regional-security system are mixed, he concludes, as the system now combines a "robust process" of political and trade integration with elements, such as a lesser concern with global stability, that threaten the peace and stability.

In chapter 3, Thomaz Guedes da Costa provides his analysis of current security and defense policy in Brazil. He writes that Brazilian strategists do not welcome a new regional-security framework that emphasizes confidence building measures and sustaining strategic and military balances. Rather, during the current era of globalization and regional integration, they favor an "evolutionary process" that respects the "traditional values of classical realism." Guedes da Costa also provides the six features of the Brazilian government's emerging proposal for dealing with the security and defense needs created by globalization.

In chapter 4, Colonel John Cope provides a U.S. perspective of strategic balance in the Americas. In an era of ever-expanding global interests, Cope writes, the United States naturally tends to seek out like-minded regional partners who will institute policy reforms and assume an international role beyond international trade and investment. New opportunities for partnerships exist for the first time since the end of the Cold War, Cope adds, and, in many areas, Washington is beginning to accept that U.S. security for the foreseeable future will be more closely tied to that of its American neighbors than ever before. The new strategic environment of the Caribbean Basin is the subject of chapter 5, authored by Ivelaw L. Griffith. Griffith contends that while global "turbulence and transformation" of recent years gives cause for assessment of the new security environment, old issues remain salient or have developed new dynamics. Drug trafficking, the primary focus of the chapter, is an example of an old issue that has been transformed by the dramatic changes in the region.

Marcela Donadio and Luis Tibiletti conclude the first section with their analysis of regional security in the Southern Cone from an Argentinian perspective, including several proposals for the development of mutual confidence. They emphasize the importance of the Southern Cone countries' transition from traditional assumptions of supremacy to considerations of common interest and coordination of policy. Increased cooperation in matters of security, the authors argue, is an inevitable consequence of an ongoing process of economic integration.

Part II opens with chapter 7, by Francisco Rojas Aravena, who examines the nature and significance of confidence building measures in Latin America. In an in-depth analysis, he explains how the nations of the region must operate—how they must focus on achieving sincerity, competency, and trustworthiness—if they are going to build a hemisphere-wide regime of cooperative security. Rojas emphasizes that movement toward this objective must be measured by clearly definable degrees of progress.

In chapter 8, David Mares examines strategic balance in the Americas with a clear eye on the lessons of history. He provides a historical analysis that focuses on three of the key bilateral relationships in Latin America. Because so many issues of core interest to the states remain to be addressed, Mares argues, taking a blanket approach to building specific confidence measures is unlikely to be successful. The discussion of strategic balance, therefore, must be country-specific with regard to remedies as well as threats. Chapter 9, by Admiral Vicente Casales, provides a Latin American perspective on strategic balance in the post–Cold War era, emphasizing the new roles armed forces can play and the need to enhance military cooperation through the Inter-American Defense Board. Casales outlines three areas in which the board can act to achieve this objective: information, regional cooperation, and peacekeeping. The key to Latin America's future effectiveness in the new world order, he contends, will depend on the ability of neighboring countries to discard long-held differences among themselves, reduce internal conflict, develop democracy, and integrate broadly with the rest of the world.

Finally, in chapter 10, Joseph Tulchin and Ralph Espach offer reflections on the various perspectives presented in the volume, and conclude that the collective efforts of the authors call for a self-conscious, deliberate effort on the part of the governments and security institutions of the region to augment the rich economic and political relations in formation since the end of the Cold War with a renewed emphasis on building mutual confidence in security relations. CBMs, they stress, are a proven instrument for the enhancement of these relations, and their implementation at the sub-regional and operational levels serves as a concrete step toward greater stability and security for the hemisphere as a whole.

The volume concludes with three appendixes that present the remarks delivered by three key practicing officials at the Regional Conference on Confidence and Security Building Measures in Santiago. Together, these commentaries place the topics of confidence building measures and cooperative security in their current context and present a clear sense of the policy ramifications of the region's strategic concerns. In addition to the insights they present, these brief commentaries are significant for the support they indicate from the powerful regional institutions these officials represent. John Holum, the Director of the United States Arms Control and Disarmament Agency (ACDA), recounts the progress that has been made in recent years in building trust and confidence among the nations of Latin America. Anticipating ideas in some of the papers, he emphasizes that Europe's experience in building its security regime will prove of little value to those parts of the world where the historical and political realities are very different. Ambassador Pablo Cabrera Gaete, in his address as chair of the Regional Conference on Confidence and Security Building Measures in Santiago, provides a Latin American perspective on the intended objectives and recent progress toward peace and security in the region. Ambassador Ricardo Mario Rodríguez, president of the Commission on Hemispheric Security at the OAS, follows by highlighting the significance of recent events in the development of that system, particularly the role of the OAS in building mutual confidence and regional security.

PART ONE

REGIONAL PERSPECTIVES ON STRATEGIC BALANCE AND CONFIDENCE BUILDING MEASURES

CHAPTER ONE

The Question of Confidence Building Measures in the Andean Subregion

FERNANDO BUSTAMANTE

The concepts of "security" and "confidence" are closely linked; indeed, measures designed to raise the level of confidence among actors are viewed as mechanisms that tighten security. In the classical "realist" concept of deterrence, each country or state attempts to demonstrate its actual or potential military power to possible aggressors. The aim is to convince an aggressor that the risks and costs of military action outweigh any potential gain. In this sense, security is based on a fixed-sum calculation. Since effective deterrence includes the latent possibility of military escalation and increasing the damage that the aggressor eventually suffers, there is no advantage to being on the defensive. Following this "Clausewitzian" logic, which emphasizes the utility of overwhelming force, security is achieved via the accumulation of quantitative and qualitative destructive capacity, and the ultimate end is mutually assured destruction.

A "worst-case scenario" assumes that an adversary has the capacity to be infinitely malevolent and has long-term intentions that are unpredictable and unfathomable. The plausibility of this assumption was reinforced in this century by the experience of two world wars. Deterrence does not consider the intentions of the potential adversary as a variable. It is not considered feasible to obtain secure or lasting guarantees with respect to intentions or to modify them in a favorable and sustained way. Therefore, prudence consists of pursuing deterrent measures capable of confronting the worst possible threat that an extremely ill-disposed enemy might pose.

Unfortunately, history has not shown this form of "security," or its resulting "balances of terror," to be tenable. In reality, the wager becomes riskier each time. Although the deterrent of great destructive capacity is most likely to endure, it is rationally flawed, considering that even a small failure could result in mutually assured destruction. This was the irrational logic behind the situation in the 1980s at the end of the Cold War.

The assumptions underlying the concept of confidence building measures (CBMs) are different from the strategy of deterrence. First, CBMs consider security to be the result of a variable sum: increasing the security of the potential adversary is a form of improving one's own security.[1] Second, the relationship structure based on the principle of self-help is relaxed, and it is assumed that security can be maximized cooperationally. This implies that adversaries have a common higher-order or meta-interest— avoiding war.[2] That is, putting an end to conflict is valued more highly than are any gains by the eventual victor. Therefore, it is not necessary to invoke scenarios of "total war"—mutually assured destruction. Everything depends on how strategic losses are appraised, which also implies that there is a high value placed on the advantages of peace. For example, even a limited conventional war among militarily weak countries (e.g., in Central America) would result in great damage to the respective economies and populations. The anticipated benefit of not entering into a war would be greater in all cases when compared to the benefits gained from military struggle.

CBMs thus imply the suspension of planning based exclusively on capabilities and the introduction of intentions as an operational variable. Security is then seen as a result of a complex articulation of capacities and intentions that can be modified at both ends of the equation. It is not necessary to assume the worst case; furthermore, it is possible to think that even malevolent intentions can be stabilized at less-threatening levels.

The question of information becomes crucial, given that the issue of security has been converted into a symbolic structure rather than something calculable by the simple measurement of relative destructive capacities. Security concerns not only calculations of firepower but also the decoding of signals and motives. This decoding can be the object of calculations, but it requires that information be shared. Moreover, it is indispensable—from a paradoxically realist and Clausewitzian perspective—that the potential aggressor counts on its adversary having the best and most accurate information about its capacities and intentions. If the game used to consist of concealing information while "stealing" it from the potential enemy, security now depends on making the defensive apparatus as transparent as possible.

In the remainder of this essay, I would like to demonstrate to what extent CBMs are applicable to the Andean subregion and to what degree the facts support assumptions regarding its rationality, given that in this part of the continent there are situations of both actual and potential international conflict. I would also like to suggest a framework using specific measures to predict the limits of deterrence to collective security. Finally, I will argue that the structure of mutual threats that confronts the Andean countries is different from the Euro-Atlantic logic of strategic realism—which implies a somewhat modified focus of the question of confidence building measures.

I will compare the construction of the Conference on Security and Cooperation in Europe (CSCE), up until its culmination in Vienna in 1989,[3] with the dilemmas and strategic problems confronted by countries like Colombia, Venezuela, Ecuador, Peru, and Bolivia.[4] I will contend that the differences are substantial and that the focus of CBMs in this area of the world should be revised with respect to the European experience following the Cold War.[5] Above all, I will emphasize the security problems that result from the lack of integration and the disintegration of the control (and self-control) of government and nation-state actors within the framework of a growing inability both to identify substate actors (another assumption of classic realism) and to consider states as unified strategic actors perfectly able to organize and control key geopolitical elements.

SECURITY PROBLEMS IN THE ANDEAN AREA

At the end of the 1980s, the intellectual, political, and diplomatic entities of the region felt that the Andean region was on its way to becoming a relatively peaceful zone. Only a few years ago it was projected that future threats to the security of countries in this area would be the result of "unconventional" phenomena, such as internal subversion, transnational illegal activities, or socioeconomic disturbances that would "spill over" borders. These hopes were grounded in two basic premises: (1) it was thought that the end of the Cold War would remove the possibility of the area being converted into a stage for conflict between the superpowers, and (2) that traditional border-type antagonisms would become more irrelevant and secondary compared to other problems that afflicted Andean societies (i.e., state disintegration, economic adjustment, guerrillas, terrorism, etc.). At the same time, the renewed popularity of integrationist schemes made plausible certain theories based on an interdependent liberalism, which assumes that the growing connections between economies and civil societies help to transcend territorial boundaries. This would, in turn, create a powerful political base that calls for proposals to bury old visions of conventional geopolitics.

Another theory that helped sustain the conviction of a less-conflictive future among the Andean states was based on the postulation that civil democracies are inherently less prone to confronting one another in a warlike manner. Military regimes, even if not involved in wars or armed conflicts, were found to be intellectually more loyal to deterrent and Hobbesian-based conceptions of national defense, which made it difficult for governments run by the military to favor collective security positions. However, given that all the countries in the region had completed apparently successful transitions to civilian regimes, it was thought that this would lead to the demise of leading international relations theories and practices based on deterrence and geopolitics. There had been a tendency to attribute to military governments a propensity to be more bellicose than civil regimes. Although this can be empirically challenged, it was evident that the new civil administrations were and still are more receptive to alternate ways of conceiving of the problem of national security.

However, recent events have clouded the optimistic projections made at the beginning of the decade. The conflict between Ecuador and Peru in the Alto Cénepa, and the recurring tension between Venezuela and Colombia in Lake Maracaibo, as well as other points, have shown that it was premature to suggest that border disputes and classical geopolitical conflicts were about to disappear, at least in the Andean area.

Likewise, the increase in interstate conflicts suggests that the assumptions about militarily nonconflictive relationships between democracies and their inherently peaceful natures are as hasty as conclusions about the pacifying effects that shared economic and social interests have on the warlike tendencies of states. It is possible that these interdependent interests have not yet been developed to the point where they can be an effective check on interstate military conflicts. It is also reasonable to think that insufficient attention is paid to the fact that deepening intersocietal relations can carry into the political processes in each country problems and struggles that are imported from neighbors or supposed partners. Perhaps not all societal interrelations promote peace and cooperation; on the contrary, they may generate new kinds of rivalries and clashes. The case of Venezuela and

Colombia is suggestive that the growing demographic and economic overlap between the two has created new discords and contradictions.

Of the imminent threats to peace, the source of conflict that should take center stage is pending territorial disputes. First, traditional deterrence assumes that states effectively have control of their own territories and are sovereign over the groups or actors that might resort to violence. Therefore, any weakening in the capacity of the state to conduct itself as an actor in complete control of its resources causes fear, and any deficiencies in governance or any internal disarticulations can cause neighbors to be more suspicious and more armed than they would be otherwise.

Second, uncontrolled cross-border activities threaten surrounding states. A neighboring conflict can be imported and internalized, and, as a result, can cause a deterioration in interstate relations. In such cases, the affected countries begin to see that it might be in their own interest to intervene in hopes of preventing insecurity by "contagion" or "spillover." This has historic precedent, clearly demonstrated by the Central American experience—most notably the various revolutionary processes both inside and outside the continent and the interventions that have occurred to "reestablish internal order" in countries in presumed disintegration.[6] In this case, the increase in international confidence moves the international community to help the country in crisis, because its neighbors cannot ignore the threat posed by the potential collapse of its political and economic systems.

A third kind of conflict pertinent to this analysis is the implantation of transnational or extraregional themes and issues. The Cold War was perhaps the epitome of such conflicts, and its end does not decrease the importance of this phenomenon. In the cases of French atomic testing, the war on drugs, and environmental issues, the original focus of the conflict is not localized in the same area, nor, ultimately, is it confined to definite limits at all. Issues about the atmosphere, for example, are a kind of unterritorialized problem, even though there can be relevant territorial factors. Concerns about weapons of mass destruction or drug trafficking are partly localized and partly not. To the extent these issues are localized, they center on policies, problems, and decisions of influential outside actors, and problems within the subregion may have to do with the various ways in which countries are linked to or articulated with the particular transregional problem. The way a country engages with its neighbors can be the result of binding itself to a foreign dispute, such as Nicaragua did in Central America and Cuba in the Caribbean during the Cold War. Hypothetical cases could include a country that agrees to create a nuclear waste depository in its territory or in an area adjoining another country, rents space for activities that are dangerous to the atmosphere of its neighbors, or makes alliances with a third party. These would all signify a fragmentation of the subregional consensus regarding transnational matters.

In such situations the theme of mutual confidence is linked to the capacity of these countries to give guarantees to their neighbors: (1) that they will maintain collective action in the face of such issues and will not exercise the option of "deserting"; and (2) that if they do diverge, they would do so in a way that limited the damage to third parties and did not harm common objectives. The countries would also have to convince their counterparts that such actions were not designed to hurt them (e.g., by offering a credible system of safeguards and protections for a project that would have a potentially transnational impact on the atmosphere).

Finally, a problem arises from predetermined domestic characteristics of the countries. There is a tendency today to consider that the political system and socioeconomic structure of a state are, in and of themselves, reasons for distrust and concern. The existence of antidemocratic governments and of highly inequitable and oppressive social systems is (or can be) threatening for two principal reasons: (1) because these regimes are perceived as aggressive in nature, and (2) because if internal conflict is high it can provoke outbreaks that destabilize not only the governments' own societies but others as well. It is not important whether this is true or not, but whether governments perceive this to be true.

Even though the relationship between democracy and security is highly debatable, in certain cases mutual confidence should be based on comprehensive agreement on commonly acceptable parameters, in which the political and socioeconomic internal order of the states can shift, and in collective mechanisms that provide effective observance of such agreement. An example of this would be a common sense of respect for human and civil rights, with corresponding mechanisms for effective administration, policing, and so forth.[7]

THE EUROPEAN EXPERIENCE AND ITS RELEVANCE TO THE ANDEAN COUNTRIES

The Euro-Atlantic system is a response to the "armed peace" between two opposing ideological factions that had the capability to unleash total destruction in a short time.[8] In an effort to avoid the start of a war due to a misunderstanding, the first CBMs focused exclusively on conventional military themes and were seen as a series of mechanisms developed to reduce the probability that potential belligerents could miscalculate the intentions of an opponent. The emphasis was on transparency and verification, on information using all available intelligence resources, on reducing anxiety in the face of unusual military maneuvers and activities.[9] It was soon evident, however, that these efforts should be reinforced by others that not only made the potential adversary's intentions more accessible, but also limited its capacity to initiate far-reaching offensive actions in a short period of time.[10] Thus, the second phase of CBMs included limitations, each time more strict, on the arms and offensive weapons systems that the factions could deploy. The Euro-Atlantic CBMs thus have two crucial and complementary components: transparency/verification and reduction/control of offensive supplies and personnel.

The CBMs referred to here did not require that the parties modify their own political system or state structure. They did not demand guarantees with respect to domestic stability, nor did they depend upon such stability. However, they did eventually call for a concurrent process of inspection of the territorial integrity of the countries. The culmination of this strategy was the Federal Republic of Germany's compromise that it would not claim the future territories east of the Oder-Neisse line that have belonged to Poland since 1945. CBMs were possible for the most part because the basis for deterrence was not territorial issues in the classical sense, and even though the nature of the domestic regime was not a condition for the advancement of CBMs, they did result in support for the development of a shared common interest in peace. This is expressed particularly well in Gorbachev's theme of European peace as a transcultural and transsystemic interest.[11]

It was extremely important that the parties were discovering meta-interests that were incompatible with the deterrent model of security. Dialogue and intercultural tolerance were not prior conditions for the development of strong economic interdependence; instead, they often appeared as a result of calculating the disastrous consequences that would befall all systems—no matter how many participants were opposed—as a result of eventual belligerence. Economic and intersocietal ties were not the reason for a favorable disposition toward CBMs. On the contrary, it was the expectation of eventual mutual advantages that transnational ties could bring that gave life to negotiations between the blocs. This seems opposite to what an economic theory of international relations would have predicted: the political project based on anticipatory hopes resulted in the desire for appeasement, while social and material ties were woven one at a time, creating a favorable climate in which political relations could develop. Societal interdependence is a desired result and not a cause. The interdependence of terror, of facing possible simultaneous destruction, motivates CBMs, while economic-political goals are secondary to such projects.

Finally, it should be pointed out that at the same time as the process of CBMs was advancing in the Euro-Atlantic context, their objectives were also changing. Initially the emphasis was on avoiding war; afterward the central theme was the consolidation and stabilization of peace. Now the goal of this process is the elimination of the basic causes of distrust that could reverse the climate of shared security between the previous contenders of the Cold War. CBMs were not seen as replacements for political negotiations in removing the causes of interbloc conflict; rather, their validity was tied to a parallel advance in negotiations on substantive differences between the parties. This should be taken into account, especially in the face of the temptation to interpret CBMs as substitutes for the settlement of serious controversies regarding the problem of security. There are certainly interactions, but it seems prudent to maintain the clear analytical distinction.

COMPARING THE EUROPEAN AND ANDEAN EXPERIENCES

First, in the Andean countries, unlike the European context, conflict between nations is not rooted in ideological or interbloc confrontation;[12] rather, the possible bases for conflict are territorial (Peru and Ecuador, Colombia and Venezuela), demographic (Colombia and Venezuela), or involve the danger of the "spillover" of internal conflicts from neighboring countries (as in the case of Colombia and Venezuela or Colombia and Ecuador). In some cases, suspicion or insecurity is not aroused by the intentions of an opposing state army, but results from the possibility that political instability will weaken the ability of the state to guarantee domestic sovereignty. In other cases, insecurity is related to the intentions of the opposing state, but the range of threats is more or less clearly demarcated and predictable. In other words, there is a strong component of the calculability of threats, given the "transparency" of information. In the Euro-Atlantic case, the complete destruction of a way of life or of coexistence itself could have been lurking behind the intentions of the opposing bloc. Here, no state fears that "total war" would destroy or fundamentally alter its own political system; rather, the situation resembles eighteenth-century Europe, where disputes were begun in order to gain territory, not to destroy an opposing dynasty or the adversary's way of life. These kinds of threats are self-moderating, inasmuch as they are self-limiting: a rudimentary form of mutual confidence. An example, given the strictly limited nature of the objectives of both parties, is the war between Peru and Ecuador in the Alto Cénepa.

Second, the problem of miscalculation is crucial when two facing armed blocs have a high level of military preparedness, a high level of fear about the intentions of the other party, and the capacity to concentrate forces in a short time and to cause massive destruction with little warning. Such a situation does not exist in the Andean context; there is no Cold War–style "armed peace." The national armies are relatively small, can only be deployed slowly, and have precarious military means and insufficient intelligence about the capacities of their adversaries (although not at a tactical level). They do not find themselves massively deployed, nor has there been a Clausewitzian tradition of experimenting with the European principles of speed and concentration of forces. The need for transparency, verification, and evaluation of intentions is not as urgent, nor is it required to be outlined in such detail as in the European case.

Third, contrary to the European case, the countries of the Andean subregion find themselves involved in a fairly old and consolidated common institutional, legal, and diplomatic network. The shared institutions of the inter-American system, evolving over the past century, constitute a relatively stable set of formal and informal practices, which attempts to tone down conflicts and allows for relatively foreseeable reactions on the part of the actors. To this is added the structure of the hemispheric power system: the Andean countries, and those of the rest of the continent, are regulated "from above" by the influence of regional hegemonic powers like the United States. This seriously limits the autonomy of the national actors to escalate conflict and project their capacity for violence. The presence of an indisputable hegemon is another de facto principle of calculability and of shared expectations that moderate power.

These three factors allow us to conclude that the system in the Andean area and South America is based in no small degree on a form of mutual confidence. The states of the region have been practicing confidence building measures—in their own ways—long before the term was coined or popularized, and the hemisphere should use this framework, which has been so firmly entrenched over the past decades, as a point of departure. It is because of this that the level of interstate violence in Latin America during the present century has been low relative to that seen in Europe and

Asia. This is related to Latin American countries' development of a security strategy that places less importance on deterrence and more emphasis on the construction of institutions and stable regimes.

The problem of arms control is much less intense in the Andean context because the armed forces of the region play a minor deterrent role, in that their role has primarily been to enforce domestic political control and national construction, instead of preparing for large-scale interstate conflict. The problem of disarmament in the Andean countries is, above all, an issue linked to the need to free resources for development, not for the peace process. The amount of weapons is not in and of itself as pressing a concern as in Europe. Expenditures on arms are small in comparison with other areas of the world, and the armed forces are not held on constant alert. Disarmament cannot, therefore, be as important a tool to contain or prevent conflicts. Its practical establishment has other important aspects but, by itself, disarmament does not seem to be a "high-return" confidence building measure.

In the European context, diplomatic and joint activities have been extremely important in increasing confidence among the respective armed forces. Knowing the strategy (ways of thinking, plans, and attitudes) of counterparts reduces uncertainty and increases predictability.[13] In the case of the Latin American countries, there is a long tradition of diplomatic relations and shared formative experiences. Uncertainty with respect to strategy is declining; therefore an increase in interaction among military elites, although profitable, does not have the same consequences as in the Euro-Atlantic case.

Domestic political stability was not a crucial issue in the process that began in Helsinki in 1975. However, in the Andean subregion it is precisely such potential threats that give rise to domestic instability and difficulties in forming domestic policy. In the European case, state control over domestic issues, the permanence of the political regime, and the regime's capacity to efficiently exercise domestic sovereignty was constant, while intentions and military capacities were seen as subject to sudden variations. In the Andean case, it is the opposite: military capacity and intentions are fixed and stable, but internal governability (the nature of the political regime and domestic stability) is seen as subject to greater variability.

Insecurity is a vicious circle. Usually CBMs are guarantees that one state makes to another; but how can one state assure another of its domestic stability when it is precisely the state's control of domestic stability that is in doubt? This is a challenge to the regional political structure. It could be said that domestic stability and sovereignty are principal measures that would contribute to mutual confidence. But these are not inherent to the states. Rather, it is societies and political systems that are able to produce those guarantees, but they bypass "normal" diplomatic-military channels. In other words, in the Andean region, CBMs in which nonstate actors play an important and active part should be developed.

CBMs were developed in the Andean countries to alleviate the insecurity arising from pending territorial issues and to reduce the level of tension they create, whereas in the European case the crucial point was ideological confrontation. It is fitting to ask in what way European-style CBMs are practicable in the Andean context, where states continue to think that vital border interests are at stake. If the European strategy is followed, the possibility of more successful CBMs would be precluded by a return to territorial disputes.

The growth of human rights and democracy was very important in Europe. It was an objective sign of the reduced level of suspicion that had resulted from the abyss between the ruling political and social systems of the rival blocs. This growth had a central symbolic value, because the rivalry between the superpowers was rooted in that intersystemic gap. This is not the case in the Andean countries. First, on the one hand, differences in the political systems, when there have been any, have not been central factors in rivalry or mutual insecurity. The presence of various regimes has not played a central role in the perceptions of either authoritarian or democratic governments. On the other hand, the differences between political systems have never been as profound and antagonistic as in the case of the Cold War. In and of themselves, confidence building measures centered on stabilizing democratic or republican systems are not valid. The measures are important only to the way in which authoritarian forms of government appear to promote internal disorder that in turn can lead to possible transnational conflicts. For instance, the Fujimori coup did not increase the insecurity of Peru's neighbors, while its success against the Shining Path, authoritarianism and all, raised the level of confidence in its subregional neighbors.

It has been proposed that economic interdependence of the Andean countries could provide an element of increased shared security. The basis of this idea is that in the center, where more groups and sectors of each country were seeing their destinies bound together, an influential political clientele could be created, designed to promote international cooperation and peace. However, the slowness and uncertainty of societal integration in the subregion does not permit verification of this hypothesis. It is not clear whether a sufficient threshold of interconnection of economic, political, and social interests has been reached; interdependence has developed apart from CBMs and the dissipation of the balance of terror. Such a sequence, in the Andean context, would resolve some antagonisms and allow for the development of intersocietal relations. However, the level of reciprocal insecurity is not as sharp or as total as in the Cold War years. It is possible to think of a development of interdependence despite standing traditional disputes. The case for interdependence may even be tried in the Euro-Atlantic region, as well as the Andean countries.

RECENT EXPERIENCE WITH CONFIDENCE BUILDING MEASURES IN THE ANDEAN AREA

The theme of how conventional threats have diminished has been addressed since the 1980s. Although recent experience reveals that such a perspective is premature, this tendency has had another effect: the expansion of confidence building measure initiatives into social and political areas.[14] The pursuit of CBMs seems justified, insofar as it is understood that the preoccupation of security is the weakening of sovereignty, not conventional realist threats that arise from the geopolitical rationale. In this conceptualization it must be kept in mind that intraregional threats are overemphasized by the unique structure of the Latin American international subsystem. It is especially pertinent to take into account the overwhelming presence of a hegemon (the United States) and the inter-American institutional system, which, with all its imperfections, provides a juridical and time-honored framework for managing tensions and conflicts in the area.

It has likewise been argued that the force of democracy and human rights is already a beneficial result of the growth of confidence. The international experience shows that CBMs do not need to depend upon this force. Perhaps this includes CBMs that are made particularly pertinent in situations in which the parties do not share political or juridical systems.[15] At the point where democracy and human rights become goods desirable in themselves, one should not forget that the desire for peace is also a justifiable independent good. Conditioning confidence using the validity of these internal political values can signify a failure to reduce tensions, which can be found even among governments of different types. Peace among nations is now, above all, a moral and political imperative that can have priority over the achievement of other desirable values.

Conventional military CBMs should undoubtedly be considered, but the different strategic context in which they are inserted should not be forgotten.[16] In the Andean region, the urgency of transparency and verification is not as great as in other parts of the world. The development of these conventional measures should not be ignored, but their return in terms of additional marginal security does not promise to be as high as in the European case.[17] Likewise, disarmament or reduction in military expenditures is not as critical, given their already low levels in Latin America. In contrast, the resolution of persistent traditional border conflicts is of great importance in light of extraregional historic experiences. In that sense the probability that a qualitatively superior climate of confidence will emerge is much greater. Peru and Ecuador, Venezuela and Colombia, Peru and Chile should all make rapid advances in the elimination of potential sources of territorial conflict.

Major civil control over the armed forces, even though it may be desirable for other reasons, does not necessarily translate into less subregional insecurity. It cannot be demonstrated that civilian governments are necessarily more pacifist. In reality, a major source of security for the armies of the region is knowing that their neighboring counterparts play a crucial role in the political decision-making process because reciprocal calculability increases between the armed forces in potential conflict. The armies of the region claim to know what their colleagues calculate and anticipate (i.e., the risks of a given strategic situation), which undoubtedly contributes to one of the concepts that CBMs seek to promote: transparency.

Socioeconomic interdependence cannot be considered a priori in reducing distrust between neighboring countries. Intensification of intersocietal relations can produce either a major overlap of state interests, a common desire for peace and the reduction of tensions, or an increase in the potential for conflict and the appearance of new dynamics of friction. It should be taken into account that the formation of political and economic blocs is found to be strongly associated with military blocs created to defend against a common enemy and are subject to strong geopolitical incentives in order to prosper common interest and economic interactions. This is not discussed in the assemblies of the Andean region or in Latin America in general, but it should be brought out before drawing any conclusions regarding the inherently pacifist virtues of the interdependence processes.

NOTES

1. Jack Child, *Conflict in Central America: Approaches to Peace and Security* (New York: St. Martin's Press, 1986); Jack Child, *The Central American Peace Process: Sheathing Swords, Building Confidence* (Boulder, Colo.: Lynne Rienner Publishers, 1992); Francisco Rojas Aravena, "Esquipulas: Un Proceso de Construccion de Confianza," in Augusto Varas and Isaac Caro, eds., *Medidas de Confianza Mutua en America Latina* (Santiago: FLACSO, 1994), 73–100.

2. See *Common Security: A Program for Disarmament: The Report of the Independent Commission on Disarmament and Security Issues under the Chairmanship of Olof Palme* (London: PAN, 1982).

3. A. Rotfeld, *From Helsinki to Madrid, CSCE Documents* (Warsaw: Polish Institute of International Affairs and Cooperative Publishers, 1983).

4. See Jean-François Monteil, "El Desafio Institucional de la Seguridad Europea," *Fuerzas Armadas y Sociedad* 4 (1991): 1–9.

5. Heinrich Gleissner, "The European CSBM Experience," in United Nations for Disarmament Affairs, *Confidence and Security-Building Measures: From Europe to Other Regions*, Topical Papers 7 (New York: United Nations, 1991), 3–7.

6. Child, *Conflict in Central America*; Rojas Aravena, "Esquipulas."

7. Virginia Gamba-Stonehause, "Alternativas para el Logro de una Seguridad Colectiva en Sud America," in *OpCiones para el Logro de una Seguridad Comun en Sud America* (Lima: Centro Regional de las Naciones unidas para la Paz, el Desarme, y el Desarrollo en America Latina y el Caribe, 1991).

8. Hugo Palma, "The Nature of Confidence-Building in the Latin American Environment," in United Nations Department for Disarmament Affairs, *Confidence and Security-Building Measures*, 141–48.

9. Rolf Ekeus, "Multilateral Measures to Increase Military Transparency and Their Alternatives," in United Nations Department for Disarmament Affairs, *Confidence and Security-Building Measures*, 55–58.

10. See Enrique Gomariz, "Las Medidas de Confianza Mutua en la Europa de Fin de Siglo," in Varas and Caro, *Medidas de Confianza Mutua en America Latina*, 31–42.

11. Enrique Gomariz, ed., *Debate Europeo Sobre Paz y Seguridad* (Madrid: MPDL-Siglo XXI, 1987).

12. Michael Morris, "Medidas de Confianza Mutua en Sudamerica," in Varas and Caro, *Medidas de Confianza Mutua en America Latina*, 101–32.

13. United Nations Department for Disarmament Affairs, *Confidence and Security-Building Measures*.

14. See Morris, "Medidas de Confianza Mutua en Sudamerica," and CLADDE/RIAL (Centro Latinoamericano de Defensa y Desarme), "Las Medidas de Confianza en el Contexto de los Sistemas de Seguridad," in *Limitacion de Armamentos y Confianza Mutua en America Latina* (Santiago, 1988).

15. Josef Holik, "Underpinnings and Adaptability of European CSBM Concepts," in United Nations Department for Disarmament Affairs, *Confidence and Security-Building Measures*, 31–40.

16. Ibid.

17. See Stephen Larrabee and Dietrich Stobbe, eds., *Confidence-Building Measures in Europe* (New York: Institute for East-West Security Studies, 1983).

CHAPTER TWO

A Chilean Perspective on Strategic Balance in the Southern Cone

MIGUEL NAVARRO MEZA

The concept of strategic balance is not new to the Southern Cone, nor is its contribution to peace and stability in the region. In fact, latent expressions of this notion can be found, in varying forms and degrees, in the foreign policy and strategic positioning of regional political actors since the middle of the nineteenth century. In addition, the ruling elites have considered foreign policy equilibrium and some level of military parity to be effective deterrents to international crises since the end of the last century.

Throughout history, the idea of strategic equality has pervaded the high politics of the major regional powers as well as the more concrete military decisions related to arms procurement and the deployment of forces in times of peace. Since the end of the War of the Pacific, relations among Chile, Peru, and Bolivia basically have corresponded to the "competition" model: two major powers attempt to gain influence over a third, less powerful, country as part of their own rivalry. Likewise, the 1902 Pactos de Mayo between Chile and Argentina clearly included the idea of a balance of power between the two nations, specifically of naval power.

On the other hand, regional strategic parity, in its purely military expression, has been apparent from the initial purchase of battleships by the Chilean navy in 1875 to the controversial acquisition of advanced fighter jets by the air forces of the Southern Cone nations. For a number of reasons this version of the model has been the most frequently used by local political and military authorities in an almost unconscious process of self-reassurance.

Until the end of the nineteenth century, strategic balance in the region, while remaining fluid, was basically bilateral in character, as were the important conflicts of the time. The entry of Argentina into the local equation (after being a latent force since the 1880s) and the significant development of Brazil provided a genuine multilateral dimension that has remained to the present day. The entire structure of the ABC countries (Argentina, Brazil, Chile) was founded to a large extent on the search for a balance among the principal regional actors, a necessary condition if the nations of the Southern Cone were to be more involved in hemispheric matters. Similarly, the idea of multilateral equilibrium has permeated power relations between the regional political actors in this century and shared center stage (although with some difficulty) with the security arrangements of the Cold War. The idea of multilateral equilibrium has revived in the last few years; with the understanding that the current regional-security system has become obsolete, the impact that real strategic balance can have on stability and peace in the region can be understood almost intuitively.

Chile is a regional actor of the first order, so its participation is essential for any local security scheme and especially for the establishment of strategic balance. In fact, the country has played—and continues to play—a pivotal role in encouraging the diverse forms of parity that have existed in the region, first in bilateral relations with Peru and later in the multilateral system within the Southern Cone.

A THEORETICAL APPROACH TO STRATEGIC BALANCE: THE CONCEPT OF STRATEGIC BALANCE

In general, all definitions of strategic balance underscore the relationship between national power and the international behavior of states.[1] In comparative studies, however, strategic balance can be understood in different ways. For some, it limits state power within the international system in the same way that domestic political balances limit the exercise of power within the state. For others, strategic balance is a political objective in and of itself, a conscious or unconscious search for balance by states through their interactions in the international arena.

Strategic balance, in its most developed form, is achieved when the total distribution of power between two or more countries is relatively equal, although it may be asymmetrical when examined individually.[2] Therefore, equilibrium is the result of the interaction in a global setting between two basic elements in international relations: power relations and conventional deterrence.[3]

Power Relations

Power is defined as the ability of one nation to proactively influence the behavior of other states in its self-interest, using a combination of its resources and capabilities. Thus, in the conceptualization of power, it is the interaction of certain factors that provides a country with the ability to influence others. Dividing the so-called power factors into objective and subjective categories is appropriate for the purposes of this chapter; but the classification is subtle. Military force is one of the most relevant objective factors in the national power equation. However, it is significant only if accompanied by the political will to use it, which is fundamentally subjective. Thus, geography, population, natural resources, industrial and technological capacity, and military capabilities are recognized as objective factors; international prestige, political leadership abilities, and the quality of diplomacy are subjective.

The interaction of these factors leads to multiple combinations of the international power equation. Thus, for the purpose of pursuing strategic balance, power relations within the international system form a fine and complex network of interrelations among the various actors, which have included international organizations in the last fifty years. It should be noted that power relations remain in effect even during periods of high levels of international political and economic cooperation, and are present in current or potential military alliances.[4]

Conventional Deterrence

Deterrence is the way that strategic balance contributes to the stability of a specific international security system. Strategic balance is a situation in which potential adversaries are inhibited from acting against one another because they lack sufficient power to achieve their objectives without suffering prohibitive costs. Ideally, therefore, for a condition of strategic balance to function properly, the actors must adopt deterrence strategies that lead to mutual inaction. Deterrence encourages an opponent not to undertake a specific action because the potential benefits do not justify the risks and costs involved.[5] The explicit or implicit threat of war has always been a diplomatic tool used to prevent one state from acting contrary to the interests of another. Similarly, presenting a credible defense before a potential adversary has been used, with varying degrees of success, to avoid military action.

Deterrence includes both the ability to defend oneself against military—or to a lesser extent, political—aggression and the ability to retaliate in the face of such aggression. This is highly functional in the concept of strategic balance, as it is based precisely on a careful separation of these two capabilities, taking into consideration the remaining power factors present in the equation. Thus, for example, in the case of two potentially adversarial countries of different size, the smaller can achieve equilibrium by developing a credible retaliatory capability with respect to its larger adversary, and simultaneously create a certain degree of defensive capability. This was the strategy developed by Kuwait with respect to Iraq during the 1980s.

THE DYNAMICS OF STRATEGIC BALANCE: TYPES OF EQUILIBRIUM

Direct Opposition

In direct opposition, rival nations increase their relative power until they reach a point where both are equal.[6] One nation has practically no power over the other, and neither nation can impose its will on the other. Although this offers a foundation for stable relations, it is highly unstable in that even small changes in the relative power of one nation can have a disproportionate effect on relations with its adversary. Therefore, this model must be constantly reestablished as it was, for example, in relations between France and Germany before 1914.

This underscores a peculiar phenomenon of strategic balance: although equilibrium brings or should bring about stability in relationships, in reality it sows the seeds of change. Nations must compete constantly unless one abandons the game and recognizes the superiority of the other. In some cases, seeking equilibrium forces the challenged nation to recognize a situation of parity and from then on to try to maintain it. The relationship between Chile and Argentina from 1885 until 1902 is an example of this model.

The Competition Model

The dynamics of this model involve two nations attempting to dominate a third, but neither having sufficient relative power over the other to be successful. The first nation is unable to dominate the third due to opposition from the second, and vice versa, but if one of the two main actors increases its power, it will be in a position to dominate the third. Historically, this model has been widely used to ensure the independence of weaker nations in geographical situations characterized by the presence of large competing powers.

The Multiple Equilibrium System

This model involves a large number of nations whose security relations are marked by competition. These nations ensure equilibrium by creating a partial network of opposition, characterized by informal alliances or, in their absence, by a country's mere physical presence—for example, the British presence in the South Atlantic with respect to Chile and Argentina. According to this model, states establish equilibrium based on the stability of the entire system and not on any bilateral parity between them. Therefore, insignificant changes in bilateral power relations do not affect the stability of the group. This system does suffer from relative instability when there are changes in alignments or when one member withdraws from the system. This model resembles collective security arrangements, but differs in that strategic balance is not necessarily the result of the deliberate political will of all the participants in the system; at times, it is the result of the distribution of real power in a given geographical area.

The Integration of Power Factors

In this model, power factors are integrated asymmetrically among the states that are part of the system in equilibrium. In other words, any given factor may be asymmetrical with respect to the same factor in a rival country, but the total of all factors tends to create a relatively balanced situation. Thus, in the ideal model a small country can combine great international prestige with adequate military capabilities that alone would be insufficient to pose a threat to the larger country. This model offers a wide range of combinations, especially in a multiple equilibrium system.

BALANCES OF POWER IN THE SOUTHERN CONE: STRATEGIC BALANCE

The development of power politics in relations between the nations of South America was an almost inevitable consequence of the emancipation process and the well-known differences in size, wealth, and idiosyncrasies of the ruling elites in the colonies. These differences gave rise to special political and economic relationships between the territories, under the general umbrella of Spanish and Portuguese domination, and, during the transformation from administrative dependencies to independent nations, relations continued as they had during the colonial period.

In general, the former colonies agreed to the principle of *uti posidetis* (literally, "as you possess"), according to which the new republics would keep the same borders as they had while under Spanish control. Although possibly the best option at the time, this solution did not completely resolve the political problems, due to the fact that Spain rarely had been concerned with setting precise borders. Furthermore, religious and jurisdictional authority had been superimposed on the political outlines of the colonies, which greatly complicated the process of establishing territorial boundaries between the new countries.

With the exception of requesting loans from Great Britain and maintaining some form of political relations with the United States, and to a lesser degree with France, the region did not have a close relationship with the rest of the world during its first years of independence. This allowed the region to concentrate on intrastate issues and to focus primarily on the internal development of its various countries. South America did display a high tendency for conflict. During the previous century there were six major wars and several minor armed conflicts—not an insignificant number considering the physical barriers, the size of the populations, and the practically endemic poverty that existed throughout the region.[7]

Within this framework it was unavoidable that some of the countries of South America began to develop highly sophisticated power politics. This process was not immediate upon independence—it began a few years later—and did not develop simultaneously in all of the countries. Three factors explain this relatively late development. First, the leaders of the independence movements were imbued with an "Americanist" concept of the region; that is, they favored a united American continent, instead of several independent nations, so their political behavior was motivated and shaped by the goal of forming a supranational entity. Second, the continent is large and the political decision-making centers of the new states were—and still are—separated by considerable distances, a difficulty aggravated by the fact that communications at the beginning of the nineteenth century were slow and unreliable. Third, in all of the new republics, independence was followed by a long period of chaos and domestic disturbances that forced the political elites to focus on resolving internal problems before turning their attention to international issues.

Another phenomenon of the first years of independence eventually influenced the appearance of power politics and strategic balance: states frequently granted political asylum to defeated *caudillos* from other countries and allowed these deposed dictators to use territories as bases for organizing new political ventures destined to undermine order in their native countries. Moreover, political leaders easily influenced and participated in the political processes of other countries in the region.

Therefore, from their very beginnings, the nations of South America realized the need to develop true power politics. This included deliberate positioning in the international system in an atmosphere of competition and using force or threats to achieve their objectives. The states also saw the convenience of establishing some type of "balance of power" to reduce the possibility for armed conflict, and the term was frequently used in official documents during the first half of the nineteenth century.[8]

Throughout the century, a number of the countries in the region shared the conviction that any significant change in the power system could affect their interests. This led them to work both to maintain the existing system so as to shield them from threat and to try to develop a power structure favorable to their particular interests. This behavior was observed in Brazil, Chile, and New Granada (later Colombia) and, to a lesser extent, in Peru and Argentina in the second half of the nineteenth century.

During the period of sectoral power politics, relations between the states, especially those along the Pacific Coast, were characterized by competition solely to gain power, the deliberate search for an advantageous power position, and the constant involvement of the internal factions of one state in the affairs of another. The most obvious example is the interaction between Peru and Bolivia between 1830 and 1843. The balance of power centered around efforts to turn Peru and Bolivia into one single political national entity and the interests of Chile and, to a lesser degree, Ecuador in preventing this from happening. Chile waged war against the Peruvian-Bolivian Confederation after realizing the danger that this union represented to its own development.

In the Río de la Plata basin, the power struggle focused on Argentina (or more precisely, the United Provinces of Río de la Plata) and Brazil in a dispute, which had dragged on since the colonial era, between the Viceroyalty of Río de la Plata and the Portuguese colony. This struggle was played out in the War of 1825–28 and led to the creation of Uruguay. However, this one political act did not resolve the power struggle, which continued for the rest of the century and ended only recently.

Relations among the South American nations took on a global perspective, a product of the "Americanist" flavor of the independence movements. Various hemispheric accords were adopted during this era; in general, however, their existence was short-lived due to frequent changes in the governments of many of the countries and differences of opinion between their leaders.[9] After 1860, power relations became interwoven, transforming the lines of confrontation that, up until then, had been regional into a system of support between the Pacific countries and the nations of the Río de la Plata basin. As a result of the War of the Triple Alliance, during which Paraguay was in danger of being wiped out of existence, the Pacific Coast nations realized that the security interests of the entire Southern Cone were inevitably linked.

From a broader perspective, the global character of the power relations in the region is a consequence of three elements: the level of national development achieved by the different countries in the system, the strengthening of individual national identities, and a formal understanding of power dynamics and strategic balances. Once power relations and the associated equilibrium were established, each of the countries in the region tried to maintain the current situation while, simultaneously, attempting to achieve a power structure favorable to its national interests. The political leaders of all of the nations involved understood the dynamics of power politics and displayed considerable will to put these dynamics into play.[10] Finally, participants in the system could modify or restructure the system themselves without foreign interference.[11]

During this period, two power struggles directly influenced the initial configuration of the regional strategic balance: the dispute among Chile, Peru, and Bolivia, dating back to 1860; and the escalating confrontation between Chile and Argentina, triggered by border tensions in 1846, which became more serious towards the end of the century and continued with varying intensity until at least 1984. The effects of these struggles have endured to some degree until the present day.

In the nineteenth century, the main goal of strategic balance or balance of power was to ensure the survival of the regional system by maintaining the political independence of all its nations—hence, for example, the irate reaction of the Pacific Coast countries when the secret terms of the Treaty of the Triple Alliance, which clearly called for Paraguay to be dismantled to the benefit of both Argentina and Brazil, were made public. This somewhat primitive notion of the balance of power was tied to the level of development of the dominant political ideas at that time and ran parallel with them. From the moment the power equation takes on a truly regional character, the concept of strategic balance begins to evolve. From a rough notion that considers only the existence of the states as a balancing factor, it grows into a more refined idea that values specific differences among them.

Moreover, during this era, candid use of "balance of power" was replaced by more euphemistic and sophisticated terms. As a result of the evolution of the concept of strategic balance, equilibrium policies gradually turned into military competitions. These resulted in the development, slow at first but much quicker later on, of arms races that continued until relatively recently. As a consequence, strategic balance has become synonymous with military equilibrium.[12]

MILITARY ASPECTS

The First Arms Races and the Pactos de Mayo

Military capability was a factor in the earliest notions of balance of power in the region. Because the independence movements involved, almost without exception, armed conflict with Spain, the new nations inherited relatively structured military organizations and certain war traditions, which were applied in initial attempts to establish regional equilibrium.

The military was seen primarily as a secondary resource, available for use in achieving international political ends only when diplomatic channels had broken down. On the other hand, the often chaotic domestic situation and the financial limitations that affected a majority of the young republics conspired against maintaining permanent military capabilities. For example, immediately following the war against the Peruvian-Bolivian Confederation, the Chilean army and navy were both discharged, a common practice at that time. As soon as hostilities ended, military and naval forces were reduced to a minimum, keeping only the indispensable troops that could be readily expanded in the case of another armed conflict.

Toward 1860 this situation began to change. The ruling elites began to associate the need for maintaining permanent military capabilities with the possibility of advancing national interests within the dominant regional political structure and balance of power. This was made feasible by an increase in public finances due to the economic bonanza and relative political stability that various Southern Cone countries were experiencing at the time.

These countries gradually began to improve their military capabilities, beginning with their navies. Given that the policy- and decision-making centers of each country were separated by great distances and by geographical barriers that severely limited the mobility of ground forces, domination of the sea was essential to any successful military campaign. Furthermore, international trade among the republics depended almost exclusively on maritime communications, a priority target during conflict. This belief was also reinforced by the experiences of the wars of independence and the first armed conflicts between the independent nations.

The military buildup initiatives inevitably led to what today would be called arms races. These competitions originally corresponded to the pattern of balances that existed at the time: Peru and Chile were balanced between about 1863 and the War of the Pacific, and the Argentine Confederation and Brazil were balanced during approximately the same time. As power relations assumed a regional perspective, so did the competitions. The most important arms race after 1880, held between Chile and Argentina, persisted throughout the remainder of the nineteenth century.

Arms races during this era were of the action-reaction type: the military buildup of one country provoked a reaction from its rival(s). For instance, Peru acquired the *Huáscar* and the *Independencia*, the two most powerful armored battleships in the region at the time, which drastically altered any previous semblance of naval parity. Chile responded by purchasing the superior ships the *Cochrane* and the *Blanco Encalada* and thus built up its navy—the results of which buildup can be seen in the outcome of the naval campaign of the War of the Pacific. The arms race between Brazil and Argentina was similar.

With the civil war that eliminated Peru from the regional strategic equation in 1883, the arms race took on a more global perspective in response to the growing confrontation between Chile and Argentina. This confrontation led to the naval arms race between the two countries during the 1890s. Chile instigated the race with its 1888 program, which temporarily gave the country undisputed supremacy in the region. Argentina responded throughout the decade with well-structured and costly programs. Chile followed with equally expensive programs, leading to a competition that easily could have resulted in open conflict. The impossibility of continuing the race led both countries to reach an agreement, calling for stabilization and the reduction of naval weapons, which was included among the Pactos de Mayo. It is interesting to note that this accord was the first of its kind in the world and directly alluded to the need to maintain a naval balance between

33

both countries and, moreover, specified that this balance constituted the basis of an arms reduction agreement.

Toward the end of the War of the Pacific near the turn of the century, the arms race between Chile and Argentina expanded to include land forces. This led to an increase in defense budgets and improvements in the professionalism of the officer corps, usually achieved by hiring foreign military trainers. This situation reflected the more global concept of military power that reigned in both countries at the time and the technological and logistical advances that made possible increased use of the army during conflicts.

From the Battleship Race to the Search for Supremacy

The next arms race in the region focused on dreadnoughts, battleships that revolutionized naval tactics and strategy at the turn of the century. This class of battleship made every other type of ship obsolete, so it was possible to begin a naval race practically from zero and even raise these nations to a par with the great naval powers.[13]

Although there had been no specific political tensions which called for such action, Brazil initiated this race by ordering the construction of two battleships in England in December 1904. These ships, the *Minas Gerais* and the *São Paulo*, completed in 1908 and 1909 respectively, were superior to all other ships, including their British counterparts. Argentina responded with the battleships *Moreno* and *Rivadavia*, built in the United States between 1909 and 1915. Brazil then ordered a third ship from Great Britain that was to be the most powerful ship of its time, though a number of factors prevented Brazil from acquiring the ship and it wound up in the British navy. Chile then joined the race, ordering the construction of two battleships in Great Britain that were each considered more powerful than those of the other countries in the region. Of these two ships, only the *Latorre* was finally incorporated into the navy; the other ship was acquired by Great Britain for use in World War I and converted into an aircraft carrier.

World War I and the extremely high cost of these types of ships brought an end to the battleship race. It is interesting to highlight once again the technological superiority of these ships, especially the Brazilian and Chilean ships, which incorporated the latest advances in the areas of propulsion and weaponry. It is also important to note that technological imperative was a contributing factor to the development of this arms race.

In the 1920s and 1930s, Argentina abandoned the idea of parity and replaced it with supremacy. This meant achieving military capabilities twice that of any potential adversary. In other words, Argentina's military capabilities were directed at successfully fighting a war on two fronts simultaneously, which could mean nothing other than fighting both Chile and Brazil.[14]

During this period, the arms race also included the army and air force, in terms of size, quality, and equipment. Between 1930 and 1940, Argentina effectively achieved undisputed superiority over both Brazil and Chile on an individual basis—whether Argentina had superiority over the two countries combined is open to debate. This was the result of an ambitious plan to rearm the Argentine navy and air force and a decade of underinvestment in defense by the Chilean government, due to the political events of the early 1930s.

Also, by this time Peru had reemerged as a military power in the region. Toward 1932 Peru began a rapid process of rearmament, specifically incorporating advanced technology into its land and air forces. A modern, and one might say bold, military doctrine was successfully adopted during the conflict with Ecuador in 1941. A curious situation was also created in which Peru and Argentina increased the power of their armed forces without fueling an arms race, because Chile did not answer their challenges. Only near the end of the decade did Chile attempt a weak response, compromised by a poor selection of equipment and by the onset of World War II, which closed access to arms suppliers.[15]

Forced Equilibrium

The end of the Second World War completely altered the strategic situation in the region. Obviously, it reinforced the unquestionable superiority and domination of the United States. Moreover, practically all of the military equipment and doctrines of the Southern Cone nations, including Peru, were made obsolete. Following some weak attempts by Argentina to maintain power politics with the United States, inevitably all of the countries formed an alliance under the strategic guidance of Washington.

This reaffirmed the trend toward a military balance in the region, which by then was the official policy of the United States. As a consequence, and due to the formal structuring of a hemispheric security system under the Inter-American Reciprocal Assistance Treaty, the United States began military transfers to all of the countries in the hemisphere, employing the criterion of strict numerical parity. Furthermore, the equipment was allocated according to the specific duties assigned to each country in the case of a worldwide confrontation with the Soviet Union instead of according to real defense needs. The majority of the countries involved were able to make this "global" assignment somewhat compatible with their own strategic needs, to some extent governed by the idea of parity with their neighbors. From the end of the 1940s until the beginning of the 1960s, the Southern Cone countries matched, in varying degrees, military dependence on the United States with acquisitions from Europe, especially Great Britain, which allowed them to maintain some semblance of equilibrium.

The Arms Races of the 1970s and 1980s

Near the end of the 1960s Argentina and Peru began military buildup programs. This brought about an arms race that involved almost all of the countries in South America to varying degrees. There were several reasons for this race, including reduced American influence, the advent of military governments in some countries, a greater availability of resources, and the reemergence of territorial disputes, which, in some cases, masked more serious disputes between the local political leaders. The arms race continued throughout the 1970s, involving Chile and Brazil especially. It subsided in the early 1980s, although it continued to some degree until the end of that decade. This era was characterized by periods of extreme tension between Chile and Peru (1974–75) and between Argentina and Chile (1978–84). Furthermore, the emergence of the South Atlantic Conflict in 1982 had a significant impact on Argentinean strength. This arms race is particularly relevant in that current military power in the Southern Cone is in large part the result of investments made during this time.[16]

A slow process of military buildup did continue in certain countries, including Chile, between 1990 and 1994. This was mainly to replace obsolete equipment, and did not constitute a regional arms race. Nevertheless, it should be noted once again that the current concept of strategic balance, at least in the opinion of regional authorities, revolves around military balance and ignores the other power factors that make up the real power equation in the Southern Cone.[17]

Arms races were associated with power politics and strategic balance as an almost unavoidable consequence of the nature of security relations in the Southern Cone and, in more general terms, in all of South America. Some were the result of mistrust and latent rivalries more than of deliberate attempts at superiority. During the first stage of the naval arms race between Chile and Peru, which was instigated by the latter country, Peru strengthened its naval power as a consequence of the financial and political options granted by a period of stability and economic boom more than from a specific attempt to gain supremacy along the Pacific Coast. This was evidenced by the episode involving the Chilean corvettes *O'Higgins* and *Chacabuco*, which tested, but was not the principal motivation for, Peru's initial reaction.[18] The same is true for the arms race between Chile and Argentina, which began in 1888. The Chilean naval program basically followed President Balmaceda's convictions that the country needed a powerful navy to protect its coasts as well as its foreign trade. In Balmaceda's opinion, significant military capabilities also provided powerful support for Chilean foreign policy. Thus, although the program was not aimed directly against the Argentine Republic, it nevertheless generated an arms race that lasted until 1902 and was characterized by growing ill will between the two nations.

This confirms the initial assertion that the arms races reflected the state of regional multilateral security relations. The existence of power politics, not weakened by cooperation, generated an atmosphere of mistrust that fueled rivalries, intensified military competition, and endured throughout the present century. The military rearmament and modernization processes in Argentina and Peru in the 1930s and in Brazil, Argentina, and other countries in the 1950s created a deep level of mistrust among the rest of the nations in the region. The fact that this did not lead to open arms races was primarily the result of domestic political events in the potentially affected countries, including Chile, which led to long periods of underinvestment in defense. After 1945, excessive reliance on hemispheric security systems also prevented open arms races. In assessing strategic balance as an element of regional stability, the dynamics of arms races must be clearly understood so that history will not repeat itself. In a balanced system, certain states may have military capabilities somewhat superior to those of the other actors, but this does not necessarily imply a threat to those with inferior military strength. An integrated process of confidence building measures can contribute decisively to this purpose.

CHILE AND THE BALANCE OF POWER

Chile was a relative latecomer to regional power politics. The struggle for independence, the traumas of the first republican era, and the chaos following O'Higgins's abdication caused the country to look mostly within. Only with the establishment of the state proper, around 1833–34, did the republic begin to participate in regional issues. This involvement ran parallel to the strengthening of domestic political, economic, and intellectual development as one single political initiative.

Almost inevitably, Chile was wrapped up in political events in Peru and Bolivia and thus in an atmosphere of distrust and animosity, dating back to the colonial era, toward the former viceroyalty. During this period in the 1830s, Chile understood balance of power as a means of insuring the survival of the various nation-states so as to impede the creation of supernations whose asymmetrical power could affect the independence of the rest. This position was undoubtedly shared by the other countries in the region, or at least by those that had already been formed. Chile did not hesitate in going to war to break up the newly formed Peruvian-Bolivian Confederation, whose potential power was seen by the Chilean ruling class as a clear threat to the survival of the republic.

The central objectives of Chilean foreign policy during this era could be summed up as: the desire to maintain cordial relations with its neighbors, to avoid their meddling in its domestic politics (a frequent occurrence during that time), and, most importantly, to increase foreign trade, which provided the resources for development. The country's ruling class now understood the advantage of maintaining equilibrium as a requisite for fulfilling foreign policy goals. On the other hand, the military triumph left Chile in the inescapable position of being the arbiter of equilibrium along the Pacific Coast, a role that it held for the remainder of the century. Chile adopted a proactive international position promoting understanding with other countries in the region. Nevertheless, foreign policy was not backed up by comparable military capabilities, a common situation during that time.

During the 1840s, Chile began to experience the first border problems with both the Argentine Confederation and the Bolivian Republic. During this same period, as Robert Burr also states, Chile became the champion of balance of power along the Pacific Coast, extending its influence to present-day Colombia and frequently introducing political initiatives in all of the countries.[19] Special mention should be made of the Chilean position on maintaining Ecuador's independence, which was constantly being jeopardized by either Colombia or Peru.

Chile, overwhelmed by hemispheric solidarity but also in line with its role as mediator in the regional strategic balance, intervened in the War with Spain. Chile suffered from this war more than either of the other countries involved, due, in no small part, to insufficient military might. On the other hand, this conflict temporarily concealed the imminent conflict on the northern border with Bolivia. At the same time, Chile began to participate in the regional power structure, specifically to show its concern over the status of Paraguay. According to the Chilean political elites, Paraguay's existence was necessary to maintain the regional balance of power. Furthermore, the gradual intensification of the border dispute with Argentina contributed to the extension of the geographical boundaries understood by Chile in its notion of equilibrium.

The War with Spain and the general dynamics of the regional balance of power forced Chile to begin strengthening its military capabilities, initially in the navy, as outlined above. The growing conflicts of interest between Chile and Peru, Bolivia, and Argentina throughout the decade created an extremely complicated situation in Chile's foreign policy. The Chilean concept of strategic balance appeared to be seriously compromised; Brazilian goodwill was insufficient to reestablish equilibrium. From 1876 onward, crises with Argentina and Bolivia developed alternately. The presence of a solid naval force lessened the danger of confrontation with Argentina but did not prevent the War of the Pacific in early 1879.

The end of the War of the Pacific left Chile the undisputed leader of the Pacific Coast, and disputably of the entire continent. The Chilean ruling class was determined to preserve this situation. Chile's army, although reduced in size following the conflict, was still powerful; its navy was the largest in the region, with the exception of Brazil, and the best trained. Profits from nitrate exports provided the funds necessary for maintaining Chile's status in the regional balance of power. The republic's search for political and military supremacy led the government to adopt a proactive foreign policy and develop programs to strengthen the military, both technologically and in terms of human resources. The main threat at that time came from Argentina, a country that, although it had inferior military capabilities, was much larger in size, had almost twice the population, and was rapidly expanding due to massive immigration from Europe. While Chile's international stance was not directly opposed to that of Argentina, it still represented a genuine interest in sustaining its privileged status in the region. Inevitably this had a considerable impact on relations between the two nations.

The 1891 Civil War in Chile did not significantly alter the scenario. On the contrary, it appeared to somewhat strengthen the country's position, especially by bringing an admiral to power, although this did not signify the installation of a military government. The presidency of Admiral Montt continued to strengthen the navy within the framework of the arms race with Argentina, which was discussed above. The Montt administration also fortified the army, as evidenced by successive laws allocating resources for national defense.[20]

The most important political consequence of the civil war was the establishment of a semiparliamentary government, which seriously diminished presidential powers and thoroughly affected the stability of the cabinet. Ministerial appointments were subject to Congress, which, in turn, was subject to the dictates of casual and short-lived majorities that lacked a broad vision with respect to national goals. This signaled the end of one of the most valuable elements of Chilean foreign policy: unanimously agreed-upon decisions, rooted in the executive branch—or, in more general terms, a high degree of national consensus. This proved fatal in the long run, as it seriously compromised the country's ability to effectively manage political, administrative, financial, and even military affairs.

At the beginning of the twentieth century, Chilean politicians and the military establishment once again began to think in terms of equilibrium. To a certain extent, this was an unavoidable consequence of the country's situation during the 1890s and its prudent recognition of the status Argentina had achieved during the same period. The new position took the form of the Pactos de Mayo (1902), in which both nations recognized a balance between their relative power and pledged to uphold the situation. This attitude continued for years, but it became increasingly oriented toward the military component. The late, but still spectacular, entry of Chile into the so-called "battleship race" was a test of this position. If Chile's arms procurements had not been affected by the start of World War I, the country could have had the most powerful navy in the hemisphere south of the Río Grande.

Nevertheless, this was probably the last deliberate attempt by Chile to maintain at least strategic parity in the region. From World War I on, a number of domestic political factors decisively affected the strategies for positioning the country within the region. With the problems of Tacna and Arica finally resolved in 1929, defense was no longer a priority for Chilean citizens. The political events of 1931–32 opened a rift between the politicians and the military establishment, reflected by the very low levels of investment in defense, for more than two decades. Still, a somewhat unconscious desire for strategic balance persisted. Scattered and disconnected military armament programs were attempted but there was no defined national policy.

Chile's participation in the hemispheric security system allowed it to benefit from military transfers from the United States beginning in 1942. However, this arrangement implied a considerable cost to its relative power position because it had to align itself strategically with the United States. This coincides with the period referred to as the "Forced Equilibrium," imposed by the United States on all of the countries in the region. As defined in the past, the idea of equilibrium remained—especially in its military aspect. Thus, Chile reacted to the arms race during the 1970s by investing an amount below that of its potential adversaries. Moreover, investment was complicated by domestic political events of the decade.

It is safe to say that the concept of strategic balance in the military sense has endured until today, within the military establishment as well as (and this is more important) among the ruling class. The high level of consensus among all political factions, regarding the need to maintain strong military capabilities in line with the strategic needs of the country and the need for permanent technological modernization of the armed forces, best characterizes the current Chilean political process.[21] For the first time in several decades, politicians are interested in international security and defense issues. Currently, a rudimentary process is under way to define an explicit defense policy that eventually will encompass all political parties and military institutions. In this context, and having taken into consideration the existence of such consensus, one may expect that the notion of equilibrium, at the least in its military sense and very possibly in its broader sense, will remain an integral part of Chile's strategy.[22]

ANALYSIS AND OUTLOOK

Balance of power has played an important role in the history of South American international relations, specifically within the Southern Cone. From its more primitive form—directed basically at maintaining independent states so as to avoid the formation of suprastates to its more sophisticated expression, balance of power has been a key factor in the interaction of the various countries on the continent.

Since gaining their independence, the South American nations have existed in an organized power-politics structure marked by a conscious policy of positioning themselves within the system and developing their own self-interests through efforts to make this system respond to their individual national goals. Strategic balance must be understood within this environment. In this equation, equilibrium has been fundamental to maintaining peace. This may seem odd considering that at least eight significant armed conflicts have occurred in the region. Nevertheless, the international situation could have been much more chaotic had the idea of equilibrium not been accepted by the local political elites. This holds true especially for the nineteenth century, when, in many cases, the existence of such balance was the only deterrent present.

Undoubtedly the legal and economic aspects of the development of the region's international relations policies have generated other elements that have contributed to peace; however, strategic parity, even in its purely military form, has been equally influential. Tensions between Chile and Peru in 1974–75, recently confirmed by President Fujimori, and the 1978 crisis between Chile and Argentina are specific examples.

Currently, the situation in South America is paradoxical. On one side, a robust process of regional integration characterized by broad political and trade initiatives is being developed, and at last, prospects for this integration are favorable. National forums are being strengthened and new avenues for dialogue and political coordination between the most important actors in the hemisphere are emerging.[23]

Yet certain factors could work against peace and stability, such as: (1) the deregulation of the international security system at the end of the Cold War, which has shifted the greater prospects for armed conflict to the peripheral regions (of which South America is one); (2) the security aspects of the integration processes, derived from the creation of large political-economic arrangements whose interests can affect other states or groups of states in the same region (even bilateral integration has its own set of security factors, which can be quite complex); (3) the end of the need for the countries in the region to seek global stability, signaled by the end of the Cold War; and (4) the trend, although intermittent, toward strengthening local armed forces through the incorporation of advanced technology, a phenomenon that was already noticeable in the arms races at the turn of the century.

The actual collapse of the formal hemispheric security system that was established by the Inter-American Reciprocal Assistance Treaty should be added to the list. The treaty had been based on the possibility of a global confrontation between the West and the Communist bloc, which no longer exists. Therefore, political and economic integration must be compatible with an equally vigorous and instrumental regional security structure. This will, without doubt, be a slow process due to the level of distrust that remains among the region's principal actors. The perpetuation of old disagreements and the emergence of new conflicts of interest among these states, and in broader terms the continuation of tenuous and subtle forms of power politics, especially in the Southern Cone, complicate efforts to reach definitive agreements and strengthen regional security.

The recent conflict between Ecuador and Peru is an ominous sign. There is the need to make cautious progress on the subject of regional security and the need to prevent the emergence of conflicts that could involve the use of force. This situation has not been ignored by regional political elites. It has encouraged the development of limited initiatives that are increasingly applicable to security, such as confidence building measures. Such initiatives are aimed at reducing the possibilities of conflict in the present time and the near future and—at the same time—at creating the broad conditions necessary for more fully addressing all security-related issues.

Strategic balance arises in this same scenario. Ensuring a certain balance between the military capabilities of the main regional actors that at the very least takes geographical realities into consideration can be a valuable aid in maintaining peace and stability. Confidence building measures blend with strategic balance to create objective conditions for maintaining stability and avoid encouraging arms races triggered by a perceived need to maintain balance.

However, the value of strategic balance to regional security goes deeper. The conscious acceptance of parity by the states does not only uphold overall stability and security, but also can contribute to a reduction in future military spending within the region. The latter point is particularly important. Historically, all local disarmament initiatives, including reductions in military spending, have failed because the relative position of each state within the local security system had not been taken into account. Military reduction cannot be linear between dissimilar countries. Only equivalent reductions that ensure parity can be made, and these reductions logically must be defined before the reduction process is begun. Alternatively, reductions must be the product of an agreement between actors in a system determined to achieve parity. This is precisely the basis of the Conventional Arms Reduction Pact in Europe.

Obviously, the formal implementation of strategic balance in the region in the long run is extremely complex. Such implementation can be hindered when balance requires considerable asymmetries between the military capabilities of the states in the system, asymmetries that, in turn, influence domestic political variables. Second, the persistent use of power politics, even though tenuous and subtle, affects the possibility of clearly formalizing the state of equilibrium.

Ideally, equilibrium in the region should extend to all of the relevant factors in the power equation for all the states in the system, although with stronger emphasis on the more important factors. An unequal distribution of the power factors in each country must be recognized by the local military and political leaders. And there should be among all of the countries in the region an explicit consensus concerning equilibrium; this consensus should involve the domestic political factions in each nation.

The task appears formidable, but it is necessary. The idea of strategic balance applied to regional security has the immediate responsibility of generating, together with other factors, a situation of stability. In the long run, it can contribute to reducing the basic causes of conflict in the hemisphere without affecting the legitimate security interests of any member of the system.

NOTES

1. This is, for example, the approach taken by both Morgenthau and Kissinger. See Hans Morgenthau, *Politics among Nations* (New York: Knopf, 1954), and Henry Kissinger, *The White House Years* (Boston: Little, Brown, 1979).

2. Definition of the author, based on "América del Sur: La Necesidad de un Equilibrio Estratégico," in A. Toro and A. Varas, eds., *La Situación Estratégica Latinoamericana: Crisis y Oportunidades* (Santiago, Chile: Institute of International Studies, 1992).

3. Although considered in the study of political science, it is in international relations that the concept of the balance of power has played a more significant role. Throughout history the desire of some states to attain a leadership position (a concrete manifestation of their relative power) and of others to resist has generated the conditions for multiple strategic balance situations, both in the military as well as in the broader arena of political equilibrium—for example, the situation in Europe, following the Congress of Vienna.

4. One example is the perception that existed in Great Britain during the 1920s that the United States could pose the biggest threat to its national interest by possibly attempting to conquer its colonies in the Caribbean.

5. Definition based on that of Mearsheimer. See John J. Mearsheimer, *Conventional Deterrence* (Ithaca: Cornell University Press, 1983), especially the introduction.

6. This idea and the competition model are both from Morgenthau, *Politics among Nations*, part 4. The multiple equilibrium system thesis is the author's.

7. Between 1825 and 1828 Brazil fought against the United Provinces of Río de la Plata. Peru and Colombia squared off in 1828–29. Chile, with some help from Argentina, confronted the Peruvian-Bolivian Confederation in 1836 and in 1839.

The Guerra Grande involved Uruguay, the Argentine Confederation, Brazil, and factions from within those same countries. Between 1865 and 1870, Paraguay fought against Brazil, Argentina, and Uruguay. Chile faced Peru and Bolivia in the War of the Pacific from 1879 until 1884. This list is taken, with some modifications, from a compilation in Robert N. Burr, *By Reason or by Force: Chile and the Balancing of Power in South America, 1830–1905* (Berkeley: University of California Press, 1965).

8. Amid many examples, see the text of the Treaty of 1856, which was among Chile, Ecuador, and Peru.

9. As in the case of the Hemispheric Congress of Mexico in 1840.

10. There are exceptions. The position taken by Chilean President Anibal Pinto in 1879 is one example from this period of time.

11. An idea similar to that expressed by Burr. See Burr, *By Reason.*

12. In this respect, see, for example, statements made by then minister of defense Patricio Rojas and the commander in chief of the Chilean air force, General Ramón Vega, with respect to the decision to acquire the Mirage 5 airplane (referred to as Elkan by the Chilean services) to replace the H. Hunter airplanes at the beginning of 1994. Both repeatedly insisted that the acquisition "would not alter the strategic balance in the region."

13. South America's participation in this arms race had, at least at the start, some elements of farce. The ships ordered by Brazil surpassed those of the British. The Argentineans built similar ships in response to the Brazilian buildup. Yet, the Chilean ships enjoyed absolute technical supremacy. There was, for a few years, the illusion of being able to match the great powers. However, only five of the more than 120 battleships built between 1905 and 1946 were South American, which clearly shows the inability of the countries in the region to compete globally.

14. Robert Scheina, *Latin America, A Naval History 1810–1987* (Annapolis, Md.: Naval Institute Press, 1987), chaps. 3 and 5 especially.

15. In relation to this material see E. Meneses and M. Navarro, *Política de Defensa: El Caso de la Adquisición de Sistemas de Armas,* Centro de Estudios del Desarrollo Working Paper no. 161 (Santiago, 1989).

16. An excellent study on this theme is C. F. José Maldifassi, *Análisis comparativo de las inversiones en defensa en latinoamérica* (Universidad Marítima de Chile). This was presented by the author at the First Ibero-American Political Science Congress, Santiago, 1993.

17. United Nations Department for Disarmament Affairs, *Confidence and Security-Building Measures: From Europe to Other Regions,* Topical Papers 7 (New York: United Nations, 1991).

18. The *O'Higgins* and *Chacabuco* corvettes, under construction in England at the beginning of the War with Spain, were seized by England until the cessation of hostilities. A similar situation occurred with Spanish ships also under construction in Great Britain. Chile was anxious to take delivery of its ships, and in order for it to do so, Chilean and Spanish agents cooperated in London, even during the conflict. These efforts were hampered by Peruvian agents who officially declared that a state

of war existed between their country and Chile, even though exactly the opposite was true. In fact, an alliance had been forged between the two countries precisely to face the Spanish threat. The incident gave rise to a noticeable deterioration in bilateral relations. Peru alleged "treason" by Chile, and Chile accused Peru of "hostility" in bilateral relations.

19. Burr, *By Reason.*

20. This is related to the costs of modernizing the army, a process initiated during the Balmaceda presidency. German instructors were hired (who joined the Congressional forces during the Civil War) and the War Academy was opened for training officers. In the technical arena, modernization included new German artillery, increases and improvements in the stockpiles of infantry portable weapons, and signaling elements.

21. For more on this topic, see, for example, Miguel Navarro, "Puntos de Acuerdo para una Política de Defensa de Consenso," *Revista Sociedad y Fuerzas Armadas* 1 (1989).

22. See, for example, the proposal made by the Liberty Institute in July 1995, in which strategic balance is directly referred to as a goal that should shape Chilean defense policy.

23. Among many works, see, for example, Boris Yopo, "La Concertación Política en América Latina: De Contadora al Grupo de Río." Working Paper, Programa de Seguimiento de las Politicas Exteriores Latinoamericanas (PROSPEL), Santiago, 1991.

CHAPTER THREE

STRATEGIC BALANCE, BRAZIL, AND WESTERN HEMISPHERIC SECURITY

THOMAZ GUEDES DA COSTA

This chapter presents a view of Brazil's strategic dynamics and interactions in the post–Cold War period and regards them in light of the traditional paradigm for international security in the Western Hemisphere as well as current proposals for change. It argues that Brazil's policy formulation regarding international security and national defense takes advantage of new opportunities to promote its national interests and includes preventive features designed to hedge against eventual unfavorable post–Cold War power struggles. A new hemispheric security regime based on confidence building measures or on arguments for the need to sustain strategic and military balances regionally is not well received by current Brazilian strategic thinkers; rather, those sectors that define the country's strategic outlook prefer a new framework for regional security that will follow an evolutionary process and respect the traditional values of classical realism even in times of globalization and regional integration.[1]

EXTERNAL UNCERTAINTIES

Brazilians were and still are disquieted by the events that precipitated the end of the Soviet Union and the dissipation of the East-West ideological

The author is a researcher at the National Council for Scientific and Technological Development in the Office of the Presidency, Brasília, Brazil. The opinions presented in this chapter may not necessarily reflect those officially espoused by the Brazilian government.

struggle, and new forms of confrontation and local tensions have developed along with economic and cultural globalization. The impact of the external events was magnified by Brazil's own effort to further open up the country to the international economy after 1990. For almost sixty years Brazil aspired to become a world power through an autarkic, nationalist, and centrally planned economic and political regime; with the failure of this model in the nineties, changes are under way. In the democratic regime under the Constitution of 1988, with neoliberal economic measures and efforts to modernize and to make the public sector more efficient, a new policymaking environment has been shaped. This new framework has had significant impact not just on internal policies but also on Brazil's interests in and attitudes toward regional and global systems.

In this context, Brazil's traditional political elite and new political actors perceive that the international system and their own political regime are suffering profound changes. Brazilians view with interest and uncertainty the rearrangements regarding the potential new configurations of world power as they watch the shock of integration and fragmentation.[2] As a consequence, public policy related to foreign affairs is tentative, with straightaways and detours, slow turns and accelerations. This produces ambivalence in the international scene about Brazil's behavior, causing many of its partners to be confused: at times they are optimistic and satisfied; at other times they are pessimistic and unhappy with Brazil's behavior.[3]

INTERNAL UNCERTAINTIES

To understand Brazil's attitudes towards hemispheric security, attention must be paid to the significant internal shifts that took place recently. The Brazilian political agenda grew enormously in the last ten years as the market for political ideas and demands expanded under the democratic regime. In a context full of contradictions, it is difficult for Brazil to produce a new national project that is internally consensual and effective and externally able to signal its decisions with precision and accuracy. If one understands strategy as a conceptual synthesis for unity and direction in decision-making, across all functions of an autonomous political entity and in an interactive environment with risks and opportunities, it is difficult to determine accurately Brazil's proposals for its future. The changes resulting from the adoption of a democratic regime instituted new power structures and introduced more transparent and competitive decision-making processes.

The new constitution transferred to the national congress the power to balance, and in many instances overcome, the prerogatives of the executive and the judiciary branches. The new political market, open to the new forces of nongovernmental pressure groups, conflicts with the formulation of public policy based on a bargaining process within a weak party system with fragile coalitions and charismatic personalities. With new actors and rules in a new political game, the decision-making and implementing processes became competitive and, by nature, unpredictable in the absence of a stable and homogenous set of national values and objectives.

The transparency of the political regime established a redistribution of responsibility among elected authorities and bureaucrats. The bargaining process opened the state to competition, changing the state's capacity to allocate financial resources, regulate markets, provide information, and respond to public demands. Government officials and bureaucrats could no longer deny responsibility for their actions, undertake covert operations, or exempt themselves from legal proceedings as they had in the past. The notion of full accountability to the legislative and judiciary powers, as well as to periodic elections, imposed greater transparency and ethical behavior. In this new democratic environment, both foreign policy and defense policy began to come under public scrutiny, with increased questioning of assumptions, objectives, and implementation strategies.

Brazil's transition to democracy created a general acceptance of constitutional order, of legal and administrative procedures, and of a new pattern of interaction between the armed forces and society. Constitutional controls are in effect under the president as commander-in-chief. Professionalization and strict criteria for career paths have eliminated the potential for *personalismo* (politics based on personal relations and favors) and militancy in the ranks of the armed forces. In addition, technical and bureaucratic budgetary measures have imposed legal limits on routine management, further reducing the autonomy of the military regarding its own expenditures. Thus, any problems with salaries, benefits, or operational funding have become insufficient conditions in and of themselves to legitimize or to justify direct intervention of the armed forces in government.

The presidency of Fernando Henrique Cardoso has stimulated the revival and refinement of concepts for Brazil's international behavior. His fame as an academic thinker in the field of international relations (he is best known for developing dependency theory), his experience in the Senate, and his past appointments as minister of foreign relations and minister of economy under Itamar Franco created space for reflection on international affairs, both in government and in the private sector. Now, such labels as "strategic insertion," "global actor," "regional integration," "hemispheric integration," "strategic partnership," and so forth must be used with care by those formulating Brazil's foreign policy, because the government is now in the hands of a president who is interested in and qualified to deal with these subjects. As to the matter of posing Brazil's international overture with strategic interactions, the president himself announced in his inaugural address that Brazilians were clamoring for work that would build the country to meet its "strategic stature." Thus, the introduction of a personality such as Cardoso caused strategists to reflect on this cornerstone of Brazil's new profile in the post–Cold War world.

Acceptance by Brazilian society of the new constitutional framework does not by itself produce complete tranquillity in national politics. A broad definition of "security" includes dealing with socioeconomic difficulties and the political problems related to income distribution, job creation, and living in a competitive market. Internal tension, both in urban and rural areas, generated by the inability of the economy to meet basic demands results in a sense of uneasiness and insecurity. This outcome can be regarded as a consequence of mismanagement of public policies or inefficient allocation of scarce resources, problems that are initially being fought with reducing inflation and public spending and proceeding with the painful macroeconomic adjustment.

Amid these economic difficulties and new prospects in transnational economic relations, there is a clear preference among government authorities and elected officials to avoid considering socioeconomic difficulties as a matter of national security. Thus, social problems no longer correlate to the former arguments that certain measures were necessary as an urgent matter of national security. By the same token, no one argues that transnational problems caused by the globalization of the economy or social relations are matters of "hemispheric security," as was also seen in the past. However, one still finds those who consider whatever the government does a matter of "national security." These proponents also argue that the need for a central, planned economy is the only *rationale* for economic and social development. Yet the pluralistic political market in Brazil—recalling the consequences of this model in the past, when results had to measure up against the winds of ideological confrontation and of political repression—does not accept state intervention as the only valid and legitimate solution to social and economic problems. Therefore, cherishing new values and attitudes side-by-side with holdover structures from the past creates a sense of confusion as to how to conduct political decisions and manage the country. As Brazilian authorities and public officials call on the country to mobilize resources to reduce social problems, these problems are seen to be of a different nature than those that they would consider matters of "national security," in the terms of their international relations in the post–Cold War period.

This change regarding security produces uncertainty. On one hand, Brazilians are optimistic about the durability of and prospects for their new democracy. On the other hand, they are unsure about the ability of their country to deal with uncertain outcomes in the global power shift. Globalization and international integration cause apprehension and contradictory expectations about opportunities and risks in a new scenario. Regional conflicts, particularly those in the former Yugoslavia and Africa, are deeply disturbing to strategists in Brazil. One can argue strongly that collective security is selective; that the major powers are not willing to sacrifice men and materials to defend the security of certain countries, national groups, or individuals unless their own key interests are affected. Transnational interests and the articulation of policies among the major powers and their allies promote the establishment of regimes that are, sometimes, ambiguous in their operational purposes. These uncertainties must be taken into consideration when trying to understand Brazilian post–Cold War policy formulation.

STRATEGIC BALANCE: OPERATIONAL DIFFICULTIES

Francisco Rojas Aravena suggests that a Brazilian view be offered on strategic balance and confidence building measures in the Southern Cone.[4] First, the concept of the "Southern Cone" is not useful because the term does not coincide with Brazil's external perception. Second, this geopolitical concept is weakened by the intensity, importance, and variety of extraregional interactions conducted by Chile with Bolivia, Peru, and the Pacific Basin and Argentina's disputes in the South Atlantic. Third, regarding the need to harmonize its foreign policy associated with the Río de la Plata basin with that directed toward the Amazon Basin, the concept of the "Southern Cone" is too dilute for Brazilian strategists who take a broader view of the country's perimeter. Thus, those who wish to understand Brazil's behavior within the limits of the Southern Cone should be advised against measuring up such approaches against the empirical evidence of strategic behavior.

Nonetheless, if this geopolitical concept must be used, Brazilian strategists can deal with the "Southern Cone" concept as a result of the increased circles of cooperation and integration developed in the Plata Basin since the seventies. In addition to the arrangement for the exploitation of the water resources in the Paraná River, the bilateral agreement between Brazil and Argentina, along with other multilateral agreements to prevent the proliferation of weapons of mass destruction, established the basis for a new sense of regional community. Thus, the Southern Cone aspect has been reduced in Brazil's international security scenarios. This view has also been reinforced by advancements in negotiations to end border disputes between Argentina and Chile and other initiatives to settle the controversies between Argentina and Great Britain. Although valid analytically, the concept of strategic balance does not find a direct correspondence either within Brazil's post–Cold War strategic interactions or in the most salient features of the country's defense concerns.[5]

The terms "military balance" and "balance of power" have been free of rhetoric in national debates as the political process and political agenda join to design formats for interacting with neighbors in the Río de la Plata, Amazon, and Atlantic sectors. Speeches by high government officials on defense issues do not show that a comparative logic about military forces, either quantitative or qualitative, has shaped national military forces in recent decades. There is such a disparity of national scales, geographic settings, interests, and arrangements in the hemisphere that Brazilian officials place little value on comparative notions of power.

Empirically, one finds that Brazil has not been immune to the impact of balancing acts. For example, from the sixties until the late seventies, new weapons systems were introduced in many areas of South America, including Brazil. The region saw the import of the second generation of jet fighters and navy frigates, and new electronic systems were brought aboard many arms systems in all major South American countries. Leaving aside numbers, however, the disparity of types and models, the diversity of logistic systems, the different deployment patterns, and distinct doctrinal assumptions would not indicate Brazil's arms procurement was either part of any action-reaction arms-race model or reflective of any hypothesis of war against a specific neighbor.

Brazil's recent defense policymaking does not show that arms procurement was undertaken to match purchases made by neighbors. When Venezuela bought F-16s in the eighties and Argentina bought and upgraded A-4s in the nineties, the reaction by Brazilian air force officials was only to wish for similar modernization of their equipment. Neither political authorities nor bureaucrats showed any reaction to these or similar events.

Refraining from escalation in arms procurement is matched elsewhere in more critical defense planning. The decision to abide by the Tlatelolco Treaty, the Mendoza Compromise, and the Quadripartite Agreement, subscribing to the respective conventions to ban both chemical and biological weapons and actively sponsoring the United Nations (U.N.) registry of conventional weapons, indicates that Brazilian authorities intend to refrain from an arms race and contribute to arms control, especially at the regional level.

But there is a somewhat paradoxical asymmetry: if on the one hand, Brazil sponsors confidence building through arms control, then on the other hand, some of its national projects may result in perceived unbalances in the regional picture. The development and modernization of military equipment has been carried out under the logic of preparing the military for standard mission capabilities for national defense. Yet this may pose a security dilemma. Many Brazilian strategists do not recognize that some national programs may cause, unintentionally, uncertainty among neighbors, which may have a synergetic reaction, and they argue in favor of the defensive nature of Brazil's strategy.[6] The most striking instance is the national program for the construction of nuclear-powered submarines. Historical experience continues to shape the Brazilian navy's desire for readiness against possible naval aggression from overseas. This happened during the Second World War, in 1963 in a fishing dispute with France, and in incidents in the 1970s with the United States; the navy also was deeply disturbed by the events of the Malvinas (Falklands) War in 1982. Strategists are also concerned by the large area of the South Atlantic, which is where 90 percent of Brazilian foreign trade flows from and to the country. Therefore, to provide a maritime operational capability that permits the Brazilian navy to be employed with greater efficacy in the South Atlantic, the Brazilian program has included an attack submarine for defensive purposes. However, viewed through the lens of "military balance," such an acquisition may disturb area relations, since other countries such as Argentina or South Africa may feel compelled to match Brazil's capacity.

The limitation of using "military balance" as a normative point of departure for regional evaluation of forces is further weakened by the fact that numbers and types of weapons do not reveal states of readiness or operational capacities. Although Brazil utilizes a modern system of aviation control, SINDACTA, to monitor and control its air space, both for civilian and military ends, there are signs that its armed forces are weak in terms of conventional readiness. As an example, the Brazilian army had difficulty recently preparing and deploying a fully equipped battalion for a peacekeeping mission in Angola. Although the Brazilian army has almost 200,000 men in uniform, the current equipment inventory was short and there were many financial difficulties in supplying and deploying the small force on short notice.

STRATEGIC BALANCE: PERCEPTION OF ASYMMETRIC STRATEGIES

According to Francisco Rojas Aravena, "strategic balance" should be seen as the relationship of tangible and intangible means of power between states or a coalition of states in an interaction in which the potential for the use of force is present. This concept also finds little resonance in Brazil's current strategic outlook. Brazilian officials prefer to consider relations according to different national realities, geographic dimensions and settings, interests, available resources, and opportunities and patterns of foreign relations. Viewed as a concept that drives initiatives for cooperation or conflict in the hemisphere, one does not find situations or historical events where perceived measurement of the "strategic balance" was a significant cause for action. On the contrary, peaceful relations and cooperative endeavors grew in situations where power asymmetry existed, including under conditions of international controversy. In a nutshell, the hemisphere contains microstates, emergent states, superpowers with extracontinental alliances, and small countries coexisting with common aspirations and drives for cooperation, not under a system of political solidarity based on principles and notions of common threats.

The presence of the United States in the hemispheric system causes the most significant asymmetry of power and interests in the region. The United States has interests everywhere, both in the economic and in the security fields. More salient, in the formation of perceptions, American security interests produce extracontinental coalitions—such as NATO—with ties that are many times stronger than those in the Western Hemisphere. The end of the Cold War dismantled the notion of regional unity under the common threat of Soviet expansionism and ideological influence. But the new proposals for hemispheric unity, either under the banner of a trade zone or security arrangements, are not robust enough to sustain the so-called continental solidarity of the "Spirit of Miami" (the inter-American conference in December of 1994).

Another facet of this asymmetry is the consequences of American attitudes towards national policies. For example, Brazil is one of the few Latin

American countries that is trying to establish national capabilities in advanced technologies. In a globalizing economy, the acquisition of such capabilities in scientific, technological, and industrial production increases a society's ability to compete, both in the domestic and the international markets. For decades, every Brazilian government has seen this challenge as a crucial platform for political action and planned national strategies and international partnerships to increase Brazil's technological might.

The critical part of this equation is that the search for advanced technology focuses on the capacity for "dual-use," having both civilian and military applications. This raises another political problem in terms of strategic balance. If one were to focus only on the boundaries of a region, the capacity to utilize dual-use technology can shape perceptions and political action. Thus, while respecting nonproliferation efforts and promoting increased transparency in national programs, Brazil seeks to promote technological development that will break the "apartheid" configuration that exists between those countries that have technology and those that do not and foster confidence among neighbors about the peaceful means of such technological development.

Finally, there are evident asymmetries even in subregional settings. Argentina has significant strategic interactions with the United States, Brazil, Chile, and Great Britain. Chile has Peru as an important card in its strategic behavior, as well as relationships with Argentina and Bolivia. For Brazil, relations with Argentina and the United States could be as important as those with Venezuela and Peru. Thus, to consider the Southern Cone as one strategic area does not reveal the importance of all the interests, agendas, and strategies in conducting security relations in South America, or in the hemisphere as a whole.

BRAZIL AND HEMISPHERIC SECURITY

Latin America is not exempt from problems, nor is the presence of the United States an assurance of confident interdependent relationships among countries. On the contrary, Brazilian officials, especially diplomats, are aware of the potential for conflicts and the flare-up of old disputes; the swift Brazilian diplomatic reaction in the most recent clash between Peru and Ecuador is an example. This awareness also results from national perceptions that are constructed from Brazil's own historical experience and the interpretation of events abroad.

The traditional security regime that has been the framework in the hemisphere since the end of World War II does not have the confidence of most Brazilian analysts. The end of the Cold War and the push for globalized interdependent relations further reduce the validity of using the "hemisphere" as a geopolitical concept to guide regional relations. The system has been incapable of satisfactorily solving interstate disputes. It has been unable to refrain the other states from choosing intervention from the United States, either to sustain ideological unity or to promote the unilateral interests of Washington. It has encouraged free-rider behavior in the decision-making and implementation of collective measures, since some states are assured that another will act in self-interest. Both the Inter-American Treaty for Reciprocal Assistance and the OAS have limited effectiveness when sharp confrontations are at hand, such as disputes in border areas or conflicts with extracontinental powers.

Nevertheless, Brazilian officials do not find strong justification to overhaul the security system centered by the OAS. On the contrary, or as a contradiction, Brazil has given support to resolution 1179/92, which establishes the first step for reinforcing the organization's role in regional security. There is in Brazilian decision-making circles the notion that, outside of the formal setup of the OAS and informal arrangements such as the Rio Group, little can be added with precision and efficacy at this point. In the overall post–Cold War setting, the main paradigm has become the U.N. In the U.N., Brazil has become active in peacekeeping, reform of the Charter, initiatives on arms control, and debates about reform of the Security Council.

Brazilians in general consider the hemisphere to be a peaceful environment, without extracontinental threats and with a plurality working for economic integration in a system of building blocks. Brazil's foreign policy measures must be tuned to avoid isolating neighbors or excluding states from regional politics, both in bilateral interactions and in multilateral initiatives. In some cases, when democratic ruling came under threat in neighboring countries, Brazil reacted forcefully; but Brazilian officials do not accept policies of foreign intervention, of changing the political culture from outside. They prefer to support political democratic evolution by arguing for policies of national conciliation. Examples of this posture can be seen in the recent developments in Peru and Paraguay, when both countries suffered political shifts and followed difficult roads in search of their own democracies.

Between Brazil and the United States there is a complex net of interests— commercial, financial, technological, and cultural—that produces a diversity of contacts. These ties are so intense that they become ambiguous in the conduct of normal relations. Brazil does not want to accept the U.S. presence in the hemisphere only in hegemonic terms, or for it to be translated into a preferential arrangement with a neighbor to the south. Most Brazilian strategists recognize the legitimacy of the United States' defense of its interests, including the establishment of an economic zone to protect American competitiveness. But this presence also raises concerns as it clashes with some of Brazil's own aspirations to be influential in the region and to defend its own interests.

Military relations between Brazil and the United States are broad and cordial, but they do not show the same closeness as during the alliance in World War II, nor the cooperation that characterized the fifties. Brazil has strong bilateral military relations with Great Britain, France, Italy, Germany, and Argentina. While Washington desires to retain some control of Brazil's military relations, Brazilians prefer to take advantage of the multiplicity of opportunities and see their relation with the United States as one in a wide menu of choices. Thus, like any other country in the region, Brazil uses its relations with Washington, moving closer or away as necessity demands.

SOME PARAMETERS IN BRAZIL'S STRATEGIC OUTLOOK

In the absence of a unified national project to promote interests and clearly define preferential strategies, the government is trying to establish a new design for Brazil's need to cope with globalization. So far, the new strategic proposal is an agglutination of ideas and interests, capabilities and new developments that can find broad support from the elite and pressure groups. It must coordinate decisions with proposals for internal reforms, new allocations of resources with the power shift, and internal development of the opening of Brazil to the world. In terms of international security and national defense, it has six features.

First is the preservation of territorial integrity, of national unity, and of the assets of Brazilian society. These principles are closely related to cherishing the notion of sovereignty and to strong opposition to foreign intervention in the internal affairs of the country. In the eyes of Brazilian strategists, collective security mechanisms are weak and the actions of the hegemonic powers and their allies are selective and discriminatory. They do not recommend that Brazil's security rely only on these mechanisms. Preserving Brazil's sovereignty in the Amazon Basin is especially important.

Since the exploration of the region is often the object of foreign criticism, the Brazilian government is stepping up measures to conduct sustainable development with a strong state presence in the area. As the government has to confront increasing illegal cross-border activities, the presence of the army has been increased and a new program for the monitoring and control of the region has been established.

Second, the problems of national development, economic stabilization, redistribution of wealth, and helping the poorer segments of the population are more important than issues of national defense. Thus, political attention and financial resources are directed primarily to social and economic functions. But this does not translate into lack of planning for contingencies. The uncertainties in the international scene demand military preparation; for that, a new effort to define objectives for national defense is under way.

Third is the strengthening of MERCOSUR, of the Treaty for Cooperation in the Amazon, and of the South Atlantic Zone for Peace and Cooperation. The search for strong ties in economic coordination and political consultation is taken both for mutual material benefit and to provide greater possibility for regional tranquillity.

Fourth, Brazil is a traditional defender of the regional status quo and expects that regional disputes can be solved under negotiated agreements, with the U.N. acting as the main vehicle to articulate this. Brazilian authorities, within the strict limits of budgetary flexibility, are committing themselves to increase the country's participation in peacekeeping. In addition, Brazil sees the channels of the OAS as a still viable means for articulating regional solutions to problems and as the best forum to promote regional confidence building measures.

Fifth, Brazil is keen to keep open a wide number of potential partners in the Americas and on other continents. Many initiatives have increased military exchanges, technological ties, and political articulation with countries such as Great Britain, Germany, France, Russia, Japan, and the People's Republic of China. Brazilian officials want to make Brazil more than a global trader; they want to make it a global actor, influential in world politics and able to create partnerships with many countries, including those that have an impact on the country's preparedness for national defense.

Finally, Brazil argues that arms control must include efforts both for the nonproliferation of weapons of mass destruction and for disarmament. The idea of an international system in which a small number of countries will retain nuclear or chemical weapons for political use, either as deterrents or as a final reserve for their respective security, is disturbing to Brazilians. In such a scenario, the security dilemma may force others in critical situations to move into acquiring weapons of mass destruction, tilting stability and threatening peace.

NOTES

1. See Gleuber Vieira, "La variable estratégica en el processo de constitución del Mercosur," *SER en el año 2000* 5 (1994): 10–11; Mônica Hirst and Letícia Pinheiro, "A política externa do Brasil em dois tempos," *Revista Brasileira de Política Internacional* (Brasília) 38, no. 1 (1995): 14–16; President Fernando Henrique Cardoso, "Discurso para os formandos do Instituto Rio Branco," *O Estado de São Paulo* (April 29, 1995): 4; Ambassador Ronaldo Mota Sardenberg, "Política de Defensa," speech to the Escola de Defensa Nacional da Argentina, August 22, 1995.

2. For debates such as these, see David Skidmore, "Teaching about the Post–Cold War World: Four Future Scenarios," *ISA Teaching Notes* 20, no. 1 (Winter 1995): 1–8; James N. Rosenau, *Turbulence in World Politics* (Princeton: Princeton University Press, 1995): 443–61.

3. Carlos Escudé and Andrés Fontana, "Divergencias estratégicas en el Cono Sur: Las políticas de seguridad de la Argentina frente a las del Brasil y Chile," *Working Papers,* 20 (Buenos Aires: Universidad Torcuato di Tella, 1995), 26–29.

4. Francisco Rojas, "Medidas de Confianza Mútua y Balance Estratégico en el Hemisfério Occidental," photocopy, June 1995.

5. Thomaz Guedes da Costa, "A Idéia de Medidas de Confiança Mútua (CBMs) em uma Visão Brasileira," *Contexto Internacional* (Rio de Janeiro) 14, no. 2 (December 1992): 297–321.

6. On the subject of naval power in Brazil, see Armando A. F. Vidigal, "Uma nova concepção estratégica para o Brasil: Um debate necessário," *Política e Estratégia* (September 1989): 317–19; Mário César Flores, *Bases para uma política militar* (Campinas: Editora da UNICAMP, 1992), 127.

CHAPTER FOUR

A United States View
of Strategic Balance
in the Americas

JOHN A. COPE

The balance of national power among neighboring Latin American and Caribbean states or between subregions of the hemisphere receives minimum attention in U.S. foreign and security policy circles. While Washington routinely assesses the relative merits of the strengths and weaknesses of American states, the intent usually is to try to ascertain the significance for U.S. regional interests rather than to make geostrategic comparisons. After all, the United States faces no potential ideological or military threat to its territory from the south, and the various inequalities among its neighbors are hardly new issues. The question of how the United States views strategic balance in the Americas cannot be answered simply, directly, or definitively.

One issue can capture Washington's passing interest in strategic balance, especially if the country involved has an active boundary dispute—U.S. arms transfers. But even with the sale of lethal weapons or weapons systems, there is a tendency to focus only on how the transfer relates to U.S. policy objectives and to pay little attention to the concerns of the subregion or the Latin American recipients' interests or priorities. The Reagan administration, for example, provided military assistance worth millions of dollars to El Salvador during the 1980s, with minimum regard for the imbalance being created in Central America. At almost the same time, the United States worried that the sale of a particular type of fighter aircraft would change the military status quo (not the strategic balance) in the Southern

Cone. It should be noted that, in practice, arms transfer decisions often turn on such other nonstrategic considerations as the sale's assumed interference with the recipients' national, political, and economic development; the parochial interests of important U.S. allies outside the region (e.g., the United Kingdom, Israel); and the possibility of U.S. Congressional involvement. In sum, even decisions on the transfer of arms to neighboring countries do not provide a sound basis for understanding how Latin American strategic equilibrium is seen from the United States.

Another way to provide a more insightful look at strategic balance in Latin America and the Caribbean is to explore the U.S. strategic approach to the region today. By examining how Washington places the hemisphere into its own global interests and commitments and how the United States pursues its security objectives in its own neighborhood, it may become more apparent how the United States sees the balance of power in the region.

INFLUENCES SHAPING U.S. REGIONAL STRATEGY

Before examining Washington's strategic approach to the Americas, four contextual points need emphasis. First, the U.S. government's principal strategic documents present an image of global commitment and a perception of equivalency among major regions of the world. President Clinton's *National Security Strategy of Engagement and Enlargement*, the Chairman of the Joint Chiefs of Staff's *National Military Strategy*, and the Secretary of Defense's *Annual Report to the President and the Congress* introduce three broad, mutually supportive policy ends—U.S. security (in a diplomatic and military sense), economic prosperity at home, and the promotion of democracy overseas—and explain how they have been adapted to the unique challenges and opportunities in each region.[1] No attempt is made to prioritize regions or countries within them. All are considered to have importance for the United States. The documents convey the sense that when the United States is engaged with any nation to preserve peace and promote democratic values, the outcome is far more beneficial to mutual and international interests than when the United States is not engaged. In practice, however, engagement is selective and concentrates less on opportunities than on challenges which are relevant to U.S. interests. Washington wants to focus government resources where they can make the most difference.

Second, domestic considerations tend to take precedence over and greatly affect how Washington interprets and deals with events outside the United

States. This often makes the line between international and domestic policy hard to define, as the Clinton administration has found with NAFTA's implementation and other economic matters. The Western Hemisphere presents a unique problem. The U.S. policy community confronts the widest array of advocacy groups and lobbies, in addition to domestic political organizations, devoted to many regions and their issues. Their primary target, Congress, also has successfully challenged the executive branch on inter-American policy many times over the last twenty years and now strictly oversees how U.S. resources are used anywhere in the hemisphere.

Third, for the United States there is no consideration of balance in its relationship with the rest of the hemisphere. Equilibrium disappeared in the latter half of the 1900s, although the total dimensions of the U.S. advantage did not become apparent until early this century. The imposing presence of the United States has found its way into the economic, political, cultural, and security lives of neighboring countries throughout the Americas. From the dollar's easy negotiability to democratic values, the world of Disney, and a nuclear umbrella, the unilateral power of the United States and its sometimes patronizing nature remain a reality for the foreseeable future. In no area of statecraft has the mismatch been more pronounced than with the military instruments of power.

As a result, finally, the United States traditionally has seen the region as a strategic zone where it could economize resources and still secure the continental United States. Washington has rarely made large expenditures to protect or promote its interests in the Americas, although military forces have had to secure them in the Caribbean Basin more than twenty times this century. The Defense Department's average contribution to the U.S. economy-of-force strategy in the hemisphere over the last decade has amounted to approximately 1 percent of the annual defense budget.

VIEWING THE HEMISPHERE IN A GLOBAL CONTEXT

The attractive idea of a distinct and superior Western Hemisphere apart from the rest of the world reached its apex between 1936 and 1940. As democracies nearly everywhere in Europe failed under increasing diplomatic and military pressure, many Americans, both North and South, came to view their own neighborhood as a peaceful and seemingly secure oasis away from the turmoil of the Old World and were attracted by the idea of a Pan-American political system. No one has described the evolution and ultimate demise of this important concept more effectively than Arthur

Whitaker in his seminal work, *The Western Hemisphere Idea* (Ithaca: Cornell University Press, 1954). Whitaker argued that the "hemisphere idea" was inseparable from another American tradition, that of isolationism, and that both lost their influence in mainstream U.S. thought as the inevitability of U.S. intervention overseas became a reality on the eve of the Second World War. With President Roosevelt's mid-1940 decision to commit the United States to Great Britain's defense with an undeclared, but nonetheless real, war against Germany, Washington committed itself irrevocably to maintaining a globalist perspective.

Since then the government of the United States has often tried to define Latin America's role in its worldwide strategic framework. From today's vantage point, the determinations made by U.S. leaders over the last fifty-five years have moved in a cycle, passing from successful multilateral cooperation during World War II through a series of strained feudal Cold War relationships, when the United States almost lost meaningful contact with the region, to post–Cold War regional partnerships in an environment marked by fundamental shifts in Latin American thinking about economic policy, constitutional democracy, and relations with the United States.

The Latin American and Caribbean experience during the Second World War attests to the fact that the inter-American region has a place in Washington's worldview. Although there were no great battles and only minor naval skirmishes (against German submarines), the U.S. Army's Center for Military History concludes that the military and economic (logistical) campaigns in the American theater were in a sense the most important of the entire war.[2] American states helped defend the hemisphere from external attack and contributed raw materials, industrial goods, and even military units (Mexican and Brazilian) to sustain the "arsenal of democracy," thereby providing a solid foundation for Allied victory. Secure at home, the United States was able to build armed forces capable of global action and developed, manufactured, and distributed modern weapons to equip both these forces and those of many of America's allies. The wartime experience demonstrates that only by being anchored economically and militarily in its own geohistoric neighborhood could the United States develop the capabilities needed to pursue shared global interests.[3]

As the Cold War's two-world concept took shape in the late 1940s and 1950s, both the Truman and Eisenhower administrations defined the Americas' role—in so many words—as a vassal in a subordinate relationship to a lord. The immediate neighborhood was one of several geostrategic areas in the free world to be protected by tenants under arms against communist encroachment. Both administrations assisted governments seeking to quell revolutionary movements that were deemed to be communist-inspired. The United States initially provided a bargain-basement shortcut to military modernization with its World War II and Korean War stocks of inexpensive but reliable arms and a wide range of associated military equipment. In the 1960s, the U.S. concept of security assistance expanded to address the social and economic sources of unrest in the hemisphere, in large part through the Alliance for Progress.

To facilitate planning for Cold War exigencies and to manage the conduct of routine military-to-military contacts, the Joint Chiefs of Staff divided the Western Hemisphere into three areas and assigned them to responsible military headquarters: U.S. Southern Command, located in Panama, focused on Central and South America; U.S. Atlantic Command, established in Norfolk, Virginia, included the Caribbean islands and the surrounding Atlantic and Pacific Oceans with its NATO duties; and the Joint Chiefs of Staff itself retained Mexico and Canada (a NATO partner) as two unassigned areas of responsibility. This basic arrangement still exists in the mid-1990s, although the boundaries between Southern Command and Atlantic Command are changing.[4]

Between 1960 and 1990, Castroism and the Cuban challenge to U.S. power caused a redefinition of Latin America's role in the U.S. global strategic framework. The region became a theater of operations in the Cold War, and Washington launched a campaign to contain the influence of Moscow's surrogate to its own neighborhood and prevent a "second Cuba" from occurring. The Nixon administration recognized that the U.S. ability to meet Soviet challenges was weakening due to global overcommitment and focused on Brazil as the "intermediate" power in the region—"as Brazil goes, so goes Latin America." The region meanwhile began to express its independence of and hostility towards the United States. During the tempestuous 1970s, the United States almost lost touch with the inter-American states as its policy shifted from support for authoritarian regimes to a focus that one historian best describes as a "mix of high principle, human compassion, belief in negotiation, and a reluctance to intervene in leftist revolutions."[5]

During the Reagan and Bush years, U.S. efforts to formulate an appropriate strategic vision experienced a transition that included the hemisphere in Washington's worldview. The initial focus in the early 1980s was on meeting the communist challenge head-on in the Caribbean Basin. The region was still a theater of operations in the Cold War. As the United States engaged revolutionary movements in different ways in El Salvador, Granada, Nicaragua, and several South American countries, Washington's geostrategic thinking evolved toward a renewed interest in democracy and market economics. The first step was the Caribbean Basin Initiative, a comprehensive trade and aid strategy that did not have a military component. At the end of the decade, as the Soviet Union collapsed and Cuba's significance for U.S. and hemisphere security altered dramatically, the Enterprise for the Americas Initiative followed the Caribbean Basin Initiative.[6] From this important and desirable economic innovation emerged NAFTA, implemented in January 1995. Almost a year later, President Clinton hosted a Summit of the Americas in Miami to celebrate a multifaceted "new movement" in the hemisphere and initiate what hopefully will be a sustained era of close hemispheric cooperation on a wide range of political, economic, and social issues and the creation of a Free Trade Area of the Americas by the year 2005.

In having to confront the shifting geopolitical and geoeconomic realities of the post–Cold War era, the United States approaches the rest of the hemisphere again, but in a sense it does so for the very first time. The hegemonic and confrontational character of Washington's past relationship with the Americas has moderated remarkably over the last ten years. Many Latin American and U.S. academic analysts and policy practitioners consider recent trends to be unprecedented. In Abraham Lowenthal's view there is "greater political and economic homogeneity across the Americas than ever before. Latin American leaders are more disposed than formerly toward harmonious relations with Washington, and the United States has greater reasons than heretofore to invest in building a regional community."[7] There has been a move toward order throughout the hemisphere with the adoption of confidence and security building measures by many governments. International organizations and treaty guarantors also have been successful in helping nations resolve long-standing boundary issues and improve local peace and security. In this hopeful milieu, the diplomat-scholar Luigi Einaudi may be correct when he observed that "NAFTA may turn out to be a first step toward a re-anchoring of the United States in its own geohistoric region. Certainly it is not since Franklin Delano Roosevelt and the policy of the Good Neighbor that the United States has moved so explicitly to strengthen its moorings in its immediate neighborhood."[8]

VIEWING THE HEMISPHERE IN A FUTURE GLOBAL CONTEXT

As the "winner" of the Cold War, the United States is the only genuinely global power today. The significance of this fact for the Americas, in Einaudi's view, is that "the United States is the only country in the world that sees itself as in some sense part of every region, from Europe and the Middle East, from Asia to Africa as well as the Western Hemisphere."[9] The ongoing, heated debate in the United States and in several European countries, for example, is about defining the appropriate role for the United States in the former Yugoslavia's crisis, rather than whether or not the United States has one. Latin American and Caribbean leaders should realize that Washington is going to continue to place its global interests ahead of purely regional ones and that, from a U.S. perspective, the American region will still be defined in this context.

A sense of global commitment pervades the U.S. government's strategic documents. In his February 1995 document *A National Security Strategy of Engagement and Enlargement,* President Clinton states: "Our national security strategy is based on enlarging the community of market democracies while deterring and containing a range of threats to our nation, our allies, and our interests."[10] Secretary of Defense Perry is more direct in his recent *Annual Report to the President and the Congress:* "These past few years have changed the security equation around the world, but one fundamental fact has not changed. The United States will remain a global power with global interests."[11] General Shalikashvili, Chairman of the Joint Chiefs of Staff, observes in *National Military Strategy* that there is "ample historical precedent in this century that regional instability in military, economic, and political terms can escalate into global conflict. Our strategy further promotes stability in order to establish the conditions under which democracy can take hold and expand around the world. We intend to use the daily, peacetime activities of the Armed Forces to pursue this effort."[12]

"Global changes have undoubtedly complicated the conceiving and conducting of U.S. foreign policy," writes respected national security analyst Richard Haass. "Ours is a period of 'international deregulation,' one in which there are new players, new capabilities, and new alignments—but, as yet, no new rules."[13] To further and protect its wide-ranging interests in this environment, the United States has had to engage not only established international actors, but also many emerging and nongovernmental players. This trend also stems from political anxieties at home. Global uncertainty and diminishing resources have caused a pervasive sense that national energies should be focused on meeting domestic needs. In many ways today's security threats and apprehensions, while often serious, do not endanger national survival but encourage a growing isolationist sentiment. Washington must move deliberately in the international arena, do so with partners, and prioritize or otherwise limit its efforts worldwide. Still, U.S. leadership continues to be sought: in the effort on behalf of NAFTA; in the conduct of diplomacy affecting the Middle East, Northern Ireland, and North Korea; and in persuading the NATO allies to support a cooperative approach toward the former Soviet Union and other former Warsaw Pact members. Since the end of Operation Desert Storm in February 1991 and the beginning of Operation Vigilant Warrior in Kuwait in October 1994, the U.S. military has participated in twenty-seven bilateral and multilateral (U.N., NATO, etc.) operations in eighteen countries. In the years ahead, global interdependence seems to guarantee that Washington will receive limitless calls for U.S. involvement overseas.

The United States neither has boundless resources nor can or should respond to every crisis and conflict. However, Washington is convinced that, to the extent that democracy and market economics hold sway in other nations, both the United States and collegial states will be more secure, prosperous, and influential, while the world as a whole will be more humane and peaceful. The United States is looking for like-minded countries with which to collaborate in engaging today's global problems. There are only two basic criteria: countries must be willing to break long-standing isolationist bonds as the United States did at the beginning of World War II and they must accept and institutionalize international standards of conduct and accountability in areas such as trade, nonproliferation of weapons of mass destruction, protection of the environment, and respect for human rights. In Washington's view, the emerging role for inter-American states in the new U.S. strategic framework is to be an engaged partner, within national capabilities, and to meet as well as help enforce international standards.

Given the importance of globalism to the United States, and its need for assistance, when a government is willing to institute policy reforms and assume an international role beyond international trade and investment, bilateral relations with the United States tend to improve. This trend is a matter of human nature rather than stated official policy. Secretary Perry, however, in a section of his annual report devoted to Latin America, does go so far as to suggest several ways in which hemispheric neighbors can share commitment elsewhere in the world. His proposals include the provision of national forces for military contingencies, support for international development and democratization, personnel or money for U.N. peace operations, and cost-sharing for U.S. deployments.[14] Many governments in the region have responded by contributing to U.N. and OAS peace operations either within or outside the hemisphere.

Argentina has shown the greatest regional commitment to globalism. The Menem administration recognizes that Argentine interests for the foreseeable future lie well beyond its borders and has initiated several forms of "overseas" engagement. As a result, relations between Washington and Buenos Aires are developing in unprecedented ways for the region. There are now strategic talks at the highest diplomatic and defense levels, regular meetings of bilateral defense and joint staff working groups, and many forms of routine interaction—all of which has significantly increased the visibility of Buenos Aires in Washington's consciousness. Similar relationships with Brazil and Chile are in early stages of development.

VIEWING THE HEMISPHERE IN ITS OWN CONTEXT

At the 1995 Summit of the Americas, President Clinton set forth the long-term strategic goal of the United States in Latin America and the Caribbean as fostering a hemisphere of democratic nations with capable, efficient governments and vibrant societies, with open, dynamic economies providing rising living standards to their peoples, and with expanding export markets for U.S. products and services. Few people would disagree with the administration's goal, but many U.S., Latin American, and Caribbean analysts would agree with Abraham Lowenthal, who believes that "the future of inter-American relations will not clarify until the United States is more truly set on a decided course [toward this goal], after a decade of drift."[15] The difference between the president's national security strategy and the Secretary of Defense's annual report in how the United States should approach the Americas suggests that Lowenthal's criticism is still valid. Both documents only establish U.S. policy objectives which, if realized, will lead to the attainment of the president's long-term strategic goal. No strategic concept emerges that would guide efforts to achieve the broad aims established for the hemisphere.

A look at the two documents reveals that the president's security strategy states that the "overarching objective" is to preserve and defend civilian-elected governments and strengthen democratic practices respectful of human rights. Four additional aims are mentioned briefly: invigorate regional cooperation (including the OAS); eliminate the scourge of drug trafficking; seek to strengthen norms for defense establishments; and protect environmental resources.[16] In the Defense Department's more traditional approach, there are two "overarching objectives": to sustain regional stability and increase regional cooperation. Success in these two areas is expected to help ensure that recent strides in democracy, free markets, sustainable development, counterdrugs, and national reconciliation continue and that further progress can be made.[17] Neither document provides a sense of how the United States sees the strategic and military balance among neighboring countries or subregions. The message to the neighborhood is that every country is important to the United States, and the United States sees its own role as important to every country. In practice, however, this has not been the case.

Historically, U.S. security interests separate the region geographically into three areas: Canada, which, until NAFTA, was thought of only in terms of Europe (NATO); the entire Caribbean Basin, which often is the source of U.S. foreign policy and domestic concerns; and the remainder of South America, with which the United States has had less contact until recently. During the Cold War, Washington focused most on countries in the Caribbean Basin. Strategic priorities included protecting access to and transit across the region, with unrestricted use of the Panama Canal; maintaining a small military presence at several bases in the Caribbean; preserving the ability to obtain essential raw materials, particularly bauxite and petroleum; and achieving solidarity within the region for U.S. positions in international forums. Intertwined with these interests has been an unstated but important aim with roots dating back to the 1823 Monroe Doctrine: ensure that the inter-American region remains secure and friendly for a U.S. commercial and military presence, power, movement, and access to facilities. In the past, this aim has entailed using diplomacy and, occasionally, military force to keep rival powers from challenging U.S. influence and its ability to keep neighborhood events from getting out of control.[18]

The hemisphere in the mid-1990s is important to the United States for a different set of reasons. The traditional strategic interests have now become secondary. The Caribbean Basin still commands the U.S. public's attention and delimits the scope of Washington's interest in the inter-American region; the United States, after all, is a Caribbean state. A short list of today's strategic interests begins with the economic imperative—particularly markets for U.S. exports and investment in neighboring states; oil from Venezuela (the largest U.S. supplier of refined product in the world), Mexico, and, increasingly, Colombia—and unrestricted paths of commerce, many of which still travel through Panama, where the retention of a reduced U.S. military presence after the Panama Canal Treaty is implemented remains an option. The list also includes the promotion of democracy, the control of illegal migration and refugee flows into the United States, and the suppression of the criminal drug trade and other forms of smuggling.

The Defense Department's Office of International Security Affairs published the "United States Security Strategy for the Americas," one of five regional vision statements, in September 1995 to explain the department's efforts to meet the challenges and seize the opportunities envisioned in President Clinton's strategy of "Engagement and Enlargement." In a sense, the document translates national security interests and objectives into defense terms. From the Pentagon's perspective, regional engagement encompasses promoting democratic norms in political-military relations; encouraging peaceful resolutions of disputes, adoption of confidence and security building measures, and implementation of nonproliferation and conventional arms control initiatives; supporting interagency counterdrug efforts with an emphasis on source countries; and deepening defense cooperation among joint and service counterparts. In addition, the Department of Defense and U.S. Southern Command are responsible for the implementation of specific aspects of the Panama Canal Treaty.[19]

The Defense Department's engagement in the Americas is interactive and diversified, encompassing a wide array of different contacts with neighboring countries. "Our strategy will be successful," writes Assistant Secretary of Defense Joseph Nye, "to the degree that its low-profile, long-range programs reduce the odds of conflict and need to deploy forces in emergency situations."[20] Reflecting Washington's basic approach to the region, the Pentagon emphasizes policy objectives rather than focusing on specific countries. A large number of its programs and activities—such as multilateral exercises, International Military Education and Training (IMET), bilateral consultations, and service-to-service contacts—support Defense aims by involving as many countries as circumstances permit. An example of this approach occurred at Fort Chaffee, Arkansas, in September 1994. Approximately 1,700 soldiers from Colombia, Venezuela, and Ecuador participated in a U.S. Southern Command–sponsored combined exercise built around a narcoguerrilla scenario. General officers from Argentina, Brazil, and Chile observed, as did representatives from nongovernmental human rights organizations. A subsequent exercise in Puerto Rico, focused on multinational peacekeeping operations, brought together Central American military units as well as civilian and military observers from over twenty countries and organizations. The 35th Unitas naval exercise in 1994 comprised a series of joint-combined bilateral and multilateral field training events over half a year by naval, marine, air force, and coast guard units from the United States and nine Latin American countries. Three European countries also participated.

Relationships between the United States and South American countries are nurtured without a deliberate focus on the relative power of the different states. The nature of U.S. security interests and current events in the hemisphere lead to contact with countries such as Brazil and Mexico more than others. At the moment, Washington's closest ties are with Buenos Aires, based largely on Argentina's commitment to international peacetime engagement. This association has caused Washington to reexamine aspects of its relationship with a long-standing ally, the United Kingdom. The potential for greater collaboration on economic and security matters with Mexico, Brazil, Venezuela, Chile, and other South American states is real and much desired by the U.S. government, notwithstanding dilatory efforts in the U.S. Congress to consider adding a highly attractive country like Chile to NAFTA.

In sum, little happens in the Western Hemisphere without the United States playing some role, even if the role is to do nothing. There is no neutrality in regional affairs for the United States, no disinterested behavior. But in the mid-1990s there is the opportunity for true partnership, which has not been possible since the Second World War. Coordination and collaboration between Washington and neighboring American capitals builds on a basis of democratic and free-market[21] transformations and shared perceptions of common security threats and apprehensions, which are defined in terms that are both transnational (narcotics, crime, migration, smuggling, environmental degradation) and traditional (territorial claims, natural resources, arms control, domestic turmoil). As a result, Washington's thinking on security matters has broadened from its earlier narrow focus only on the Caribbean Basin, although this subregion remains very important for the United States.[22] Evidence of the shift can be seen in the current counterdrug strategy, for example. Since November 1994, the principal focus of U.S. drug enforcement agencies and supporting players, such as the Defense Department and the U.S. intelligence community, has been on drug production and trafficking in several Andean source countries instead of exclusively on the northern transit of cocaine and its entry into the United States. In the area of narcotics, and in many other areas, Washington is beginning to accept that U.S. security for the foreseeable future will be more closely tied to that of its American neighbors than ever before.

The one exception to this view is U.S. policy toward Cuba, which has not adjusted to the new reality. Clinging stubbornly to a policy of containment and isolation that was developed for the very different world situation of thirty years ago, the United States has little influence in Cuba, no contact with current or potential future leaders, and no way to precipitate change on the island except to hope that the economic embargo will cause Castro's government to fall. Cuba no longer presents a strategic threat to the United States. The collapse of the Soviet Union and its external support eliminated Cuba's ability to conduct international adventurism; at the same time, changes in the post–Cold War world made Cuba's revolutionary model and foreign assistance undesirable. Today this neighbor presents many of the same problems and opportunities that Washington has faced in other Latin American countries.

IMPLICATIONS FOR THE WESTERN HEMISPHERE

The original question pursued in this chapter asks how the United States sees the balance of power in the Americas. After examining Washington's attempts to place the inter-American region in its global framework of strategic interests and commitments and after looking at how the Defense Department pursues U.S. security objectives in the hemisphere, the concept of a balance of power as it might be applied in this region does not emerge as relevant for the United States. Strategic documents identify U.S. interests and objectives and underscore the recent desire to share responsibility for global and regional peace and security. Defense programs and initiatives endeavor to support these ends wherever possible, without a sense of priorities among nations. Geography and history will always give Mexico, Central America, the Caribbean Islands, Venezuela, and Colombia an edge in dealings with the United States; this has nothing to do with such foreign policy considerations as maintaining or changing a local or subregional strategic balance.

Writing about traditional U.S. policy in the Americas, Robert Kagan, former Deputy Assistant Secretary of State in the Bureau of Inter-American Affairs, observes that "successive American leaders sought to ensure that this hemisphere would be one place where Americans could travel and do business free from arbitrary power, economic warfare, or threat of violence. America's ability to create such a climate near its borders was greater, its tolerance for disruption and interference smaller, than in most other parts of the world."[23] The quest for stability and the opposition to chaotic change, lawlessness, and violent upheaval have remained constant and the narrow, paternalistic thinking seen in the U.S. approach in the past has begun to disappear. Today's emphasis is on strengthening regional partnerships and solving common problems. In the 1995 Ecuador-Peru border conflict, for instance, neighboring states did not choose one side or the other to support. Rather, they bolstered the four guarantor countries—Argentina, Brazil, Chile, and the United States—in their efforts to work with the belligerents to find a final solution to this lingering headache, a solution that avoids rekindling a reflex arms race between the two Andean states.

In the long run, a balance of power mentality is not conducive to either regional stability or cooperation. Nor is the implied fine-tuning of national capabilities among competitive neighbors consistent with U.S. interests. "Future success 'beyond NAFTA' will be neither exclusionary nor isolationist," Luigi Einaudi observes about the hemisphere's future, "but rather GATT [General Agreement on Tariffs and Trade] compatible in economics, democratic in politics, and universalist in spirit."[24] To this he could add committed to security and confidence building and respectful of national sovereignty. Active U.S. interest in the region in the years ahead and its willingness to continue grappling with the thorny question about where the hemisphere fits into the broader U.S. view of security can help to ensure movement toward Einaudi's vision. If Washington finally looks hard enough, it will discover that this region is the crucial, mutually dependent variable in its strategic equation.

NOTES

1. Six broad geographic regions are addressed in William J. Clinton, *A National Security Strategy of Engagement and Enlargement* (Washington, D.C.: The White House, 1995): Europe and Eurasia, East Asia and the Pacific, the Western Hemisphere, the Middle East, Southwest and South Asia, and Africa.

2. Charles E. Kirkpatrick, *Defense of the Americas, U.S. Army Campaigns of World War II* (Washington, D.C.: U.S. Government Printing Office, 1991), 20.

3. The Inter-American Defense Board is a monument to this moment of consultation and collaboration. Established in Washington in 1942, the board has allowed each American government the means to voice its own concerns and ask neighbors for assistance in dealing with them.

4. One recent change to Department of Defense's Unified Command Plan united, on order of the Secretary of Defense, all of Latin America (except Mexico), the Caribbean, and the sea/air approaches to the region under U.S. Southern Command on July 1, 1997. Under Defense plans implementing the Panama Canal Treaty,

its headquarters relocated from Quarry Heights, Panama, to Miami on September 25, 1997.

5. Michael I. Kryzanek, *U.S.–Latin American Relations*, 2d ed. (New York: Praeger, 1990), 66–67.

6. The Enterprise for the Americas Initiative promised a reduction of Latin America's official debt owed the U.S. government, offered help to facilitate investment in the region's economic recovery, and held out the prospect of free trade agreements.

7. Abraham F. Lowenthal, "Latin America and the United States in a New World: Prospects for Partnership," in Abraham F. Lowenthal and Gregory F. Treverton, eds., *Latin America in a New World* (Boulder, Colo.: Westview Press, 1994), 237.

8. Luigi Einaudi, "Security and Democracy in the Western Hemisphere," in L. Erik Kjonnerod, ed., *Hemispheric Security in Transition: Adjusting to the Post-1995 Environment* (Washington, D.C.: National Defense University Press, 1995), 173.

9. Ibid.

10. Clinton, *A National Security Strategy*, 2.

11. William J. Perry, *Annual Report to the President and the Congress* (Washington, D.C.: U.S. Government Printing Office, 1995), 7.

12. John M. Shalikashvili, *National Military Strategy of the United States of America, 1995: A Strategy of Flexible and Selective Engagement* (Washington, D.C.: U.S. Government Printing Office, 1995), 4.

13. Richard N. Haass, "Paradigm Lost," *Foreign Affairs* 74 (January/February 1995): 43.

14. Perry, *Annual Report*, 4.

15. Lowenthal, "Prospects for Partnership," 246.

16. Clinton, *A National Security Strategy*, 30.

17. Perry, *Annual Report*, 4.

18. Washington has not redefined the Cold War and balance-of-power concept "rival powers" for its neighborhood for either the near term or the future. In today's atypical security environment, some nonstate actors, such as drug cartels and international smuggling rings, are in fact rival powers, at least in terms of wealth and a willingness to use it to protect and promote strategic interests. A future challenge could come from an extra-hemispheric economic competitor interested perhaps in dominating the trade of a subregion, which in turn leads to significant diplomatic leverage in hemispheric affairs.

19. The companion Neutrality Treaty gives both the United States and Panama the unilateral right to defend the Canal and keep it open to ships of all nations. There is no time limit on this treaty.

20. Department of Defense, Office of International Security Affairs, *United States Security Strategy for the Americas* (Washington, D.C.: U.S. Government Printing Office, 1995), 19.

21. Latin America and the Caribbean and the United States are the fastest-growing markets for each other's exports. Two-way trade with the region has more than doubled since 1983, from $67 billion to roughly $153 billion in eleven years.

22. Economic stagnation in several Caribbean countries, weak state systems, government mismanagement, and a general acceptance of corruption make this subregion vulnerable to narcotics trafficking and some drug production. Political unrest and a bleak economic outlook provide incentives for illegal immigration, which national governments are either unable or unwilling to prevent. Use of countries in the Caribbean Basin as conduits for the international smuggling of illegals is increasing.

23. Robert Kagan, "There to Stay: The U.S. and Latin America," *National Interest* (Spring 1990): 61.

24. Luigi Einaudi, "Security and Democracy in the Region," *Joint Force Quarterly* 11 (Spring 1996): 68.

CHAPTER FIVE

THE CARIBBEAN IN A NEW STRATEGIC ENVIRONMENT

IVELAW L. GRIFFITH

The cumulative dynamics of developments within nations and across regions over the past decade have made credible the characterization of contemporary world politics as both turbulent and transformational. Scholars and statesmen are not quite clear about what the turbulence and transformations portend, but they no longer have the luxury of trying to interpret the world before attempting to change it. Now part of the challenge involves having to manage change while interpreting events and outcomes.

This chapter seeks to interpret global events and consider how the Caribbean "stands" in the new environment. The analysis here suggests that while the new strategic environment is the result of global turbulence and transformation, some "old era" issues still retain their security salience, while others have developed new dynamics. In the latter regard, drug trafficking—a nontraditional security issue—stands out, and considerable attention is paid here to some of its dimensions.

THE NEW STRATEGIC ENVIRONMENT

There are at least three structural and operational features of the still-transforming global environment with direct implications for the Caribbean: the changed structure of global military and political power, alterations in economic relationships, and policy reprioritization by states with traditional Caribbean interests.

The collapse of world communism and the concomitant end of the Cold War are at the center of the transformation in the first area. The bipolar character of global military-political power has been replaced by the reemergence of a multipolar global system. Not only is there evidence of multipolarity, but some scholars point to the development of the multidimensional basis of global power. One discerns the development of different currencies of power affixed to different poles of international power: military, economic and financial, demographic, and military and economic. One can see the poles varying in their productivities, with demographic power as more of a liability than an asset, and the utility of military power being reduced.[1] Another respected scholar, now a policymaker, views the structural and operational aspects of world power differently. He sees the distribution of power being "like a layer cake," with the top, military, layer being largely unipolar, the economic, middle, layer as tripolar, and the bottom layer of transnational interdependence showing a diffusion of power.[2]

This post–Cold War structural-operational transformation has at least two major implications for the Caribbean, both of which pertain to the realities of U.S. geographic proximity, power, and interests. The first is that U.S. policy and action toward the Caribbean will be shorn of the previous East-West ideological cloud, thereby altering the character, if not the scope, of U.S.-Caribbean relations. Although it is true that to the extent Fidel Castro is able to remain adamant in the pursuit of communism in Cuba there will be some U.S. concern about an ideological threat, "the communist threat" is virtually nonexistent, partly because of regional changes in Nicaragua, Grenada, Guyana, and elsewhere.

The East-West military-political fixation of the United States not only colored its relations with Caribbean countries on a bilateral basis, it influenced multilateral relations as well. During the Cold War period, the interests and conduct of some Caribbean countries caused them to suffer the consequences of U.S. displeasure, while others received the benefits of its approbation in the context of institutions such as the International Monetary Fund, the World Bank, and the Inter-American Development Bank. However, there is already evidence that the end of the Cold War has led to appreciable change in U.S. attitudes and behavior toward Caribbean countries in these multilateral arenas.

The second implication is related to the American military presence in the region. The nature and scope of U.S. military deployment and posture

in the Caribbean, part of its geopolitical game-plan for countering the Soviet Union, has already begun to change. This is contributing to a lesser U.S.
military presence, reduced International Military Education and Training
Program assistance, and reduced arms supplies and sales to countries that
were either U.S. allies in the East-West conflict or considered otherwise important to U.S. national interests.[3] Moreover, as Jorge Domínguez has
rightly observed (and this is partly because of the two implications mentioned above), the Caribbean now has lesser military importance in world
affairs, although there remain some significant military issues in the region.[4] Yet the end of the Cold War does not obliterate the strategic value of
the Caribbean. As several Caribbean specialists have shown, the region's
strategic significance is reflected in economic, geographic, and communications attributes that have transcended East-West geopolitics, even though
they were affected by it during the Cold War.[5] And, as will be seen below,
the Caribbean is not only of strategic importance to states, but also to nonstate actors, notably the drug barons.

Allied to the military-political changes attendant upon the end of the
Cold War are alterations in the structure and operation of economic power
relationships. The profundity of actual and anticipated economic power
changes has been such that one security specialist was able to quickly popu-
larize a concept he coined about the scope and depth of economic power relations in the new global environment. The term is geo-economics: the mix-
ture of the logic of conflict with the methods of commerce. Edward Luttwak
is convinced that the new strategic environment will be such that "as the
relevance of military threats and military alliances wanes, geo-economic
priorities and modalities are becoming dominant in state actions."[6] He expects that both the causes and instruments of conflict will be economic.

The movement toward the formation of economic blocs around the
world is one important manifestation of global economic power alteration.
The European Union now boasts a unified market of 320 million consumers, and the Association of Southeast Asian Nations agreed in January
1992 to create a free trade area as a precursor to the establishment of a
common market. Closer to home we have NAFTA, with annual production
of over six trillion dollars and 320 million consumers. One appreciable consequence of this megabloc phenomenon for the Caribbean is the potential
reduction or even loss of economic assistance, foreign investment, and preferential trading arrangements. Concerning NAFTA, for example, there is
justified fear that the anticipated increase in trade resulting from the removal of trade barriers in Mexico will help displace U.S. trade with Carib-

bean countries and reduce the benefits of tariff preferences under schemes like the Caribbean Basin Initiative, the General Scheme of Preferences, and Section 936 of the U.S. Internal Revenue Code, which gives tax credit to U.S. businesses that invest in the Caribbean Basin. And this is only one of several policy and institutional concerns with economic and political security implications.

The megabloc phenomenon with its multiple implications comes at a particularly unpropitious time for the region, given the cumulative impact of the global and regional turbulence, which includes depressed banana, bauxite, and sugar production, high public debt, and high unemployment. A former Deputy Secretary-General of the Latin American Economic System has observed: "The dawn of a new era of heightened economic competition in which industrial countries are adopting a less concessional approach to developing countries on trade and economic matters generally coincides with an almost loss of geopolitical appeal for Caribbean countries. . . . It is important for Caribbean Community societies to recognize that the nature of the challenge goes even beyond NAFTA. . . . It relates much more to the requirements of the current global economic environment of increased competition, to which NAFTA is itself a response."[7]

The military-political changes due to the end of the Cold War and the megabloc phenomenon have had both causal and consequential linkages to the third general feature of the new strategic environment that is critically important to the Caribbean: the issue of policy reprioritization by large and mid-sized powers that either once considered the Caribbean to be important to them and/or were countries on which Caribbean states placed importance. The noteworthy countries in this respect are the United States, Britain, Canada, the Netherlands, and Venezuela.

The reprioritizing by these countries is the result of several factors, sometimes acting in combination. These include leadership changes which may or may not cause policy reevaluation, budgetary constraints, economic recession, the demand by domestic constituencies for more attention on the "home front," aid reallocation, and shifting foreign policy focus. In tangible terms, these situations mean reduced aid, readjustments in preferential trading arrangements, reduction in foreign investment guarantees, and diplomatic downgrading of Caribbean countries.

For example, the withdrawal by the British of their military garrison in Belize has been prompted by both budgetary difficulties and a review of British foreign and security policy towards Central America and the Caribbean. The action has had a dual effect: it has increased the vulnerability of

Belize to territorial and political sovereignty violation by Guatemala; and it has reduced the capacity of Belize to render credible responses to narcotics production and trafficking. When the U.S. slashed its 1990 aid package to Jamaica to augment its aid to Poland, more important than the sum of money involved—US$20 million—was the symbolism of the action. Moreover, in May 1994 the U.S. State Department explained that it planned to close embassies in Antigua-Barbuda and Grenada because of the strategic insignificance of those countries and partly "to shift resources to Eastern Europe and the former Soviet Union." It took Congressional pressure, especially from the Black Caucus, to reverse the decision in relation to Grenada; the embassy there will remain open—for the time being.[8]

Not all countries of importance to the region have been reducing their tangible interaction with it. Mexico, France, and Spain are notable in this regard, although Spain's involvement has been narrowly focused, mainly on Cuba and the Dominican Republic. There are also a few countries that are taking new or renewed interest in the region, Japan and South Korea being two of them. Nevertheless, the value of the lost interest seems to far outweigh that of the new and renewed relationships. More than this, the Caribbean's diminished importance based on reprioritization is not limited to actions by states. Some nonstate actors, such as foundations and multinational corporations, are also acting accordingly.

THE PRESENT LANDSCAPE: TERRITORIAL DISPUTES AND DRUG TRAFFICKING

As might be expected, the turbulence and transformations mentioned above have affected the region's strategic landscape, precipitating changes in many areas. Yet some issues of the previous era remain important. One area where salience has been retained is territorial disputes; one where the dynamics have been accentuated pertains to drugs. Territorial disputes and drug trafficking are not the only items on the Caribbean security agenda; however, they are among the most critical ones.[9]

The outbreak of hostilities between Peru and Ecuador on February 26, 1995, not only threatened to shatter the "Spirit of Miami" six weeks after it was created, but it provided sobering testimony of the continued importance of territorial and border disputes in the Americas. Moreover, while there had been an accentuation of peace initiatives in the hemisphere even before the Summit of the Americas, the collateral consequences of the Peru-

Ecuador conflict include a jolting of memories about the number of similar disputes in existence and a rekindling of nationalist sentiments about the prosecution of claims.

For instance, the aftermath of the Peru-Ecuador war led to apprehension in Guyana over troubling signals coming from Venezuela. In relation to its Guyana claim, which is for two-thirds of the country, Venezuela's Foreign Minister, Miguel Burelli Rivas, visited Guyana in March 1995 and asked that priority attention be given to the issue. More troubling, though, he called on Guyana's president, Cheddie Jagan, to have "a proposal to be pursued in practical terms" ready for Jagan's meeting with Rafael Caldera in fall 1995. Guyana flatly refused the diplomatic arm-twisting. Because of the response, Venezuela now seems unwilling to set the date for the Jagan-Caldera summit.[10]

Global transformations have left intact other significant disputes involving Caribbean countries, notably the claim by Suriname for 15,000 square kilometers of Guyana's territory; and that by Guatemala for the entire territory of Belize. While Guatemala recognized Belizean sovereignty in August 1991, it has not renounced its claim, although its posture has changed remarkably. It is useful to note, though, that while the structural and operational post–Cold War changes might not have affected the salience of territorial disputes, they have helped to create an environment in which peace and reconciliation are emphasized and which has made a difference in approaches to conflict resolution.

The Caribbean lies at what Jóse Martí once called "the Vortex of the Americas," making it a bridge or front between North and South America. Soon after the 1492 encounter between Europe and the Americas, European leaders recognized the strategic importance of this vortex, which has persisted over the centuries and which was dramatized in geopolitical terms during the recent Cold War. However, the strategic value of the Caribbean is not only geopolitical, as viewed by state actors engaged in systemic conflict and cooperation; in recent years the region has also been viewed as strategic by nonstate drug actors, also with conflict and cooperation in mind, but in terms of geonarcotics.

The concept of geonarcotics posits that the narcotics phenomenon is multidimensional, with four main problem areas—drug production, consumption-abuse, trafficking, and money-laundering—that give rise to actual and potential threats to the security of states around the world, and that the drug operations and the activities to which they give rise precipitate conflict and cooperation among various state and non-state actors in the international system. Over and above this, the term geonarcotics captures the dynamics of four factors: drugs, geography, power, and politics.

Geography is a factor because of the global spatial dispersion of drug operations, and because certain geographic features facilitate some drug operations. Power involves the ability of individuals and groups to secure compliant action. This power is both state and nonstate in source, and in some cases nonstate sources exercise relatively more power than state entities. And politics, the fourth factor, revolves around resource allocation in the Lasswellian sense of the ability of power brokers to determine who gets what, how, and when. Since power in this milieu is not only state power, resource allocation is correspondingly not exclusively a function of state power-holders. Moreover, politics becomes perverted, and all the more so where it already was perverted.[11]

THE CARIBBEAN'S STRATEGIC PLACEMENT

Several aspects of the Caribbean's geography make it conducive to drug trafficking; the two most important pertain to island character and proximity. Most of the Caribbean countries are island territories, and some are plural island territories. Indeed, the Bahamas are an archipelago of 700 islands and 2,000 cays. This island character permits entry into and use of Caribbean territories from scores, sometimes hundreds, of different places from the surrounding sea, from the Atlantic Ocean in the case of Guyana, Suriname, and French Guiana and from the Caribbean coast in the case of Belize. The inability of Caribbean countries to provide adequate territorial policing makes their vulnerability to trafficking more readily appreciated.

Proximity is dual: there is proximity to a major drug supply source—South America—and to a major drug demand area—North America. On the supply side, the world's cocaine is produced in South America, with Colombia alone producing about 80 percent, although only about 20 percent of worldwide coca-leaf cultivation is done there. A significant proportion of global heroin and marijuana production also comes from South and Central America, especially from Colombia, Mexico, Peru, Paraguay, Brazil, and Guatemala.[12]

On the demand side, the United States has the dubious distinction of being the world's single largest drug-consuming nation. An analyst at the Congressional Research Service reported in 1988 that: "America is consuming drugs at an annual rate of more than six metric tons (mt) of heroin,

70–90 mt of cocaine, and 6,000–9,000 mt of marijuana—80 percent of which are imported. American demand therefore is the linchpin of one of the fastest-growing and most profitable industries in the world."[13] By 1993, State Department estimates placed consumption of cocaine alone at 150–175 mt, valued at US$15–17.5 billion.[14] In April 1995, the head of U.S. Southern Command estimated that about 300 mt of the approximately 575 mt of cocaine available worldwide in 1994 were consumed in the United States.[15]

There is not much distance either between the Caribbean and South America or between the Caribbean and the United States. Most Caribbean countries are less than 2,000 miles from Miami and less than 1,000 miles from Caracas or 1,500 miles away from Bogotá, Cali, or Medellín. The distances involved are often quite short: for example, Bimini is just 40 miles from the Florida Keys; it is merely seven miles between La Brea, Trinidad, and Pedernales in northeastern Venezuela; and the town of Lethem, Guyana, is only 75 miles away from the city of Boa Vista, Brazil.[16]

Europe is also a large drug-consuming area, with cocaine, heroin, and marijuana imports coming through and from the Caribbean.[17] However, despite the relatively great distance between them, the Caribbean is a major transit area for drugs bound for Europe. Because French Guiana, Guadeloupe, and Martinique are Départments d'Outre Mer (DOMs) of France; Anguilla, Bermuda, British Virgin Islands, Cayman Islands, Montserrat, and the Turks and Caicos are British dependencies; and Bonaire, Curaçao, Saba, and St. Maarten are integral parts of the Netherlands, certain customs, immigration, and transportation arrangements and facilities between these territories and their respective European "owners" are used by traffickers to good advantage. Some of the arrangements are similar to those involving the United States and Puerto Rico and the U.S. Virgin Islands, which also facilitate traffickers aiming for destinations in the continental United States.

TRAFFICKING PATTERNS AND METHODS

Apart from trading their own marijuana in the United States, some Caribbean countries are important transshipment centers for South American cocaine, heroin, and marijuana bound for Europe and North America. For more than two decades the Bahamas, Belize, and Jamaica dominated this business. In the case of the Bahamas, its geography makes it an excellent candidate for drug transshipment, given its 700 islands and 2,000 cays and strategic location in the airline flight path between Colombia and South Florida. For a typical cocaine trafficking mission, aircraft depart from the north coast of Colombia, arriving in the Bahamas four to five hours later. The cargo is dropped, either to waiting vessels or for collection later to be placed on vessels, and then the final run is made to a U.S. point of entry. However, this is not the only modus operandi. As one report indicates, traffickers use other tactics, including use of Cuban waters to evade Operation Bahamas and the Turks and Caicos efforts, drop-offs by aircraft making only momentary landings, and the development of a cocaine route through Jamaica.[18]

The geography and topography of Belize also make that country ideal for drug smuggling. Apart from a long coastline and contiguous borders with Guatemala and Mexico, two major heroin and marijuana producers, there are dense unpopulated jungle areas and numerous inland waterways. Moreover, there are about 140 isolated airstrips and virtually no radar coverage beyond a thirty-mile radius of the international airport at Belize City. While there still is air trafficking, recently there has been an increasing use of maritime routes. Whereas 141 kilos of cocaine were seized in all of 1994, two seizures in January 1995 alone netted 636 kilos of cocaine.[19] Crack cocaine, in particular, has been featuring more prominently in the drug trade.

Jamaica has long been key to the drug trade, given its long coastline, its proximity to the United States, its many ports, harbors, and beaches, and its closeness to the Yucatán and Windward Passages. Trafficking takes place by both air and sea. For the maritime traffic, use is often made of pleasure boats with storage compartments to ferry small quantities of drugs. Large loads are put aboard commercial cargo and fishing vessels. Both large and small amounts are also smuggled by air. Jamaicans also have another asset as far as South American operators are concerned: a long track record of marijuana smuggling.

Jamaica Defense Force (JDF) sources indicate that both legal and illegal airstrips are used for trafficking. Apart from landings on strips designed or adapted for drug operations, landings have been made on roads, in cane fields, and on legal strips owned by bauxite and sugar companies. The JDF has destroyed some eighty illegal airstrips and fields (up to December 1994), but as the JDF Chief of Staff explained, given the heavy limestone in many of the popular landing areas, operators are often able to make fields serviceable within ten days of destruction.

Indications are that most of the cocaine air operations using Jamaica involve San Andres and Bogotá in Colombia, the Bahamas, Panama, and

Curaçao. Traffickers do not rely only on illegal flights; legal commercial flights are also used. Particularly popular, and problematic for Jamaican officials, was the commercial link between San Andres and Montego Bay. That connection was suspended in September 1994, but there are still commercial flights linking Jamaica and Bogotá. Now, according to military intelligence sources, the drugs go from San Andres to Bogotá and then to Montego Bay or Kingston.[20]

Jamaican drug seizures are sometimes dramatic because of the quantity of drugs seized. In April 1989, 5,000 pounds of marijuana were seized in Gramercy, Louisiana, on board *MV Kotor*, which was there to deliver a shipment of Jamaican bauxite. The drug consignment was discovered after violent clashes by two rival gangs over ownership. According to the 1995 *International Narcotics Control Strategy Report* (*INCSR*), during 1994, 179 kilos of cocaine, 47 kilos of hashish oil, and one kilo of heroin were seized. There was also a large seizure on March 6, 1995: 4,000 pounds of marijuana along with weapons and ammunition in the St. Paul's district of Manchester.[21]

Although the Bahamas, Belize, and Jamaica are still important drug trafficking centers, countermeasures there and in South and Central America have prompted traffickers to seek and develop alternative routes, bringing eastern and southern Caribbean countries into greater prominence since the early 1990s. The shifts are of such a magnitude that in November 1994 Puerto Rico and the U.S. Virgin Islands were designated by the U.S. drug "czar" as High-Intensity Drug Trafficking Areas (HIDTAs), a designation surely appropriate to other areas in the region. Moreover, because of the increased drug activity, in July 1995 the Drug Enforcement Administration (DEA) upgraded its presence in Puerto Rico from "Office" to "Field Division," increasing its staffing and assigning a special agent—Félix Jiménez—to oversee the Caribbean, a job formerly done from Miami, and report directly to Washington, DC.

The Netherlands Antilles and Aruba are said to serve as vital links in the transshipment of cocaine and heroin from Colombia, Venezuela, and Suriname to the United States and Europe. Aruba, Bonaire, and Curaçao are very close to Venezuela, from which much of the drugs confiscated in these islands come. Trafficking in the Dutch Caribbean generally involves the use of commercial and private airlines, air cargo flights, and cruise ships, although ship containers have also been used. Several features of the Dominican Republic also make that country a trafficking candidate: proximity to Colombia, the Bahamas, Puerto Rico, and the southern United States; a long, often desolate, border with Haiti; and poorly equipped police and soldiers. Moreover, drugs are smuggled over the border from Haiti using the same techniques and routes used to smuggle petroleum into Haiti during the embargo.[22]

Guyana has recently become an important center of operations. Like other Caribbean countries, Guyana saw its trafficking use graduate from marijuana to cocaine and heroin. The earliest known trafficking case was on June 16, 1979, when a trader from the bauxite-mining city of Linden arrived from Jamaica with sixty pounds of compressed marijuana.[23] Cocaine and some heroin now enter Guyana from all three neighboring countries: Brazil, Suriname, and Venezuela. Cocaine seizures in 1993 totaled 463 kilos—1,000 percent higher than in 1992. This exceptional figure was due to one dramatic seizure: on June 4, 1993, 800 pounds of cocaine were dropped from air into the Demerara River, along with US$24,000 and huge quantities of Colombian and Guyanese currency. Several Guyanese, Colombians, and Venezuelans were implicated in the affair.[24] On January 4, 1995, 5,000 pounds of marijuana valued at US$2 million were discovered behind a false fiberglass wall of a container about to be shipped from Georgetown to Miami.[25]

The air, sea, and land routes developed for smuggling contraband into Guyana from Brazil, Venezuela, and Suriname during the economic crisis of the 1970s and 1980s have now been adapted for narcotics trafficking. A further complication is the fact that the borders with these neighboring countries are very long: 1,120 kilometers shared with Brazil; 745 kilometers with Venezuela; and 600 kilometers with Suriname. Moreover, traffickers are able to take advantage of the country's large size (214,970 km^2), the coastal habitation, and the absence of adequate manpower and equipment to police the territory.

Given the country's physical and social geography and the corruptibility of some officials, traffickers sometimes aim at establishing their own physical base in a big way. In one case some Colombians and Americans were able to enter the country illegally and bring a generator, a water pump, two airplane engines, six transmitting sets, tool kits, arms and ammunition, and other supplies in over a four-month period. The plan was to build a processing and transshipment center at Waranama, in northeastern Guyana, 400 miles from the capital, Georgetown, to be part of an international network involving Colombia, Guyana, Trinidad and Tobago, and the United States.[26]

Like elsewhere in the Caribbean, trafficking in Guyana is not done only by air runs dedicated to drug delivery or collection; commercial flights are also used. In one dramatic case, on March 15, 1993, a Guyana Airways Corporation (GAC) plane—flight GY 714—arrived in New York from Guyana with 117 pounds of cocaine in its paneling. The U.S. Customs imposed a fine of US$1.8 million for this violation, which led the GAC to offer a million-dollar (Guyana) reward for information leading to the arrest and successful prosecution of the people involved in the affair.[27] This was the first time that a Caribbean airline had been forced to resort to such desperate and dramatic action to deal with commercial trafficking. The case was unsolved as of August 1995.

Guyana's physical geography makes it also vulnerable to maritime trafficking. One could readily appreciate this when it is noted that Guyana, whose name is derived from an Amerindian word that means "Land of Many Waters," has hundreds of inland rivers and creeks. Moreover, there are thirteen huge rivers that flow into the Atlantic Ocean, and each of those rivers has a network of tributaries. Maritime trafficking is also facilitated by the fact that the network of rivers also runs into Brazil, Suriname, and Venezuela.

The Guyana situation is clear evidence of the vulnerability of Caribbean countries to drug trafficking and other operations. Geography apart, a contributor to this situation is the absence of adequate military and police resources to offer credible countermeasures. In effect, the state lacks the power to exercise proper political and territorial jurisdiction over the nation. Top army, coast guard, and police officials in many parts of the region have expressed frustration not only at their inability to adequately protect their countries' borders against trafficking, but also at being the pawns of traffickers who often create successful small interdiction diversions in order to execute large operations.[28]

CONVEYANCE AND ORGANIZATION

Drug trafficking brings out the creativity and ingenuity of drug operators and the people who collude with them. People have used every possible orifice of the human anatomy, every possible piece of clothing, all manner of fruits and vegetables, and a variety of craft, furniture, and other things for the conveyance of drugs. Even dead and living birds and animals have been used to convey drugs.[29] One official recounted a situation where a guitar was made entirely of compressed marijuana,[30] and one *New York Times* report highlighted some incredible and creative cases, including 1,000 pounds of cocaine packed into hollow plaster shells shaped and painted to resemble yams.[31]

People of all ages and of both sexes are involved in trafficking. Old women are sometimes used since they do not fit the trafficker profile used by law enforcement agencies. But some are caught. In one case, a sixty-three-year-old Honduran-born American citizen was arrested in Guyana with six pounds of cocaine in her underwear. She was one of several "granny mules" arrested during 1993 and 1994 in Guyana and Trinidad.[32] Children have been used, because their tender age and innocence are often good camouflage, as well as cadavers.[33]

Some trafficking is done on an individual basis, but most of it is based on simple or elaborate organizational structures and networks. Some operations are very sophisticated, using digital encryption devices, high-frequency transmitters, cellular telephones, beepers, radar tracking devices, flares and sensors for air drops, and other equipment. Some operators are trained in armed combat, counternarcotics surveillance, evasive driving, and other areas. And, of course, traffickers are able to buy the services of specialists such as lawyers, pilots, and accountants.

Most of the structures and networks could not exist and deliver without the collusion of people in government and private agencies in various positions and at all hierarchical levels: people in shipping companies, customs and immigration agencies, warehouses, police forces, the military, airlines, export and import companies, stores, cruise ships, fishermen, trucking companies, farms, factories, bus and taxi operators, etc. Some officials collude by acts of omission: they just fail to perform certain acts, go to certain places, or return to their posts at a certain time. And considering their earnings for "doing little" or "doing nothing," one could appreciate how many people are susceptible to the corruption, especially in places with poor salaries specifically and/or economic deprivation generally.

CONCLUSION

In sum, while the recent global turbulence and transformations have altered the strategic environment in many ways, because of the continued salience of some issues and the heightened dynamics of others, the Caribbean strategic environment still holds some clear and present dangers.

Drug trafficking presents some of these dangers. The implications of trafficking go beyond merely the consequences of being transit centers, partly because not everything intended to go through the region actually does so. Some of the cocaine and heroin remain, both by default and by design, as payment for services, for example. There is a correlation between cocaine trafficking and cocaine consumption and abuse: the countries with high cocaine addiction are the very ones that are major cocaine trafficking centers. Moreover, throughout the Caribbean there are the attendant problems of crime, arms trafficking, and corruption, and these are only some of the dangers of combining the dynamics of drugs, geography, power, and politics.

NOTES

1. Stanley Hoffman, "A New World Order and Its Troubles," *Foreign Affairs* 69 (Fall 1990): 115–22.

2. Joseph S. Nye, Jr., "What New World Order?" *Foreign Affairs* 71 (Spring 1992): 88. Nye is now Assistant U.S. Secretary of Defense for International Security Affairs.

3. For a discussion of military changes, see Humberto García Muñiz and Jorge Rodríguez Beruff, "U.S. Military Policy toward the Caribbean in the 1990s," *Annals of the American Academy of Political and Social Science* 533 (May 1994): 112–24; and Gen. John J. Sheehan, "Lessons of 1994; Outlook for the Future," presentation at the LANTCOM—NDU—North-South Center Caribbean Security Symposium, Miami, Fla., April 18, 1995.

4. Jorge I. Domínguez, "The Caribbean in a New International Context," in Anthony T. Bryan, *The Caribbean: New Dynamics in Trade and Political Economy* (Coral Gables, Fla.: University of Miami Press, 1995), 2.

5. See Andrés Serbín, *Caribbean Geopolitics: Toward Security through Peace?* (Boulder, Colo.: Lynne Rienner, 1991); Ivelaw L. Griffith, *The Quest for Security in the Caribbean* (Armonk, N.Y.: M.E. Sharpe, 1993), 175–216; and Michael Morris, *Caribbean Maritime Security* (New York: St. Martin's Press, 1994).

6. Edward N. Luttwak, "From Geopolitics to Geo-economics," *National Interest* 20 (Summer 1990): 20.

7. Henry S. Gill, "NAFTA: Challenges for the Caribbean Community," in Bryan, *The Caribbean*, 49.

8. See Steven A. Holmes, "Less Strategic Now, Grenada Is to Lose American Embassy," *New York Times*, May 2, 1994; and "U.S. Embassy for Grenada," *New York Times*, May 15, 1994.

9. For an assessment of the region's security agenda, see Ivelaw L. Griffith, "Caribbean Security: Retrospect and Prospect," *Latin American Research Review* 30 (Summer 1995): 3–32.

10. See "Indecent Proposal," and "Venezuela's Ultimatum," *Guyana Review* 27 (April 1995): 2–6; and "Rohee Says No," *Guyana Review* 29 (June 1995): 7.

11. See Ivelaw L. Griffith, "From Cold War Geopolitics to Post–Cold War Geonarcotics," *International Journal* 49, no. 1 (Winter 1993–94): 1–36.

12. For a discussion of Latin American drug production in a global context, see United Nations, *Report of the International Narcotics Control Board for 1994*, 29–36; Bruce M. Bagley and William O. Walker III, eds., *Drug Trafficking in the Americas* (Miami, Fla.: University of Miami Press, 1994); and *International Narcotics Control Strategy Report* [hereafter INCSR] (Washington, D.C.: Bureau of International Narcotics Matters, 1995), 63–155.

13. William Roy Surrett, *The International Narcotics Trade: An Overview of Its Dimensions, Production Sources, and Organizations*, CRS Report for Congress 88-643 (October 3, 1988), 1.

14. INCSR (1993), 16.

15. Presentation by General Barry McCaffrey, "Lessons of 1994: Prognosis for 1995 and Beyond," at the 1995 Annual Strategy Symposium cosponsored by the Southern Command and the National Defense University, Miami, Fla., April 25, 1995.

16. I am grateful to Brig. (Ret.) David Granger of the Guyana Defense Force for the Guyana-Brazil and the Guyana-Venezuela information, and to Ricardo Rodríguez, Minister Counselor at the Venezuelan Mission to the OAS for the Trinidad-Venezuela information, all provided during May 1995.

17. For a recent assessment of European drug operations and their Latin American, Caribbean, and other connections, see INCSR (1995), 303–98, 513–21; Scott B. MacDonald and Bruce Zagaris, eds., *International Handbook on Drug Control* (Westport, Conn.: Greenwood Press, 1992), chaps. 14–18; and Rensselaer W. Lee III and Scott B. MacDonald, "Drugs in the East," *Foreign Policy* 90 (Spring 1993): 89–107.

18. INCSR (1995), 160.

19. INCSR (1995), 119.

20. Interviews with Rear Adm. Peter Brady, Chief of Staff; Lt. Col. Allan Douglas, Staff Officer (Operations and Training); and Captain Desmond Edwards, Military Intelligence Officer, JDF Head Quarters, Up Park Camp, Jamaica, December 19, 1994.

21. "Jamaica under Drug Siege," *New York Carib News* (May 2, 1989): 4; "Questions Surround Air Jamaica Drug Find," *New York Carib News* (May 16, 1989): 3; and "Major Ganja Find in Manchester," *Gleaner* (Jamaica) (March 8, 1995): 3A.

22. INCSR (1994), 184, 185; and INCSR (1995), 168–69.

23. Interview with Winston Felix, Assistant Commissioner of Police (Crime), Eve Leary Police Head Quarters, Georgetown, Guyana, June 30, 1994.

24. See Mohamed Khan, "Drugs Dropped by Mysterious Aircraft," *Stabroek News* (Guyana) (June 8, 1993): 1, 11; and "23 Held in Air-dropped Cocaine Probe," *Stabroek News* (June 9, 1993): 1, 11.

25. See INCSR (1994), 189; Alim Hassim, "Marijuana Container Valued at US2M," *Stabroek News* (January 6, 1995): 1; and "Three Charged for Trafficking," *Stabroek News* (January 16, 1995): 1, 24.

26. See "Illegal Airstrip Case: Three Colombians, One Guyanese Charged," *Guyana Chronicle* (January 29, 1989): 1, 4.

27. See Anand Persaud, "117 Pounds of Cocaine Found on GAC Plane," *Stabroek News* (March 18, 1993): 1, 2; and "GAC Offering G1M Reward for Cocaine Find Leads," *Stabroek News* (March 19, 1993): 1.

28. Interviews with, among other officials, Brig. Joe Singh, Chief of Staff, Guyana Defense Force, Camp Ayanganna, Georgetown, June 30, 1994; Lt. Cmdr. Gary Best, Acting Commander, Guyana Coast Guard, Coast Guard Headquarters, Georgetown, July 1, 1994; Jules Bernard, Commissioner of Police, Trinidad, Police Headquarters, Port of Spain, July 8, 1994; Orville Durant, Commissioner of Police, Barbados, Police Headquarters, Bridgetown, July 19, 1994; Rear Adm. Peter Brady of the JDF; Supt. Reginald Ferguson, Head of Drug Enforcement Unit, Bahamas Police Force, Nassau, December 22, 1994; and Alvin Goodwin, Deputy Commissioner of Police, Antigua-Barbuda, in Port of Spain, Trinidad, January 21, 1995.

29. "NY Drug Agents Find 10 Cocaine-filled Condoms inside Dog," *Miami Herald* (December 6, 1994): 3A; and "Man Sentenced for Bid to Smuggle Coke in Dog," *Miami Herald* (April 27, 1995): 3A.

30. Deputy Commissioner Goodwin, Antigua-Barbuda Police Force.

31. Jessica Spart, "The New Drug Mules," *New York Times Magazine* (June 11, 1995): 44–45. The tomato sauce case was reported in the *Miami Herald* (June 16, 1995): 17A.

32. "10 Years in Jail for Honduran," *Stabroek News* (November 1, 1993): 1.

33. Interview with Captain Edwards of the JDF, December 19, 1994.

CHAPTER SIX

STRATEGIC BALANCE AND REGIONAL SECURITY IN THE SOUTHERN CONE

MARCELA DONADIO AND LUIS TIBILETTI

This chapter seeks to incorporate the notion of balance into the debate on the necessity and viability of a system of regional strategic security (RSS) in the Southern Cone from an Argentine perspective.[1] It tries to avoid the tendency to confuse, as has been done in the past, the consideration of the concept of security with strategizing about all areas of relations between nations and peoples. This tendency emerges because the problems that seriously affect the survival of our region are political, economic, and social in nature, not the result of an external military threat. Therefore, this chapter will distinguish the concept of security as a response to the danger posed by these broader problems from the concept of security specifically related to the area of military strategy.

This chapter presents a reflection of RSS as a multilateral system that is constructed from the multinational geographic spaces of the American continent, whether the aim is to consolidate peace or to reestablish it where it has failed. This approach does not attempt to encompass all aspects—political, economic, ecological, social, and criminal—that are normally included in the broad meaning of security. Nor does it attempt to weaken the concept of security. Rather, it is limited strictly to the possible use of military power, understood as the "hard" nucleus of so-called hemispheric security.

Preventing wars implies not only the capacity to deter a potential aggressor, but also to convince the aggressive country that a greater return can be had through mutual peace. The essence of RSS is to prevent the escalation of interregional conflicts that lead to the use of military force. Thus, "regional ecological security" (the responsibility of environmental specialists), regional anti–drug trafficking security or regional antiterrorist security (the responsibility of police forces and specialized organizations), and so forth all fall within the concept of this multifaceted and multidisciplinary system of hemispheric security, albeit not necessarily under the auspices of military security.

There are numerous activities aimed at building such a subsystem of security, particularly the interaction among the political, military, diplomatic, and academic arenas; the efforts to revise the defense doctrine; the scientific/technological and productive cooperation in matters of goods and services for defense purposes; mutual confidence measures; and/or prevention of conflicts. But the problem of balance in Argentina remains an underlying issue as far as the development of those activities is concerned.

Some feel the need to give special consideration to the idea of "balance of power" when dealing with the issues of integration and security. Others make reference to "strategic balance," which at times also is referred to as "military balance." This chapter seeks to achieve some theoretical precision with respect to this issue, through which the peculiarities of the Southern Cone and the perspective of developing mutual confidence measures as an instrument for regional integration and stability can be analyzed.

Three key concepts—balance, equilibrium, and stability—that will be used throughout this chapter require further clarification. Their applicability here is, of course, more figurative than literal. Balance may be seen as a relationship that is static and more quantifiable, whereas equilibrium need not refer to a state of being simply equal, but can be a relative concept. The definition of stability is less clear. Is stability the result of a balance that permits equilibrium, or can stable systems exist even without equilibrium? What relationship is there between a system of local stability, at the subregional level, for example, and a regional or global system? If one speaks of dynamic equilibrium, does this imply accepting a degree of instability? How do each of these situations affect the ideas of military balance and equilibrium in the enunciation of subregional security policies?

The remainder of this chapter treats the notions of balance and equilibrium as they have generally come to be used; that is, we will accept the failure to distinguish clearly between the two terms. The question remains for the future whether a deeper distinction between them should be drawn.

THE CONCEPT OF BALANCE OF POWER IN THE
DEVELOPMENT OF INTERNATIONAL RELATIONS

Realism

The notion of balance of power as a general principle had its origins in the philosophers of India, China, and ancient Greece; it appeared later in Machiavelli and Hobbes; it guided the actions of great statesmen like Richelieu, Cromwell, and Bismarck; and it reached the level of theory thanks to the crowning work of Hans Morgenthau.[2] As one scholar wrote: "For more than two thousand years, Morgenthau's 'political realism' has constituted the central traditional thought in the analysis of international relations in Europe and its offshoots in the New World."[3] It is not possible here to give a detailed analysis of the key role played by the concept of the equilibrium of power in the development of the school of realism, but the basic principles will be covered.

In the realist's view, peace (understood as the absence of war) can only be maintained to the degree that sovereign nations competing against each other in the international scenario succeed in establishing an equilibrium or balance of power through military force, international law, and the art of diplomacy.[4] This perspective is based on five pessimistic assumptions: 1) the international system is anarchic; 2) each state (nation) has the military capacity to harm or destroy others; 3) no state knows the intentions of the other with certainty; 4) the basic impulse of a state is to survive and to maintain its sovereignty; 5) states strategically (rationally) think of how to survive, and as a result they are necessarily aggressive because they fear each other (they are not sure they can deter potential adversaries; because of this, they prepare for war), they pursue survival in a context of "just save yourself" (alliances are temporary and are a result of this need to survive), and they seek to maximize their relative power, basically through military force.[5]

Morgenthau's central idea, along with the idea of equilibrium of power, is that nations are always moved by national interest: "Nothing in the position of the school of realism goes against the assumption that the present political division of the world into nation-states will be replaced by larger entities of a different nature, more in accord with the technical potentials and moral demands of the contemporary world."[6] Likewise, it is worth remembering—as Padilla does—that Morgenthau assigned a very special role to a "new type of diplomacy" needed to maintain peace. He was not referring to collective security utopias but, rather, to the development of a new kind of equilibrium that takes into account the points of view of other nations and uses negotiation as a means of conflict resolution.[7]

What has happened to the concept of equilibrium of power in theoretical developments since Morgenthau? The hypothesis of this chapter is that it developed into an idea that was accepted without question and, in its practical use, became increasingly complex.

The School of Scientism and the Balance of Power: Behaviorism and Systemic Theories

Perhaps because their analysis is based on the explanation of conduct in decision-making, the behaviorists did not focus on the analysis of the equilibrium of power, although the concept of equilibrium was certainly taken as a given. Within the school of scientism, when discussing systemic theory, we focus on Morton Kaplan, who propounded these ideas in his study of international relations. As Kaplan stated, "each system is at the same time structure and process, that is to say that it is maintained and modified, stable and dynamic."[8]

In this view, therefore, equilibrium should not be confused with stability. There are systems in a state of stable equilibrium (that fluctuate between given limits), but one may also face situations of unstable equilibrium.

The Neorealism of Kenneth Waltz

Waltz bases his theory on a critique of the earlier currents of the school of realism, whether they be traditional or linked to the school of scientism. He faults them for attempting to interpret the performance of the system solely through the analysis of the units represented by the nations (states). His analysis applies the concepts of system, structure, and structural causality to international relations. However, by specifically leaving out nongovernmental actors, he limited the study to political relations, that is, to power relations.

Thus, with respect to what constitutes the ultimate interest for a nation, Morgenthau pointed to power, Waltz to security. Waltz also maintains that "being sovereign and dependent are not contradictory situations . . . a State is sovereign when it decides by itself what is the best way to confront both its external and internal problems, including whether or not to seek help from other parties and thus restricting its freedom."[9]

Waltz also emphasizes the idea of "structural causality." If a fixed distribution and disposition of power indeed exists in the structure of the system, and this has a direct impact on the possibilities for action of each one of the units (states), what space remains for the bilateral game of balance of power between two states that are not potentially capable of changing the structure of the system? Can it exist autonomously or will it always be an expression of that structure? From Waltz's theory, one could interpret that the structures are defined not by all the agents within it, but by the actions of the principal parties.[10]

The Neoliberal Institution and the Balance of Power

The idea of the neoliberal institution and the balance of power was introduced by the now-famous work on complex interdependence by Robert Keohane and Joseph Nye and further developed in other studies, such as Keohane's *International Institutions and State Power*. Here, the theory from the school of realism provides an essential point of departure for the analysis of international policy. Although it should be further defined, it rejects the fact that such policy is always somewhat institutionalized: "In understanding the behavior of a Nation, we not only have to take into account the capacity for physical power of a State and to acknowledge the absence of hierarchic authority, but we should also comprehend the global political institutions, formally organized and explicitly codified side by side."[11]

Along with this position, we come across the difference with respect to Waltz's neorealism, because his idea of structure remains incomplete and thus is not dynamic: "The capacities, for Waltz, principally refer to the economic resources and the productivity of a State, on one hand, and to its military power on the other. . . . However, I believe that the conventions in the political world are as fundamental as the distribution of resources between the States."[12]

From this logic, Keohane discusses the concept of Waltz's equilibrium of power, introducing the question of how one explains why states that feel secure do not seek to maximize their power, maintaining that "the theory of the equilibrium of power is incongruent with the assumption . . . of what a State 'does to maximize its power,' if it is understood that power alludes to tangible resources that can be used to persuade other agents to do what they would not do by any other means, through threat or imposition of losses. A State concerned about self-conservation does not seek to maximize its power when it is not in danger."[13]

From this basis, Keohane concluded in 1988 that the challenge for the next decade is to determine the influence of these ideas on issues of security and cooperation.

Neoidealism and the Theories of Research for Peace

We have specifically excluded Bjorn Moller from the group of thinkers of the school of neorealism, despite the fact that he is defined as belonging to this group.[14] In this fashion, we have kept the analysis within what would be called "mid-conservatism" in the analytical continuum of idealism and realism. From the neorealism defined by Moller in his formulation of defensive sufficiency—or the mutually assured defensive superiority that he proposes for strategic relations between Argentina and Chile—to "the art of living in peace," in which Pierre Weil talks about the crisis of fragmentation of the Cartesian-Newtonian paradigm, we find philosophers of the stature of Galtung, Haas, or Wallenstein.[15]

Considering the development of peace studies and the efforts of a group of experts from eighty-eight countries that have worked in the U.N. on the redefinition of security since 1985, the concept of strategic balance may be considered vis-à-vis the implementation of the idea of cooperation. Undoubtedly this is distinguished by the normative character of the U.N. reports, but their increasing influence on its member states should be acknowledged. The idea of linking the maintenance of peace to development and justice between peoples has been incorporated to the modern formulation of the Social Doctrine of the Catholic Church since Vatican II.

THE RELATIONSHIP BETWEEN THE EQUILIBRIUM OF POWER AND MILITARY EQUILIBRIUM: STRATEGIC BALANCE

Much has been written about the various meanings given to the word *strategy*;[16] we will use definitions from Luttwak: "The art and science of developing and using political, economic, psychological, and military forces . . . to increase the probabilities and favorable circumstances of victory and lessen the chances of defeat" (U.S. Joint Chiefs of Staff); and "the art of the theory of wills that use force to resolve their conflicts" (General André Beaufre).[17]

If this definition is accepted, how can these strategies be compared as a way to combine means, time, and space if they are not compared by their results? Who dares to explain how to balance two interpretations of a confronting idea? To measure balance or strategic equilibrium is a difficult task to accomplish; it implies weighing not only quality but a definitive combination of issues. It would be different if we measured an idea or strategic doctrine by its costs or by the real likelihood of its implementation in terms of efficiency and efficacy. But what type of concept would we weigh this idea against? It seems more adequate to talk about balance of power and military balance as two separate issues.

The notion of strategic balance played a fundamental role in the logic of a total confrontation between two states. As far as relations among countries were concerned, it was essential to seek to establish the ability of each nation to display its full power when confronting another state in battle. This is considering that the confronting party had in turn displayed its full potential for battle as well.

This scenario of competing displays of power was the most classical interpretation of strategic balance. The strategies pursued under this classical view included not only an estimate of the military forces that could be deployed at any given time and place, but also all those other elements of national power that could also be set in motion.

Slowly, these interpretations grew increasingly complex.[18] The political and psychosocial components of national power were added. These included religion, nationalism, ethnic origin, poverty, social ills, internal conflicts, the personality of some leaders, relations between the civilian and military sectors, the level of institutionalization, the operating structure of the country's organizations, international and regional status, defense patterns in the history of the country, and an array of elements limited only by the imagination of strategic analysts.

In addition, the different ideas about the use of force began to increase the specific weight of other elements in the strategic balance. We refer here to the strategic dimension or depth associated not only with surprise tactics but also with the notion of strategic surprise.

The next question, then, is: When does military imbalance imply a strategic imbalance? Is it always the case? Not if we consider some examples. Would it be a change in balance if Ecuador were to have a larger air force than Brazil? Regarding the "balance" between these two countries, how great would the military imbalance have to be before the abysmal difference in their national potential was forgotten? And how does the old saying from the school of realism—that a difference in military potential can create armed conflict—apply here?

CONCLUSIONS OF THE THEORETICAL ANALYSIS

Based on the preceding discussion, one can draw the following theoretical conclusions, which will prove helpful in a subsequent analysis of the Southern Cone: 1) the concept of balance of power is a result of the experience gained by the successive world powers throughout the history of international relations; 2) therefore, the countries that define the international system determine the theory of its implementation and its factual analysis; 3) in this sense, "balance" is a product of the system that impacts every nation, whether its importance is average or small or whether its geostrategic location is central or peripheral;[19] 4) in particular, there is no development of a theory or factual analysis in terms of peripheral states that goes beyond how the balance of power impacts them or what shape this balance takes and how it behaves in the regional or subregional schemes; 5) specifically, there has been no analysis other than the transfer of principles applied by the main parties and their direct application to the South American region (as an example, the elements that distinguish the Latin American situation described by José Paradiso—the American character of the region, its peripheral location, and permanent relation with a hegemonic power in the region—were never mentioned in the classic geopolitical analysis papers from the period when overlapping strategies were being designed);[20] 6) there is no agreement among writers over the cause-and-effect relationship of imbalance of power and war. Thus, while some believe that strategic balance makes war less possible, others believe that the existence of an imbalance renders war more possible. Some even consider that such a correlation does not exist and therefore balance does not affect the possibilities of peace.[21]

THE SPECIFIC FEATURES OF THE SOUTHERN CONE

The nations of the Southern Cone have a long history of mutual distrust and mutual suspicion, curiously not inherited from previous wars but, rather, fed by the perceptions of threats that each one has over the other—to the point that they are part of each country's national, social, and cultural traditions. As a reaction to the changes of the post–Cold War era, and to the current globalization and integration trends, our countries designed policies in three main areas.[22] First, there was "market-country" policy, the search for a model for "independent development," in which economic growth and raising the standard of living were seen possible only under the control of an independent and autarkic nation. In this instance, global integration would work *if and only if* it was possible to influence this integration.

Second, policy was considered in terms of national society and culture. Maintaining separate identities is the basis for the affirmation of culture itself; the promotion of these differences has encouraged distrust throughout history.[23] The third area was the political-military approach of the nation, which was guided by the hypothesis of confrontation with a neighboring country. This has customarily led to the development of military forces and resources.

The balance of power was the tool for this logic of confrontation, guaranteeing the achievement of this autonomous and distinct model. The objective was to limit the ability of other states to alter their own history—principally through military means—by strengthening their own capabilities or weakening those of their opponents. From a geopolitical perspective, two crossing axes were constructed along which the dynamics of this equilibrium were at play—Buenos Aires/La Paz/Lima and Brasília/Asuncion/Santiago. They represented the search for regional equilibrium masking the supremacy pretensions of the principal parties on each axis.

The East-West conflict was superimposed on this situation. The doctrine of national security and the presence of the armed forces at the higher levels of power reinforced this vision both in external relations and towards internal enemies. This created a paradoxical situation: at the same time that the militaries—at the request of the United States—acted jointly and amicably in the repression of "communism," they continued preparing to fight against each other.[24] The most crucial effects of this historic search for "equilibrium" was the near war between Argentina and Chile in 1978 and the controversy between Argentina and Brazil over Itaipú-Corpus in 1979.

The presence of actors from outside the region acted as a counterweight to shift the "balance" from one side to the other and has been the other contributing factor to this politics of the equilibrium of power. The strength of the United States, a hegemonic power in the world and specifically on our continent, and Great Britain's nuclear power, in addition to its unresolved conflict with Argentina, have been influential factors in the search for regional control. Coupled with any future decisions made by the actors in the region, this presence could become a destabilizing factor in the region's strategic equilibrium; or it could be beneficial to gain some advantages otherwise out of reach. Although the logic of confrontation is not abandoned, it becomes a destabilizing factor that encourages mutual suspicion and perceptions of threats among the militaries of our countries. For example, how does one explain to a member of the Brazilian armed forces that the alignment of Argentine security objectives with those of the United States does not represent a design to obtain better weapons or a goal of serving as a "beachhead" for a U.S. landing in the region?[25] Or how does one explain to Argentine military personnel that Great Britain will not use Chile as a base for the exploitation of the Malvinas (Falkand) Islands in exchange for support of their territorial claims and conquests? How can one do this when the constant supply of arms to Chile from Great Britain is set against the maintenance of an embargo on Argentina, and the search for unilateral decisions—as in the exploitation of oil and fish—is set in the context of a conflict that still remains unresolved?

Confidence opens the way to abandoning the logic of confrontation, and the policy of equilibrium of power locks the region in the "prisoner's dilemma," while any possibilities for action and integration into the international context are diluted day by day. The new international conditions that our nations face have converted these types of concepts into tools for maintaining dogmas and sectional privileges, but not into a strategy for development. As Beltrán says, "If you are preoccupied with *geopolitics*, it is certain that your borders will be impenetrable. If you have a *geoeconomic* concern, try to make your borders as porous as possible, so that commerce flows. If you are preoccupied with *geopolitics*, you see your neighbors as enemies that you must keep at bay. If you have a *geoeconomic* concern, you want to integrate with your neighbors."[26]

A free-market country, a national social culture, and a legal-political-military state must adapt to the demands of the globalization of the economy, to the models of international society and culture, and to the regional political and military scenarios of this new world context.

THE CONTEXT OF TRANSITION IN THE SOUTHERN CONE

In addition to the change in the external expression of the strategy that stemmed from the end of the Cold War and the need to adapt, the Southern Cone added an internal transformation produced by the establishment of democratic regimes after decades of alternating between military and civilian governments. In a changing context, in which the basic nature of conflicts has varied significantly and conventional threats seem to have lost the importance they had during the Cold War, ideas regarding military resources are oriented toward the design of the countries' security structures. Troop reductions—in the United States as well as in Europe—were the measures first adopted in following this line of thought. Such thinking also applies to the transformation of existing structures into forces capable of working under new circumstances and facing new risks.

In the Southern Cone, this change is more drastic because the armed forces were set up in response to the threat represented by an internal enemy as well as conventional aggression, either from neighbors or from countries outside the region. Now we have not only the loss of effectiveness of the covert, subversive aggression that characterized the East-West conflict and the trend toward integration among neighbors; we must also consider the processes of economic and technological adaptation as fundamental to integration with the rest of the world. The region, moreover, exhibits a particular characteristic: its strategic irrelevance in the global context (unlike, for example, the Caribbean). There are some questions on this issue that still remain unanswered. Why maintain armed forces if no threats exist that portend their use? Should not funds destined for military expenditures be used for social development policies? Does the search for military balance make sense?

Political, military, and—to a lesser extent—academic circles have proclaimed the nonexistence of military threats to the region, arguing instead that the major problems of the region are political, economic, and social. However, the armed conflict between Ecuador and Peru has demolished this argument, just as the Gulf War and the ethnic conflict in former Yugoslavia squashed the theory of "the end of history," which presupposed the end of military conflicts. The Southern Cone currently recognizes that the disarmament process, overcoming distrust, theories such as "cooperative security," and control of the armed forces are essential elements of an agenda for the maintenance of peace.

The process of democratic transition and consolidation in the Southern Cone is different in each country, even though they all share the common bond that this is a recent experience that needs to be implemented with caution by the civilian governments. From a civil-military point of view, the main issue to be resolved in the region is the effective subordination of the armed forces to the political leaders to guarantee the stability and predictability necessary for the development of mutual confidence and honest relations. In short, the internal process in each country should be related to the discussion of strategies, not to those who elaborate the strategies—or, simply speaking, not to "who does it" but rather to "what is done."[27]

The budget restrictions on the defense department in each country, the result of both economic crisis and lack of growth in the region, are also seen in other areas of state transformation. This leads into a situation such as the one envisioned by Dreifuss. Obsolete military equipment, outdated technology, and nonoperational equipment, due to lack of funds for maintenance, are some of the problems that impact national defense in the Southern Cone. These problems are aggravated in countries where a process of major reform is under way, as is the case in Argentina.

In this context, the search for cooperative security as promoted by the OAS, a system of common security under the umbrella of MERCOSUR, and the implementation of mutual confidence building measures (such as those that reduce the perception of threats that results in increased military spending in the search for military equilibrium) are options that contribute both to greater efficiency in the use of military resources and to a more efficient national defense at the lowest cost to each party.

These considerations become valuable when certain facts are taken into account, as in the case of Argentina, where only 5 percent of the country can be effectively controlled by radar.[28] As far as the army is concerned, no one really knows how to afford the costs of a volunteer army. Maneuvers and training of the three forces have been so reduced that many of the enlisted soldiers have unofficially stated that the country is almost "defenseless."[29] Redesign of the armed forces appears to be the path to follow; soliciting great sums of money without restructuring does not seem to be a sensible alternative. At the present time, the political tendency, at least from the point of view of congressional defense commissions, is to make the armed forces more efficient and to generate a rational defense spending policy in accordance with Argentina's economic reality.[30]

If the Southern Cone is seeking, now that it is being integrated into a dynamic world, to avoid being isolated and marginalized, it must take into account certain conditions (which are as much positive as negative) for moving forward, which can be described as follows:

At the global level:
  • generalized acceptance of humanitarian principles and of the principle of resolution of disputes by peaceful means;

- clarification of the uncertainty that surrounds the area of security, rendering obsolete the old and rigid doctrines of the use of military resources, and a reformulation of the mission and duties of the armed forces;
- discussion of the possibilities for action within the framework of international organizations, and the decline of individual action;
- acknowledgment of democratic ideals as a style of government;
- high technology in military resources;
- influence of the media and public opinion on decisions dealing with international and national security.

At the subregional level:
- reduced probability of an increase in resources available for acts of violence, stemming both from the agreements on arms reduction as well as from economic and technological shortcomings;
- a low level of conflict among countries;
- a low probability of aggression from outside the region;
- a new institutional role for the armed forces, and the repercussions of this role in the area of defense policy.

Institutional transformations have changed the strategic relationship of the Southern Cone internally and within the global context. This has mitigated points of friction in its interaction with the world, particularly in the area of human rights. The relationship has expanded, incorporating aspects such as political parties, trade union associations, electoral activities, and the production of the current economic relations.[31] There is room for expansion into the areas of security and defense as well.

STRATEGIC BALANCE AND MUTUAL CONFIDENCE MEASURES: FROM CONFRONTATION TO COOPERATION

MERCOSUR and the Extension of Security Frontiers

If during the world wars and, although with certain limitations, during the Cold War the physical conquest of other countries was an indication of the potential for national growth (or a way to add the wealth of another to one's own), today this kind of action is not only strongly condemned by the international community; it also does not appear to be income-producing.[32] Knowledge is the fundamental weapon nations need in the present and will need in the future.[33] In this regard, it is technological development that opens the doors to integration into an ever more selective international system.

In addition to this, the nations of the Southern Cone must add to their agendas other concerns about the economy and society. In the case of Argentina, these concerns ensure that its people can remove from their daily lives thoughts about "making war" against its neighbors, a war whose cost—in lives and money—could be infinitely greater than any possible benefit. This was evident in the resolution of differences with Chile over the Beagle Channel in 1984, whereby Argentina expressly renounced, via referendum, any possibility of repeating experiences like that of the Malvinas (Falklands) War.

This is not a casual example: the two wars, internal and external, endured by Argentina constitute the effective subordination of the armed forces to political power. The wars are influential factors in the search for a vision that includes not only the removal of any possibility of armed conflict, but also the rationalization of military resources and a restructuring of the defense system.[34]

In this regard, in Argentine political, military, and academic circles a step has been taken toward what could be summarized as a concept of expansion of the frontiers of security.[35] This idea is based on the concept of a development and geographic continuum, which defines the Southern Cone as a "geographic continuum that includes hundreds of millions of people, whose basic needs remained unfulfilled and that therefore constitute a phenomenal potential market from an economic/commercial point of view," which could be integrated into the global economy through a strategy of combined development and common marketing.[36]

In this context, the expansion of the borders of security signifies that, as a result of political agreements, any threat to a neighbor's security becomes a threat to one's own security. Threats to security would only come from beyond the region, thus reducing the possibility of any bellicose actions by the parties to the agreement.

Yet it should not be assumed that no attempt has been made in the Southern Cone to reach common agreement in political decisions as well as in national defense structures. Efforts have been made, based on a common strategic interest, on the belief integration does not in any way involve the abandonment of sovereignty or the merging of national identities. These efforts are aimed at constructing, despite the differences among the actors, a regional bloc capable of capturing the potential—as a group—of individual capacities.

The need to respect differences among countries is accepted not only in regard to sovereign political decisions, but also to the distinct potential of each country. For example, Argentina cannot deny the distinct regional potential enjoyed by Brazil, which shares borders with almost every South American county. Nor can it deny the capability and challenges resulting from the huge extension of its territory and its large population. Trying to match this reality, to compete for a supposed supremacy in the region, is to take the path contrary to the realistic notion of joining together in progress for the benefit of both parties.

In this same context, it is fitting to recognize—within the framework of this process of association—certain policies that slightly interfere with the capacity and maneuvering room of a neighbor. In 1988, referring particularly to the relationship between Argentina and Brazil (but with ideas that can be expanded to the entire Southern Cone), Virginia Gamba, an Argentine specialist, stated that:

> The world should be viewed as is and not as we would like it to be; every Nation wants a tolerable status-quo, always and when its security is not seen affected by its passivity; and rationality implies that all statesmen will always desire to limit the damages and costs to his own State, and that the adversary statesman will desire exactly the same. In addition to these assumptions it is possible, therefore, to negotiate, find agreements, and to seek to limit the effects of conflict and/or escalation of conflicts between two international actors. By these same principles, it is possible to see that a realistic dialogue must be sought in the geostrategic relationship between Argentina and Brazil. The willingness to analyze the situations of our countries, both from a regional perspective as well from outside the region, will allow us to find areas where we can work jointly. Once we establish agreements, we should work to consolidate them, but in the case of disagreements, we should not try to change the other party's ideas without respecting them. We should generate a language of deterrent signals, so that both countries acknowledge the warning lights when, inadvertently, the geostrategic level of one interferes with the most basic level of the other.[37]

The policy followed by Argentina and Brazil on nuclear issues serves as an example. Respect for differences has allowed Argentina to accept in recent years a Brazilian position different from its own in relation to adherence to the Non-Proliferation Treaty. With the signing of the Tlatelolco Treaty, Argentina guaranteed its security while Brazil maintained a political position that implied more guarantees. This is a clear example of what we could call a realistic peaceful coexistence, in which the pressure to change positions respects certain limits and is part of the process of political negotiations between countries.

At the same time, the "warning lights" to which Gamba refers begin to flash when Brazil continues its nuclear submarine project, the objectives of which for Argentina are unclear. The project "creates friction at its most basic level," since it involves the security of the South Atlantic. This is where the search for agreement and security guarantees for both parties should begin to work. Would Brazil be able to put that submarine at the service of the patrol and defense of the South Atlantic? Would Argentina be able to collaborate with its technological knowledge? Without claiming that these questions are part of any future reality (it is doubtful that the project will remain cost-efficient), they provide an example of how—following the logic of cooperation—divergent views that affect the perception of threat can be converted into a joint undertaking.

NATIONAL INTEREST

This analysis of the concept of equilibrium and/or balance of strategic military power is based on accepting a neorealistic position in which states legalize their international action in accordance with the "value-category" scale of national interest.[38]

There is no doubt that today Argentina's key interest is development. A strategy for economic development does not yet represent an autonomous model but, rather, is necessarily complementary. And even when the fight is over integration into international markets, this potential can be realized only by strengthening the type of continuum in development and geography that produces conglomerates.

This national interest, one that currently requires a stable situation in the neighboring country as well as in one's own country, changes the perspective on strategic balance. One should not necessarily perceive a strategic relationship with one's neighbor in terms of a total confrontation. This means that, during the transition from the hypothesis of conflict to confluence, it is not necessary to maintain a preventive national security system.[39] What is relevant here are the confidence building measures, which will be referred to later.

The nations of the Southern Cone, therefore, no longer manage their strategic balance in terms of a possible total confrontation but, rather, maintain a defense capability that prevents strategic surprises and helps preclude any crisis (resulting naturally from the process of integration) from escalating uncontrollably. This explains why Argentina proposes a *defensive* strategic attitude,[40] although not without internal discussions with those that support an autonomous course of development.

The space for military balance can be analyzed from this new reading of the problems that affect security in the Southern Cone. In this context, it is assumed that the notion of equilibrium means to avoid one country being endowed with a military capacity that affects the defense capability of another, that is, with the capacity of mass destruction or a surprise attack of such force and magnitude that it implies an intention of territorial conquest.

It is important to remember here that the logic of a military balance that does not affect strategic balance is based on the following principles. First is the total acceptance of the premise of shared development. This acceptance is specifically manifested in the acceptance of confidence building measures of a second degree, or hard measures (specifically aimed at the perceptions of threat), including intrusive measures, such as verification, when they are imposed as a result of an autonomous decision within the region.[41] Second, the process of economic, political, and cultural integration of the Southern Cone is of a transitional nature. Third, there should be no implication of any limits on the modernization of the armed forces. On the contrary, the logic allows this modernization to take place and renounces the search for arms systems of mass destruction or deployment for the territorial conquest of the neighbor.

MUTUAL CONFIDENCE BUILDING MEASURES: THE LOGIC OF COOPERATION

Mutual confidence building measures are the tool needed to move from the logic of confrontation to the logic of cooperation. They do not constitute an end in and of themselves, nor should they occupy the space allotted to political agreements that guarantee predictability and transparency in the relations between states. In our regional context, to think of the implementation of mutual confidence building measures isolated from a political will with broader objectives to advance progressively but firmly towards cooperation is equivalent to condemning such measures to failure or irrelevancy.[42]

It is important to emphasize the inadvisability of inserting the European experience in matters of confidence building measures into a strategic scenario like the one we find on our continent. There is little doubt about those differences; one has only to think of the internal wars that weakened Europe throughout the centuries and the logic of mutual fear that resulted. Even today, that history influences the way confidence building measures are used by those nations. However, one cannot ignore that a passage from the logic of confrontation to that of cooperation requires a gradual modification of the perceptions of mutual threat; only through these small steps are we able to modify the perception of the other actor. The size of those steps and the means used to take them are determined by the regional actors themselves.

To deem this unnecessary is to bow to the danger of accepting an idealistic and utopian position. In such a scenario, the perception of threat would disappear by the mere presence of the idea of integration.

If "the objective of confidence building measures is to contribute to the reduction, or in some cases, the elimination of the causes of distrust, fear, tensions, and hostilities" between states, it is fitting to ask if, in fact, the conditions for advancement in this area exist.[43] One fundamental gain is the generation of confidence in nonproliferation, as developed by successive governments of the region, which has removed any threat of using unconventional weapons. The nuclear nonproliferation agreements and the accords forbidding the production of chemical and biological weapons are an important measure of confidence building in our region, despite some persistent misgivings.[44]

Although progress has been made, the dynamics of mutual confidence as developed in Europe—for example, through a system for inspection of military installations and units and information measures concerning military resources and troops, which imply a commitment to eliminating the feeling of distrust—are still difficult to apply in the political and military context of our region. The Southern Cone has worked on the so-called "first-generation," or "soft," measures, principally through contacts and initiatives between the armed forces of our countries. The real challenge— one that would allow the perceptions of strategic balance to be modified— is the progress to be made in the "hard" measures, a task to be assumed by the political leaders.

The "great confidence measure," represented by MERCOSUR, should in the future, so as to be more effective in eliminating mutual pretensions of supremacy, be followed by other important political measures, such as the search for coordination of decisions in external affairs that affect the region. The unilateral alignment of Argentina with the United States, the suspicion that Great Britain can find room in Chile for action to avoid resolution of the Malvinas (Falklands) conflict and to continue its unilateral policy in this regard, and Brazil's decision to continue developing sensitive technology are negative and counterproductive factors for the development of confidence.

Security agreements—multilateral or bilateral—can represent the development of another fundamental measure of confidence. If, for example, Argentina and Chile signed an agreement, based on the Treaty of Peace and Friendship, which would establish joint agreements on what is referred to as the threat to common interests by a third party, the search for military balance would begin to lose relevance as a security guarantee. If we eliminate the existence of a hypothetical threat from a neighbor, the resources allocated to national defense could instead be allocated in terms of emerging threats that will almost certainly be common to both countries.[45] In the same sense, the perception of threat would be substantially modified by discarding the military potential of the other country as a reason for discord and mutual suspicion.

Even as far as relations with the United States are concerned, a path for these kind of ideas seems to be opening up. This could be seen in the recent declaration by the Chief of the Southern Command of the United States, General Barry McCaffrey: "The government of the United States can endorse cooperative security agreements that reduce tensions and mutual suspicions and assist Latin American armed forces in the development of roles and missions appropriate to their new circumstances. We can aid them in creating doctrines to guide them in multinational peace operations or in the cooperative administration of border issues."[46]

If we concentrate on the concrete level of weapons systems, we can use as an example the case of the Argentine and Chilean air forces. The people and political leadership of Chile have given priority to their defense capability instead of their geostrategic situation. The effort to avoid a strategic surprise from Argentina—in particular by the forces stationed in Río Gallegos and Mendoza—is permanent. Thus, Chile has spent enormous resources on its early warning systems. However, a red light appears in this logic of balance not because of the capacity for detection and/or interception but, rather, because of two new arms systems. First, there has been a significant increase in the capability to refuel planes while in flight; and, second, we have seen the emergence of an early warning system mounted on the Boeing 707 Falcon airplane, with Israeli electronic equipment, which also allows the support of offensive actions in the midst of Argentine territory.

At the same time, however, on the Argentine side there is a geostrategic vulnerability—the dispersion of its land and sea borders. This makes a deterrent defense system based on a real capacity for early warning and interception very costly, and creates the need to maintain an offensive air force component that is able to exercise a minimum level of deterrence.

In the proposed model, what could be the alternatives to this situation? The intense thought given to a shared development-security model undoubtedly corresponds to thinking of a joint system of electronic satellite intelligence able to detect and intercept any threats to the air space in the subregion of the Southern Cone. In the transitional thinking that we propose, the first measures would be basic. These would include, first, redeployments and restructuring of resources, and this would imply the ability to renew discussion on the budgets and/or cost-benefit analyses that today do not seem to support this idea.[47] A second group of measures could be aimed at promoting confidence. In the past, the creation of a system of observation and permanent communication between the bases of the air forces of Argentina and Chile has been proposed. Every professional is familiar with the most elementary signs of military action; the concern for mutual strategic surprise would be set aside.

The example of an observation and communication system simply represents an attempt to apply the proposed logic. The complexity of the technical analysis would require a much greater development of this notion. The idea is simply to suggest a new kind of work for those techniques.

At the level of concrete proposals for the immediate future, there is a vast scope of action within which these mutual confidence building measures can be developed. Argentina's orientation should be directed at the political and military objectives listed in the paragraphs that follow.[48]

The increase in cooperation on matters of security in the region is an inevitable consequence of the growth of the integration process in progress, represented by MERCOSUR. This process should grow in three directions: first geographically, to include, at least in a first expansion phase, Chile and Bolivia (in this regard, when dealing with issues of security, we prefer to refer to this area as the Southern Cone); second commercially, so that the benefits of agreements reach equally every productive sector and region in order to avoid aggravating the isolation of specific territories of a nation; and third in other noneconomic dimensions that require its enunciation, such as the institutional, political, cultural, and social areas.

It should be understood, however, that cooperation in security matters ought not to generate mechanisms that could be transformed into the self-destruction of the defense capacities of each one of the states. It should be advanced by the coordination and harmonization of defense policies and along the path of bilateral and multilateral confidence building measures.

In this respect, it is necessary to move toward institutionalizing existing confidence building measures to render them more effective and to keep them from remaining only the informal initiatives of the armed forces. The political powers constituted in each country—in the case of Argentina, through the ministry of defense—should take it upon themselves to develop confidence building measures

The creation of a research center for security and peace in the Southern Cone can be converted into an adequate framework to confront such a task. Its main role would be to generate agreements in principle on security matters with the potential to develop a body of common doctrine; to set forth security policies of the governments of the region and their consequences for the maintenance of security; and to promote its research activities and results in the region with the aim of cooperating in making policies clear and increasing awareness of the issues.

It is necessary to initiate various activities at the educational level, such as joint meetings of congressional commissions specializing in education and defense, in order to analyze elementary and secondary education curricula—the content of which corresponds more to a period of affirmation of national identity as a means to differentiate a country from its neighbor—such that new generations of students are trained with the idea of an identity that is capable of thinking cooperatively with another; to legitimize the functions of defense and security in accordance with the new challenges facing the nation-states—not in any way to militarize education but, rather, as a complement to the previous point; and to increase the quotas for exchange scholarships both at the university level, in order to link the centers that study this issue, and in interinstitutional relations related to defense in general and armies in particular. In the case of Argentina, there is a need to create a Center for Strategic Studies at the ministerial level similar to that of the Secretary of Strategic Matters in Brazil.

Regarding relations between military institutions, a standard agreement should be signed giving continuity to the important efforts that have already been made and helping avoid the breaks in this type of activity that we have seen historically. In this fashion, year after year, there would be the need to reunite members of a follow-up commission for the agreement, which would determine what activities would continue, decide which were to be increased, and evaluate the results. Given that it would be a standard agreement, it would not imply any strict obligation for the institutions. An example might be the agreements signed between the ministers of defense of Argentina and Spain—with the participation of the congressional commissions—on the themes of military administration and technological cooperation.

Related to the above point, projects for joint development should be identified, favoring those with low costs and whose tactical use could continue generating a capacity for development, production, and joint commercialization.

Applying the European model to our region, it seems possible to clarify the reasons behind the military redeployments carried out by any given country and behind the restructuring of military resources (such as Argentina is currently attempting). The goal is to eliminate all possibility of suspicion that such redeployments obey the hypothesis of conflict with a neighbor. Along the same lines, we must make available information regarding military movements and exercises in border regions.

Clear information on military spending is another "hard" measure. As a measure for the exchange of information, the development of a White Book of Defense for each one of the countries of the Southern Cone has been proposed. This would also stimulate a uniform and standardized system for measuring military spending at the regional level.[49]

CONCLUSION

Advances in the transformation of perceptions regarding strategic balance in the region need to be supported by the deepening of the democratic transformations of the countries. This will promote a positive evolution of civilian-military relations and the enunciation of a stable political culture. The latter will help institutionalize cooperation in security matters, in accordance with the advancement of MERCOSUR.

Likewise, these concepts will have to be articulated through the U.N. and OAS frameworks. They would be complementary to the security alternatives outlined by the United States, the fruit of joint cooperation between civilians and the military, and not just the result of political agreements made without the support of those parties who must institute the decisions. Equally important, we must learn from the European integration experience that we should not bureaucratize the realm of security through the use of a variety of institutions with poorly defined areas of responsibility.

At present, the most viable outlook for integration is found in the deepening of confidence building measures as a way to eliminate distrust and strengthen agreements among countries. As such measures are converted into real instruments, we will be taking a basic step that will allow us to consider the future integration of defense policies and, consequently, the construction of a regional strategic security system.

NOTES

1. See Gustavo Druetta, Luis Tibiletti, and Marcela Donadio, "Los Nuevos conceptos de seguridad Estrategica Regional," *SER en el 2000* 1 (1992).

2. Hans Morgenthau, *Politica entre las Naciones: La lucha por el poder y la paz* (Buenos Aires: Grupo Editor Latinamericano [GEL], 1986).

3. Robert Keohane, *Instituciones Internacionales y Poder Estata* (Buenos Aires: Grupo Editor Latinamericano [GEL], 1993).

4. Luis Padilla, *Teoria de las Relaciones Internacionales: La Investigacion sobre la paz y el conflicto*, Serie Cooperacion y Paz, vol. 4 (Guatemala: IRIPAZ, 1992).

5. Virgilio Beltrán, "Contribuciones para una concepcion estrategica en el cono sur de America," Paper presented at the second Encontro Nacional de Estudos Estrategicos, São Paulo, Brazil, August 16, 1995.

6. Morgenthau, *Politica entre las Naciones,* 21. Nevertheless, we need to admit that Morgenthau says nothing about the process of transition from a system of a division of nations into one of larger units. We might then wonder what happens to national interest in that transition. It seems reasonable that the existence of contradictions between the many national interests of each country—between those that want to accelerate the process and those that do not—is proper of this transition process.

7. Although it might seem ludicrous, it is tempting to establish a relationship between Morgenthau's statement regarding the need to respect the point of view of others with the notion of lateral thinking that Edward Del Bono develops in his writings about the basis of criticism—thinking undoubtedly shared by Pierre Weil—to the logical Western paradigm, so useful for scientific development in terms of allowing an identification by differentiation and so dangerous for the pursuit of peace. See Edward Del Bono, *Conflictos una major manera de resolverlos* (Buenos Aires: Sudamericana Planeta Editions, 1986).

8. Padilla, *Paz y el conflicto*, 137–38.

9. Kenneth Waltz, *Teoria de la politica internacional* (Buenos Aires: Grupo Editor Latinamericano [GEL], 1988), 143.

10. See Keohane, *Instituciones Internacionales*, 93.

11. Ibid., 7. See also Robert O. Keohane and Joseph S. Nye, *Power and Interdependence: World Politics in Transition* (Boston: Little, Brown, 1977).

12. Keohane, *Instituciones Internacionales*, 24.

13. Ibid., 75.

14. Bjorn Moller, *Common Security and Non-Offensive Defense: A Neo-realist Perspective* (Boulder, Colo.: Lynne Rienner, 1992).

15. See Padilla, *Paz y el conflicto*, 67–107.

16. Gustavo Druetta and Luis Tibiletti, "Cooperacion regional para la paz," *Nuevo Proyecto* 7/8 (Buenos Aires: CEPNA, 1991): 67.

17. See Appendix 1 in Edward Luttwak, *Strategy: The Logic of War and Peace* (Cambridge: Harvard University Press, 1987), 239–41.

18. This complex approach has been widely developed in all military and strategic intelligence projects. In regards to the field of international relations, a more modern vision that includes the elements of wealth, organization, and status can be found in Marshall R. Singer, *On the Dynamics of Power in Weak States in a World of Superpowers* (New York: Free Press, 1972), 71–79.

19. For a more extensive paper on how the balance of power affects all nations, particularly those not at center stage, see Michael Handel, *Weak States in the International System* (London: Frank Cass, 1990), 173–87.

20. This description is part of an ongoing project lead by the director of the School of International Relations of the University of El Salvador (Argentina), José Paradiso.

21. See Wagner R. Harrison, "Peace, War and the Balance of Power," *America Press Society Review* 8 (September 1994).

22. These categories have been taken from René Armand Dreifuss, "Impactos globais e percepcoes fragmentadas," *Premissas* 9 (April 1995): 75–130. This author makes an analogy—with the exceptions of the case—between the current trends and the development of the nation-state. The three categories guiding this development would then be transformed into globalization (an expansion beyond the borders of the production and consumption base), internationalization (dissemination of traditions and familiarization with cultural means), and planet-wide expansion (transnational integration and a new formula for all nations).

23. For example, school teachings in this context are guided by an assertion of the national identity with those neighbors seeking to occupy territory in another country, or to "infiltrate" a nation through migration. The failure to consider the neighbor as a relevant player in a country's own history and development is also another trait of this societal development, as it is replaced by the consideration of players from outside the region. Even today, in Argentina, for example, students dedicate many years and programs to studying European and North American history, while the history and culture of Brazil or Chile don't merit more than short paragraphs during a given school day.

24. The findings of recent years about how prisoners were exchanged, and that even commando groups from the neighboring country operated within the national territory, leave no doubts about this close collaboration.

25. Or, of "self-imposed subordination," as stated by José Paradiso in *Debates y Trayectoria de la Política Exterior Argentina* (Buenos Aires: Grupo Editor Latinamericano [GEL], 1993), 200. In an interview, this same author asserts: "From the economic point of view, both the model based on principal exports as well as industrialization by substitution imply parallel courses and individual advantages, which at the same time contribute to the logic of the balance of power. On the other hand, the industrialization of exports and the search for competitive advantages in a scenario where countries work together in blocks or quasi-blocks, are in support of joint and convergent processes that neutralize or diminish the excessive attention given to considerations of balance. Nevertheless, temptation could arise again through the search of special relations, by one party or the other. A privileged relationship between hegemonic powers compromises the potential for a strategic alliance." See "The Path of Foreign Policy," *Current Files* 1 (Fall 1995): 147.

26. Beltrán, "Contribuciones," 16, quoting Noordin Sopiee, emphasis mine.

27. The resolution of this discussion in Argentina has resulted in the acceptance by the armed forces of the role the government gave them while redesigning national policy; in terms of increased participation in international policy, it has resulted in irritating decisions such as the one to abandon the Cóndor II missile project and accept the agreements with Chile and Great Britain. In the domestic area, 1995 was the stage for the armed forces' recognition of their illegal activities during the dictatorship, something unheard of until now in Latin American history.

28. As stated by a chief officer of the air force during the seminar "Relaciones Cívico-militares," organized by the University of Quilmes, Buenos Aires, May 9, 1995.

29. Although an official version might record the reactions of the military chiefs to the last budget cuts of August 1995, which in their opinion will cause "the curtain to be closed."

30. The Chief of Staff of the Argentine air force himself declared, in a radio interview on August 11, 1995, his understanding of the priorities that the government sets in accordance with the economic circumstances prevailing in the country. The previous day, in his speech celebrating Air Force Day, he had asserted that "it has been clearly stated that the leadership of the Armed Forces has fully admitted that the development of defense cannot be unrelated to the global development of the Nation and respond, definitively, to the country's concrete possibilities."

31. An American academic says: "A critical source of the region's changing environment is found among the region's vigorous major actors, despite a series of unending domestic political and economic tensions. Brazil is now ranked as one of the world's top 10 nations across an array of economic and political-geographic attributes, while Argentina has claimed international attention in recent attempts to climb out of a serious national decline. Other regional states are also significant. Chile has structured a complex web of international relationships and obtained considerable respect for its style of economic management and successful transition

back to democracy. . . . Even the Southern Cone's smaller players have in recent years established a sharper multinational focus, exemplified by Uruguay's involvement in the 'Group of 8' (now the Rio Group) support effort to the Central American peace process." See Georges Fauriol, "The Future of the Western Hemisphere," in Erik Kjonnerod, ed., *Evolving U.S. Strategy for Latin America and the Caribbean* (Washington, D.C.: National Defense University Press, 1992), 4.

32. See Beltrán, "Contribuciones," 2.

33. Although we should note here that in the case of the superpowers this seems to be based on the possession of nuclear arms as a last resource for deterrence.

34. While this chapter was being written, in August 1995, a series of public hearings was beginning at the National Congress regarding the restructuring of the defense system, initiated by the chair of the defense commissions of both chambers, both senators and representatives.

35. We include this concept by Jaime Garreta, "Regional Strategic Security in the Integration of the Southern Cone: A Case of Security and Peace Building," paper presented at the first Latin American Congress on International Relations and Peace Research, Guatemala, August 1995.

36. Ibid., 7.

37. Virginia Gamba, "La perspectiva argentina I," in Mónica Hirst, comp., *Argentina-Brazil: El largo camino de la integracion* (Buenos Aires: Legasa, 1988), 146–47.

38. At the opening of the public hearings mentioned in note 34, Senator Eduardo Vaca proposed to replace the formula of "national interest" for one of "defense of the people," which was adhered to by many of the high officials present. Beyond this comment, the need to work on the theory of this concept is undeniable.

39. This distinction is established in the Argentine Law of Defense no. 23.554.

40. As stated by the president of the Defense Commission of the Argentine Senate, Senator Eduardo Vaca, at the fifty-second plenary meeting of the seminar "Towards the Armed Forces of the Year 2000," July 3, 1995.

41. Augusto Varas named them this way; see "Un nuevo regimen de seguridad hemisferica," *SER en el 2000* 7 (March 1995): 24.

42. In Europe the mutual confidence building measures (MCMs) worked within the logic of confrontation, but had a role of ensuring that the feared mutual destruction did not take place; and in the end they became an efficient tool to provide guidelines for cooperation.

43. Secretary-General of the United Nations, *General and Complete Disarmament: Confidence Building Measures*, Document no. A/36/474 (New York: United Nations, 1981).

44. In spite of statements indicating that its goal is not to operate in the region, the fact that Brazil is going ahead with a nuclear submarine project undoubtedly represents a source of concern for the rest of the countries. Argentina appears to have accepted Brazil's nonadherence to the Non-Proliferation Treaty, through

Tlatelolco and the Bilateral Agreement with OIEA (Organismo Internacional de Energia Atomica) inspection. This might be a clear example of a security agreement seeking common interests while respecting the other party's differences.

45. A fundamental task for the future will be the definition of the shared strategic interests for the region, a subject that we have not approached any further while we proceed with the main objective of this chapter. These interests exist, although they are not perceived by our countries either in the same fashion or with the same priority. For more on this, see Marcela Donadio, "Política de Defensa y Misiones de las Fuerzas Armadas en el Marco de la Integración Regional y del Nuevo Contexto Internacional: Argentina y el Cono Sur" (Defense Policy and Mission of the Armed Forces in the Context of Regional Integration and the New International Context: Argentina and the Southern Cone), report presented to CONICET (Consejo Nacional de Investigaciones Científicas y Technicas), Buenos Aires, June 1995.

46. *Clarín*, July 22, 1995, 15.

47. This issue began to be widely discussed in the specialized circles of Argentina as a result of the proposal presented by the EURAL (Europa America Latina) group of researchers, outlined by Gustavo Cáceres and Thomas Scheetz, eds., in *Defensa No Provocativa* (Buenos Aires: Editora Buenos Aires, 1995).

48. The feasibility for a future application of these measures can be perceived in the fact that some of them were even accepted by both Argentines and Brazilians at the fourth Meeting of the Brazilian Institute of Strategic Affairs (IBAE), held in São Paulo in February 1995, and the conference SER en el 2000, held in Buenos Aires in March 1995.

49. This measure was agreed upon at the preliminary meeting of the Meeting of Defense Ministers, held in Buenos Aires in June 1995 under the auspices of FLACSO Chile, SER en el 2000, and the Woodrow Wilson International Center for Scholars.

PART TWO

CONFIDENCE AND EQUILIBRIUM IN THE INTER-AMERICAN SYSTEM

CONFIDENCE BUILDING MEASURES AND STRATEGIC BALANCE: A STEP TOWARD EXPANSION AND STABILITY

FRANCISCO ROJAS ARAVENA

Strategic balance is designed to prevent crisis situations in which force would play a major role. On the one hand, it is a way of measuring and establishing deterrents that can help maintain a desirable situation. On the other hand, it allows measures to be taken when a negative situation develops, especially regarding security. Strategic balance establishes a level of parity in terms of potential force that makes dissuasion effective; that is to say, it includes the ability to do significant damage to prospective assailants. From this perspective, strategic balance is related to transparency and predictability, two conditions that are reached by developing confidence building measures.

Strategic balance is a clear perception of the relations of strength, potential, and capacity among two or more actors. It is the sum of power in the relationship and its relative proportion among the actors so as to avoid either confrontation or submission. This balance refers to more than just the balance of armed forces. Even though there are no ideal models, each situation of balance must be expressed and understood as a function of its specific geographic, historic, military, or cultural context. An evaluation of these factors determines the degree of "satisfaction" or "dissatisfaction," including a level of "preoccupation," with a specific strategic relationship. This evaluation will analyze the perceptions about security, as each actor will make decisions as a function of its perceptions.

Confidence building measures seek to create a climate that establishes transparency in the relationship, ensuring that there is no threat to security or that perceived threats can be controlled by maintaining the strategic balance. As instruments for preventing conflict, CBMs will permit the strategic situation to be viewed objectively, will allow for predicting behavior, and will help to avoid miscalculations that can trigger tensions. In order to be effective, CBMs should develop as part of a general climate of improving relations and should be accompanied by processes to verify the degree of compliance with agreements.

The balance is precisely defined and can be analyzed for a current situation. It also is projected onto future situations and defined in relation to future events. However, the primary factors in the analysis are those from the past, an approach that makes the incorporation of changing situations difficult. What was the balance previously, and how has it been modified? If a situation of imbalance is evidenced, there is also a recognition of vulnerability. This can be anything from a danger to a threat. Are the perceptions and the analysis accurate? What past history would allow the situation to be defined in a different way? How does one come up with an adequate response? These continue to be some of the basic questions.

Consolidating the alternatives of peaceful resolution to controversies is as important as maintaining a level of sufficient dissuasion in order to create an effective diplomatic space. It is here that we should look for an effective link between confidence building measures and strategic balance.

THE END OF THE COLD WAR: PRINCIPAL HEMISPHERIC TENDENCIES

The confrontations in the jungles of Alto Cénepa, in the heart of South America, and the accompanying tensions along the borders of other states in the region rekindled the theme of security in the Western Hemisphere. Similarly, the search for accords at the Defense Ministers of the Americas meeting and the debates in the Special Commission on Security for the Organization of American States prove that consensus on the definitions of security and the mechanisms to prevent conflict still do not exist in the hemisphere. The debates among international organizations and between academics and intellectuals also make manifest differences about how to characterize the new context and new demands in the area of security and how to go about defining and establishing consensus on the new dangers. The strong combination of international and domestic influence on the definitions and political alternatives complicates the debate and impedes the process of reaching accord.

Where do we focus on energies and dedicate resources following the fall of the Berlin wall? The threats in Latin America were essentially local and ideological. Those threats were replaced by the new ones like drug trafficking and environmental degradation. The traditional themes, however, remain significant. How to define the new hemispheric context? Is it necessary to build new institutions? Should practices and actions tending to avoid the use of force be systematized in an international regime? Working within this framework to define and conceptualize confidence building measures in the Western hemisphere will permit policy coordination to continue, culminating in the creation of a new Cooperative Agreement on Hemispheric Security.

The process of Latin American redemocratization began in the mid-1980s and culminated in the end of the Cold War. Today, democracy characterizes Latin American political regimes and is the core value advocated by its political elites and governments. The states of the region have sought to establish support mechanisms to sustain democracy in an international framework; the Santiago Compromise of June 4, 1991, was an expression of this tendency. The states that make up the OAS declared this compromise indispensable for the defense and promotion of democracy, and with it they established a framework of legitimacy and renewed strength in the hemisphere. This political alliance to promote democracy has served as an efficient deterrent in the face of threats of authoritarian regression.

The end of the Cold War led to great expectations with respect to the possibilities of swiftly eliminating the principal sources of conflict in the region. At the same time, it helped establish, almost automatically, new international mechanisms that replaced the Cold War institutions. In the Western Hemisphere, these mechanisms emerged in the form of the Inter-American Reciprocal Assistance Treaty. The disappearance of the outside threat and the perception that democracies tended to resolve their differences without the use of force reaffirmed these positive perspectives. The resurgence of territorial conflicts, however—which amount to differences in resource endowments among countries—combined with the emergence of new dangers and threats, presented a more complex panorama by the middle of the 1990s.

These conflicts and tensions made clear the need for strong political will combined with effective action to prevent the continued emergence of conflicts and their possible escalation. The transfer of instability is one of the dynamic effects of interstate confrontations, or any conflict that affects the bases of state power and the interests of their inhabitants. Although the Western Hemisphere has been one of the most stable regions in the last few decades, this does not mean that conflicts do not exist. One of the most serious errors occurs when situations that are conflictive or that generate distrust are believed to be resolved when they actually continue to exist. It is even more dangerous when the hemisphere lacks a security policy.

It is necessary to acknowledge tensions, areas of divergent interests, and points of conflict as well as to manage and control them and to take preventive measures to keep these situations from transforming into crises. This means preventing situations in which actors, perceiving a threat to their concrete interests, tend to generate responses with a higher probability of resorting to the use of force. In a crisis situation there are few options. Consequently, uncertainties are increased and decision-making processes develop in a context of great subjectivity. Such uncertainties reaffirm the need to construct a new comprehensive international security regime in the Western Hemisphere.

The end of the Cold War has had mixed effects on the Americas with regard to security. For the United States, it signified an essential change that has led to the redefining of U.S. global policy and a significant process of reduction and demobilization of forces assigned to regional matters, in particular the Southern Cone. In this context, the United States has changed the orientation of its policies toward multilateral organizations, both global and hemispheric, as well as toward Latin American and Caribbean countries.

In Latin America, the effects of global change are as diverse as the subregions that make up the mosaic of its nearly thirty states, and the changes are expressed differently in each subregion. In Central America, the end of the Cold War ended the discussion about the main external condition affecting security, making possible a more profound process of national reconciliation; it also made possible a substantial change in political regimes and institutions, including the armed forces. The process of demobilization and demilitarization has been profound in this region as well. In the Caribbean, certain key characteristics of the Cold War continue to exist, which condition many of the courses of action in that area. This is especially seen in U.S. relations with Cuba. In a general way, this situation affects the perceptions of security in the Caribbean. Many new dangers have acquired special importance in the area and created a new type of vulnerability. In South America, the end of the Cold War did not have a central impact on the perceptions of threat and the way in which key security issues are defined. The themes related to relations with neighbors have had, and continue to have, priority. The major change is linked more to the processes of integration and political coordination than to the impact of the end of the Cold War.

It is in this general framework that Latin America can possibly open up space to participate in defining the new international system. Few states in the region have sufficient power to be solely capable of influencing the course of global action, but the collaborative definition of common goals would provide a greater opportunity. The process of agreeing upon objectives reinforces the need for dialogue within the region and with the principal actors in the international system. This need for communication translates into a major opening for "multilateralism." Globalization is increasingly obliged to define fundamental international norms for cohabitation. The transfer of rivalries from the exclusively national arena to the international arena is a tendency that had already been in force before the fall of the Berlin wall.

The end of bipolar conflict creates a chance for Latin American countries, if they are able to achieve common objectives, to become involved in the design of a new global system. On the contrary, if the countries of the region do not seek to coordinate their central interests, the danger of marginalization increases. The current period is critical for reconciling positions and defining policies and courses of action. There is greater space for involvement, and there are better opportunities for constructing efficient courses of action.

THE CHANGING REGIONAL CONTEXT

The regional context in the mid-1990s is not clearly defined. The principal tendencies are found fully developed and have not yet been synthesized. Regional diversity is being reaffirmed. Five crucial aspects together affect the definition of security: democratic processes, economic development, processes of integration, regional stability, and ties with the United States. In the 1990s, the region provides examples of both progress and decline in each of these phenomena, and each includes characteristics and specific developments related to security and defense.

The above implies a broad approach to the factors that are involved in security. The concept of security, however, should be most focused on themes dealing strictly with defense. That is to say, the analytical framework should incorporate all the significant factors, in addition to those referring to specifically military aspects. This perspective will allow the development of a political context that seeks stability and peace, based on the capacity to operationalize actions specifically in the area of defense. Otherwise, it involves the development of a whole group of measures, in the various fields of action, that will create a bloated military. In other words, interstate crises in the areas of politics, economics, society, etc., can have ominous consequences; however, a military crisis involving the use of force has irreparable consequences, the historical memory of which lasts for generations.

Democratic Processes

Although democracy is the principal regional political tendency, most of the countries still have weak democracies, and very few are consolidated. There is a tendency to equate elections—which are more or less open—with democratization. Problems of governing—understood in the double meaning of the capacity to govern and the ability to exercise good government—are manifest in many states of the area. No distinction is made on the basis of subregion, size, or influence of the state. Linked to this notion of distinction is a high degree of political and functional autonomy that the armed forces have in many countries. This reality influences the form as well as the basis of civil-military relations. The effects of this situation spill over into the national arena and influence local perceptions concerning international security in the region.

On the other hand, the recent Ecuador-Peru military conflict in Alto Cénepa proves that even democratic regimes, or those regionally recognized as such, can have armed confrontations. This war is more than just an exception to the rule that democracies do not confront one another; it has caused a fundamental rupture in that argument.

Economic Development

Although the region is recovering, the fall in the gross national product in the "lost decade" was so severe that a long period of sustained growth will be needed to recuperate completely. The crisis in Mexico—the "tequila effect"—reveals some existing vulnerabilities and the great interdependence of perceptions toward the region. Linked to this situation is the crisis and burden that poverty poses for the region as a whole, and the great inequality it exhibits. This situation affects and reinforces the tendencies that the lack of governability has demonstrated.

Integration Processes

Integration processes, the grouping of countries into free trade areas, denote major advances in just a few years. The constitution of NAFTA, MERCOSUR, CACM (Central American Common Market), and renewed integration in the Caribbean (CARICOM) show the vigor of these processes of commercial opening. Nevertheless, it will be a while before they can be consolidated. A major coordination of macroeconomic policies is required, at a time in which states are reluctant to free themselves from the few instruments of economic policy that support them. The consolidation of these processes requires actions in other areas in order to pass from commercial to economic integration and to achieve a better position in the global system.

Regional Stability

Regional stability is viewed by how it is affected by various situations. Crisis in one country creates the perception of more general crisis in the subregion or the entire region—that is, there is a transfer of instability. This occurs with greater force than the inverse process; that is to say, the successes of a country or a subregion are not so easily transferred. Three elements stand out in this process of transferring instability: the expansion or the overflow of a national situation into the neighboring states, a lack of sovereign state control over a part of national territory, and the absence of the territory issue in new threats.

Links with the United States

Although U.S. policy tends to bring the region together, the end of the Cold War has aided in a reduction of the instruments of action. There is a decline in aid, but mechanisms that allow the growth of open and free trade have not been developed. A goal has been set, but there are no tools to build the path to it. Domestic power issues take such priority that they have further reduced the region's influence in the context of defining international policy. The lack of common regional positions reduces the capacity for involvement. Similar or clearer situations can be expressed in relation to other international powers.

OVERCOMING THE COLONIAL INHERITANCE

Building a space for agreement requires not only policy choice, which was expressed by the Rio Group, but overcoming distrusts that are rooted in problems of defining territories. To resolve the question of borders is to overcome the colonial inheritance. Until this occurs, the general climate of relations will not change qualitatively, nor will it be expressed in collaborative policies. The perception of threats linked to territorial sovereignty is expressed in the concept of "zero sum" conflict. Conflict situations, however latent, produce distrust and perceptions of uncertainty and vulnerability, especially regarding the issues of sovereignty and territorial definition.

Latin America experiences relatively low conflict as a result of a certain international recognition of state boundaries; in addition, the states have established dissuasive policies that have succeeded in demonstrating that the costs of conflict inhibits its occurrence. However, history shows that the danger of conflict is always present. Although the risks are not high, they have generated recurring cycles of tension between states in the various subregions. Without overcoming the colonial inheritance, the region continues to be a zone of danger and distrust.

THE PERMANENT SEARCH FOR PEACE

The region has developed various mechanisms and commitments that tend to defuse tensions. Significant multilateral agreements have been sought to remove the specter of destruction caused by armed force, especially by weapons of mass destruction—atomic, chemical, and biological. Most notable among these are the Tlatelolco Treaty of February 1967, which by 1993 had been endorsed by all Latin American countries, and the Mendoza Compromise and the Declaration of Cartagena, both of which prohibit the development, production, storage, acquisition, and transfer of weapons of mass chemical or biological destruction. The first was signed on September 5, 1991, by the governments of Argentina, Brazil, and Chile, which were later joined by the government of Uruguay; the second was signed on December 4, 1991, by the presidents of the Andean countries.

Declarations by heads of states and governments have sought to establish favorable conditions for the stability and international security of the region, whose countries adhere to the principles and norms established by the multilateral global and hemispheric bodies—the Constitution of the United Nations and the Charter of the Organization of American States. Also in this group, despite not having achieved full ratification, is the Bogotá Pact for the Peaceful Solution of Controversies and the Declaration of a South Atlantic Zone of Peace and Cooperation, proclaimed by the U.N. in 1986.

Among the principal declarations regarding security are the Declaration of Ayacucho (December 1974); the various declarations of the Contadora Group (1983–87); and the Declaration of Acapulco, proclaimed by the first Presidential Summit on the Permanent Mechanism for Consultation and Political Cooperation (Rio Group), of November 1987. Since that meeting, each Rio Group Summit has issued proclamations concerning international and regional security. Recently, the Miami Presidential Summit of December 11, 1994, as well as the meeting of the Defense Ministers of the Americas—the Williamsburg, Virginia, conference of July 25, 1995—reaffirmed the desire and necessity for peace and stability in the hemisphere.

Moreover, there is a thick network of contacts and declarations among professionals in the military institutions. Among the armed forces of the hemisphere, regular bilateral and multilateral meetings are taking place, the latest of which have been institutionalized in the Annual Conferences of the Chiefs of the Army, Navy, and Air Forces.

However, despite the intentions of these declarations by civilian leaders and high military officials, tension, conflict, and crisis recur in Latin America. Although the intensity may be less than in other regions, and the means of force employed more modest, the consequences to regional stability and peace are significant. Each crisis produces a strong regression in confidence, at a time when the perceptions of traditional threats are being reinforced.

For these reasons, a set of practical measures needs to be established to prevent misinterpretations that might produce tension and the attendant danger of escalation. Developing a preventive plan allows for early action and for taking particular actions in the face of tension-producing situations. The central element of cooperative security is the basic comprehension of the sense of relativity that the idea of security encompasses. The security of any state depends upon the perception of security by itself and by others. From this perception, policy coordination is transformed into the key to cooperative security. A second essential element is that concrete measures are developed within an expanding global policy framework that includes political, economic, social, and cultural aspects. In the same way, promoting a general policy framework is not sufficient by itself; it should be highly focused and operate on specifically military or other relevant areas of defense. The general framework of democratic understanding and economic rapprochement is favorable to the development of specific policies in the area of defense and military relations. It is here that confidence building measures have their greatest application.

CONFIDENCE BUILDING MEASURES

Confidence building measures are bilateral and multilateral actions designed to prevent situations of crisis and conflict. They seek to strengthen peace and international security, contribute to communication between and among actors, and create a favorable atmosphere for establishing a framework of understanding that mitigates the perception of immediate threat and prevents possible elements of surprise. CBMs presuppose the existence of differences of interests and of low confidence in relations. Their application is essential when the attainment or defense of differing ideas would be expressed in the use of force. In those situations, misinterpretation could result in unwanted conflict.

What we should emphasize first is that confidence building measures are "acts" that usually are preceded or accompanied by favorable declarations of peace, understanding, and harmony among peoples. This means that we seek to make these actions known to the international audience so that the world can serve as a witness, giving greater force to the measure.

Confidence building measures are reciprocal, hence "mutual." This distinguishes them from the tokens of goodwill that one state issues for the benefit of another, which are unilateral and therefore not binding. The obligation of CBMs does not only mean that both states are developing the same action—which can occur in some cases—but also that they are equal and concurrent. The withdrawal of military forces from an area of conflict on the part of one of the actors, for example, has its counterpart in the reduction in the arms inventory of the other actor.

In this sense, CBMs are not only "declarations" or "commitments"; they are also effective actions, capable of being evaluated and verified. The transformation of commitments into actions allows the construction of specific international regimes. This is a key point. Declarations are not confidence building measures; we can believe their content or not, or have confidence or not in the promises that they make. But they can strengthen actions and reaffirm the building of political will. A declaration does not change reality by itself; renouncing the use of force does not make a military threat just disappear. The announcement of maneuvers along the border allays the feeling of imminent threat. Changing deployment at the border is an action that transforms both the perception of a threat and its material reality.

Confidence building measures are an instrument, a technique for maintaining peace. They do not resolve conflicts or differences of interest; they make communication possible and they make the courses of action of the various actors involved more transparent and predictable. The process presupposes good faith and the desire to avoid confrontation. Otherwise, CBMs could be used to gain time or to intentionally conceal the real interests of one actor from the another, and to create a false sense of security. Confidence building measures seek to prevent escalation as an automatic response. It is therefore fundamental to generate confidence, establish networks of communication and of interpretation of actions, and create space for verification. The circulation and delivery of basic information concerning courses of action, which is then reinforced by action, makes it possible to regulate certain forms of behavior and misinterpretations that could lead to the outbreak of conflict.

Reducing uncertainty and increasing predictability are two central objectives of CBMs. By establishing a communications network and promoting the growth of actions that demonstrate a tendency towards peaceful resolution of conflicts of interest, a window of opportunity is opened to develop actions in other areas, principally politics and diplomacy. Furthermore, if there are solid diplomatic commitments and a system of real CBMs is constructed, the space for establishing arms control and limitation measures is generated in areas defined jointly by the parties involved.

The objective of CBMs is to act above risks and above threats. They have preventive value. They make communication possible and information mechanisms effective. CBMs are not arms-control measures, and neither are they arms-limitation measures. Nor do they constitute disarmament measures, even though the development of CBMs can form part of a process that includes these kinds of measures. It is difficult to think that arms-control and -limitation measures, and even disarmament, can be developed in the absence of a climate of confidence—and without CBMs.

CBMs are designed to influence the course of events. They transform declarations of goodwill into effective actions. They allow an evaluation of the actors' conduct from where the risk is generated or the threat is perceived. The first level of action is defined by overcoming distrust generated by specific fears. A second level of action is aimed at establishing a framework of trust that permits the reevaluation of dangers on the basis of new information. A third level refers to the creation of a base of confidence that makes possible the development of collective action and association.

Confidence is sustained through diligence amid a high degree of intangibility. Trust is built gradually, incrementally. But it can be lost suddenly. CBMs seek to establish a pattern of relations that grants credit to declarations of intent. They are designed to help determine which acts will and will not tend to affect security, integrity, or any other vital interest. This represents the essential link between CBMs and the verification processes.

There has been much debate over the flexibility or restrictiveness of CBMs. Some interpretations view them in the broad context of the development of security, including political-military aspects and aspects related to the economy, culture, and social relations. They emphasize political, governmental, and parliamentary contacts, along with open intergovernmental cooperation, diplomatic contacts, and activities in the field of education and culture. Other views focus on defense and the development of essentially military measures. Among these are the exchange of military information, the development of consultation mechanisms in the face of unusual military activities, cooperation in matters of military incidents and accidents, notification of military maneuvers, observation of specific military activities, training and education, etc.

In the case of Latin America, systematizing accords in different spheres should include a major focus on defense, which is where CBMs possess their central value in what is referred to as security. Nevertheless, given that the regional diplomatic style is suitable, the debate should not be polarized over the degree of flexibility. Rather, a pragmatic response should be sought. Establishing the origin and substantive elements of each situation of risk, tension, or threat makes it possible to develop a set of political, diplomatic, economic, and military measures in response. The success of CBMs applied in the area of defense will depend upon the general framework of relations. Thus the design, limitations, and speed of implementation of particular CBMs will depend upon the ease or difficulty of resolving the differences among the interests of the parties involved. The view should be set toward reaching mutually beneficial results and in constructing a framework of trust in the relations.

Sources of distrust are varied and tied to diverse rivalries (political, territorial, ethnic, military). Of these, the territorial and geographical conflicts, together with ethnic problems, play a major role. The historic transmission of distrust crosses generations and reaches into the social arena.

Confidence building measures have ten characteristics. These features are provided with examples in the following paragraphs.

Transparency and openness seek to establish the "clarity" of objectives pursued or actions developed. Transparency is basic; it seeks to make courses of action obvious, to demonstrate a logic of action. Transparency does not respond to aggression by other actors. Verification is an essential part of establishing transparency. Compliance with the delivery of information to the U.N.'s Registry of Conventional Arms is a confidence measure of this type, as is the exchange of information on military estimates.

Predictability seeks trustworthy and reliable conduct. Its specific function is to make evident "aggressive" conduct that contrasts with the pattern of established relations or with the commitment to act in a predetermined way. Notification of military activities on the ground and the exchange of plans concerning significant military maneuvers are examples of this point.

Reciprocity and equivalence should be found in actions that should follow developments between the parties; there should be a basic symmetry in the commitments, or at least a balancing. Reciprocity allows actors to become involved in the process. This differs from unilateral actions, which ultimately put distance between the parties. The exchange of information, established formally or bilaterally by multilateral organizations, serves as an example here.

Adequate communication enables the confidence building measures' design to establish conversation, allow for interaction that promotes the understanding of actions and intentions, and establish a professional dialogue to reinforce transparency. The meetings of high commanders and authorities from the defense ministries are examples that demonstrate the emphasis on communication and conversation.

The establishment of a relationship is a factor, and patterns in the relationship should be established. Measures should have a permanence over time. Stability in execution allows a better understanding and evaluation of courses of action. The annual meetings for the exchange of views and analysis serve as clear examples in this regard.

Feasibility is important, as measures should be realistic in their execution. Simplicity is essential. In their design, as much as in their exchange, verification measures should exhibit a high degree of feasibility, taking into consideration the speed and costs of implementation. Installing a remote sensor system can be more efficient than a peacekeeping force. An observation satellite is able to deliver adequate information, but at a high cost; a group of observers can, in some cases, complete a mission more effectively.

Coherence is essential for making sure executed measures coincide with other policies. Lack of coherence could be viewed as an intention to use CBMs as a subterfuge. Coherence reinforces other aspects of the relationship and the global climate of the relationship. An aggressive and even hostile discourse on the domestic front would not be coherent with proposing a series of measures to promote confidence.

Verification of CBMs, as they are actions, not declarations that one may or may not choose to believe, must be possible. Verification proves compliance. A schedule of actions to be completed by a specific time; the establishment of a demilitarized zone within a given period; the development of inspections on request without the possibility of being denied; and authorized flyovers are all examples of verification.

Social support of the measures should be given strong domestic legitimacy. The domestic consensus will reinforce the institutional policies, providing transparency in compliance and ensuring its stability at the same time.

Finally, variability according to number of actors is a characteristic of CBMs, as they can be bilateral or multilateral. Multilateral arrangements require a majority consensus and are based on the least common denominator. Given the diversity in the Western Hemisphere and the differentiation and asymmetries of powers, interests and practices should outline subregional measures versus those of a global character. In general, the latter measures relate to the exchange of information: the U.N. Registry of Conventional Arms, for example. In neighboring and subregional areas, the notification of maneuvers and the presence of observers have the greatest significance.

CBMs seek to establish a pattern of conduct that can be evaluated. That is to say, the judgment that we make about the future behavior of another actor can be developed on the basis of specific practices, expressed and executed in actions that we can observe and analyze over time.

The formation of confidence therefore is a process in which we permanently assess the conduct and the courses of action of the actors whose credibility we seek to establish. Three elements can be evaluated: sincerity, competency, and trustworthiness.

Evaluating sincerity focuses principally on the degree of coherence—the comparison between public and private discourse and the difference between the domestic discourse and the international message. Furthermore, the degree of coherence can be seen in the difference between executed actions and words and in the correlation between promises of execution and their quality of execution, or the degree and punctuality of compliance. Sincerity will reflect good faith, which is based on the degree to which commitments are met.

Competence is the capacity to make the commitments effective and/or the conditions and material capacities available to put them into practice. The development of state policy in the defense area indicates a greater level of competence as compared to the consideration of government policy exclusively. The evaluation of political competence—political capacity—is significant in democratic regimes where the balance of power can block initiatives or veto their execution. For example, the ratification of an agreement by parliament will demonstrate a level of competence in building political consensus.

Reliability seeks to evaluate the historical consistency, the pattern of long-term conduct, experiences in previous situations, and the level of coherence with established courses of action.

Confidence building measures seek to transfer stability to relations, establishing a process by which these measures will give concrete satisfaction to the commitments made. CBMs seek to change the history of distrust that characterizes the ties between countries of the region. This implies a high degree of risk for a situation in which, given the actions we are evaluating, we achieve stability and later expand on it. If we keep looking at the past, we will not have options for the future. If we trust only in declarations, we base the future on a question of faith. If we develop CBMs as part of a process of creating a climate of confidence, we will be able to interact in a way that is more transparent and predictable. A greater space for diplomacy and policy will be made possible. Confidence building measures will allow us to offer guarantees. Here the difference between faith and confidence takes root. With guarantees we will be able to establish an objective pattern of evaluation, independent of our faith in the degree of compliance.

The development of CBMs is a substantive part of the process of establishing a Regime of Cooperative Hemispheric Security. The Peace and Security in the Americas program has defined the concept of cooperative security as a system of state interactions that, by coordinating governmental policies, prevents and contains the threats to national interests and avoids the tendencies of states to transform their perceptions into tensions, crises, or open confrontations.

For development to occur, there must be progress in ten areas: prevention of crises and the maintenance of the status quo, modernization and regional balance, mutual confidence measures, arms control and limitation, disarmament, security regimes, bilateral responses, institutionalization of cooperative hemispheric security, constructive involvement of the United States in the development of a system of hemispheric security, and the role of the U.N.

The process of building confidence can advance by clearly distinct degrees, beginning with eradicating distrust. Measures must seek to establish a framework that would eliminate suspicion and fear by generating transparency. Verification is determined by giving complete satisfaction on this point.

Building an area of confidence comes next, as a relationship of predictability should be maintained over time and demonstrate the construction of a new type of relationship that allows certainty and confidence in meeting commitments.

Deepening trust is the next step in the strengthening of relations. A pattern of relations that points toward greater association has now been created. The design of collaborative actions and joint practice characterizes ties.

Recognizing interdependence follows—when the collaborative projects acquire a greater presence, interdependencies are recognized and institutional limits for coordinating policies are established. Simultaneously, there is progress towards the creation of supranational institutions.

The confidence building process is a lengthy one. In the case of Europe, it took more than two decades. There, at the Helsinki Conference in 1975, basic measures were established to overcome distrust. The development and launching of the first-generation mechanisms took ten years; second-generation measures were developed between 1986 and 1989. The changes made under *perestroika* and *glasnost* were an important advance. In 1990, third-generation measures were presented at the Vienna Conference, and parallel the endorsement of the Paris Letter concerning the new Europe. These measures allowed for the code of military conduct that exists today and for joint agreements that have reduced the fear of historical interstate conflicts. These developments have made it possible to limit the transferral of the instability the Balkan conflicts generated.

Confidence building measures permit the construction of a history of satisfied promises and fulfilled commitments, the establishment of practices for expanding them, and the shaping of a pattern of relationships that gives certainty and predictability to relations. Strengthening those processes will enable the definition of specific measures in the area of arms limitation and control, including disarmament. That is to say, only when we see proven certainties are we able to search for concerted measures destined to change the strategic balance. The reduction of the potential for conflict in a parallel, simultaneous, and balanced way, around which strategic balance is established, will be possible only in an atmosphere of trust and stability. This must embrace bilateral ties, yet also consider the area where the balance is developed.

The present democratic context and the growth of integration are positive for the construction of the political space that permits a movement from distrust to cooperation in the region and across the hemisphere. In this way, we can build the foundation that is essential in developing a regional strategic balance. It is this balance that will allow us to influence the design of the new world that opened with the end of the Cold War.

BIBLIOGRAPHY

Bomsdorf, Falk. "The Third World, Europe and Measures to Establish Confidence." Paper presented at the Workshop of the International Academy of Peace, London, October 23–24, 1984.

Castro, Carlos, and Francisco Rojas Aravena. "International Crisis: A Key Concept for Making State Decisions." *Trabajo de Investigación* (Research Work). Santiago: National Academy of Political and Strategic Studies, 1994.

"Confidence-Building Measures." *The Arms Control Association Fact Sheet,* April 1995.

Document of Budapest 1994. "Towards an Authentic Partnership in a New Era." Statement of the Budapest Summit, February 2, 1995.

Document of Vienna 1990. Vienna, 1990.

Echeverría, Rafael. *Ontología del Lenguaje* (Substance of Language). Editorial Dolman, 1994.

Flores, Fernando. *Creando Organizaciones para el Futuro* (Creating Organizations for the Future). Santiago-Dolme Editions, February 1994.

Krepon, Michael, ed. *A Handbook of Confidence-Building Measures for Regional Security.* Henry L. Stimson Center, Handbook No. 1, January 1995.

McFate, Patricia Bliss, Douglas A. Fraser, Sidney N. Graybeal, and George R. Lindsey. "The Converging Roles of Arms Control Verification, Confidence-Building Measures, and Peace Operations: Opportunities for Harmonization and Synergies." *Arms Control Verification Studies,* NR 6, Department of Foreign Affairs and International Trade, Canada, October 1994.

Palma, Hugo. *Confianza, Desarme y Relaciones Internacionales* (Confidence, Disarmament and International Relations). Lima: CEPEI, 1991.

———. *Medidas de Confianza Recíproca* (Mutual Confidence Measures). South American Peace Commission, Working Document, Santiago, March 1988.

Paz y Seguridad en las Américas (Peace and Security in the Americas). "Policies for a Partnership of Hemispheric Security: Policy Recommendations." No. 1, March 1995.

Schoultz, Lars, William C. Smith, and Augusto Varas, eds., *Security, Democracy and Development in U.S.-Latin American Relations.* North-South Center, University of Miami, 1994.

Varas, Augusto. "The Post–Cold War Partnership in Hemispheric Security." Santiago: International and Military Relations Area, FLACSO-Chile, 1994.

Varas, Augusto, and Isaac Caro, eds., *Medidas de Confianza Mutua en América Latina* (Mutual Confidence Measures in Latin America). Santiago: FLACSO, Stimson Center, SER, February 1994.

STRATEGIC BALANCE AND CONFIDENCE BUILDING MEASURES IN LATIN AMERICA: THE HISTORICAL UTILITY OF AN AMBIGUOUS CONCEPT

DAVID R. MARES

Strategic balance is a fundamental consideration in any context in which bargaining occurs, be it voluntary or coerced, implicit or explicit. Strategic balance consists of all the elements that make up bargaining power, which include not only domestic resources but also the international resources upon which a nation can call when the need presents itself. Domestic resources include such things as economic, social, political, and military capability; international resources include not only formal alliances but also reputation and strategic assets. Any of these may influence other states to come to another's aid in a confrontation. For example, since 1948, Costa Rica has been able to draw upon its reputation as an unarmed country to convince both the United States and Venezuela to assist it in minor military confrontations.[1]

Although "confidence building measures" is a relatively new label, having come out of the Helsinki process (1975–89), the concept has been around for a long time.[2] Due to the anarchic nature of international politics, a state that has competitive security interests but that would like to cooperate in order to diminish or resolve them exposes itself to potentially high costs if the other states involved renege on cooperation (e.g., Munich in 1938). Since "talk is cheap," the credibility of international commitments is always an issue.[3] Confidence building measures, consequently, are designed to enhance the context for cooperation.

The relationship between strategic balance and confidence building measures is complex. On the one hand, strategic balance itself may be designed to increase confidence between two adversaries such that, in moments of crisis, neither side will be tempted to use military force to resolve the issue. On the other hand, since strategic balance itself is not entirely objective (see discussion below), it may be useful to think about ways in which one can instill confidence in knowing that the distribution of strategic resources is in fact stable. The emphasis on defensive over offensive weapons in developing a strategic balance is an example of this type of thinking.

Although strategic balances are composed of many resources, in the context of a discussion of confidence building measures it makes sense to focus the historical discussion on the question of military balance itself. Throughout Latin American history the military factor in strategic balance has been dominant in interstate disputes. The first section of this chapter discusses the question of strategic balance itself. The ambiguity of the concept, in both its military and nonmilitary components, is highlighted, and theoretical possibilities are explored to discover why the concept has been so useful despite the uncertainties of what it claims to measure. The second section looks at the historical record as it relates to the distinctions made in the first section, and demonstrates the importance of different versions of strategic balance in intra–Latin American relations. The concluding section addresses the policy relevance of this analysis, and argues for the need to link any serious discussion of confidence building measures to broader conflict avoidance measures; in the context of unsettled border problems, even democratic governments may be reluctant to give up any potential advantages. Blanket recommendations that do not recognize differences in bilateral contexts may actually serve to undermine strategic balance, thereby inadvertently increasing the lack of confidence between the two parties.

AMBIGUITIES IN CONCEPTUALIZING STRATEGIC BALANCE

Strategic balance is a *relative* measure, the importance of which can only be understood in the context of relations between nations. It is important to understand what is likely to occur if two nations become entangled in a dispute in which both sides perceive important interests to be at stake. A focus on the *absolute* capability of a nation is inadequate for discussions concerning how much is enough to provide an acceptable level of security.

The appropriateness of a measure of the balance depends on both the strategy being confronted and the strategy being utilized in defense. There is no inherent measure of strategic balance that is useful in all scenarios. This can be illustrated with examples of miscalculations concerning the relevant components of strategic balance. The United States had prepared for a conventional war of attrition against the Soviet Union, possibly escalating to a nuclear confrontation; but its advantages in these military aspects served it poorly when it confronted guerrilla warfare in Vietnam. In Panama, General Noriega appeared to expect that the diplomatic advantages he had in the OAS in opposing a U.S. intervention would help keep the United States at bay; however, the position of the OAS on this issue was not considered important enough by the United States to constitute a veto on its action. In short, "strategic balance" must be contextualized, and that requires exploring theoretical possibilities and relating them to the historical record of conflict in the region.

Which resources are relevant to strategic balance depends upon whether the strategy being implemented or confronted is offensive, reactive, or diversionary. This categorization does not imply intent, but rather focuses on the conflict dynamics that could lead to the use of military force. Thus, an offensive strategy may be utilized for strictly defensive purposes—"the best defense is a good offense." Each strategy will render distinct components of the strategic balance relevant. Failure to appreciate the difference can make a country incapable of successfully confronting a challenge or produce inadvertent conflict escalation.

Offensive Strategies

These are the most difficult to deal with peacefully because of the dangers of being wrong in the anarchic international realm. To choose an offensive strategy implies that one believes that offense has an advantage; that is, whoever strikes first wins. Under anarchic conditions, therefore, the incentive is to strike first.[4] This limits the time for crisis negotiation and makes it more difficult to implement confidence building measures before a potential crisis. Blitzkrieg, limited aims, and coercive diplomacy are offensive strategies.

In blitzkrieg, one quickly penetrates deep past segments of the enemy's army to destroy lines of communication and render the army on the front lines incapable of fighting. Successful performance of this task requires well-trained personnel and mobile resources concentrated on one or a few potentially vulnerable points of the defender's front. Successful examples of blitzkrieg strategies in Latin American history include the U.S. invasion of Mexico in 1847 and Peru's invasion of Ecuador in 1941.

The goal of a limited aims strategy is to seize a segment of the adversary's territory and hold it for incorporation into one's nation or as ransom for a coercive diplomacy strategy. Resources are concentrated at the vulnerable point for taking the territory and subsequently defending it. Resources in the strategic balance that affect the ability to concentrate and defend forces in the targeted area become relevant in analysis of limited aims disputes. Most Latin American militarized conflicts in the twentieth century have had one side that was playing a limited aims strategy.

Coercive diplomacy is reactive in principle but relies on an offensive capability to make it effective. The goal is to persuade an opponent to stop short of its goals once it has achieved initial successes, or to undo the actions it has already undertaken. To be successful the coercion must inflict high levels of pain, be it via diplomatic and economic sanctions or militarily induced casualties.[5] The U.S. response to Castro's Cuba is a case of failed coercive diplomacy, while the Sandinistas' demise in Nicaragua represents a success.

Reactive Strategies

These can be either defensive or deterrent. In defense, the goal is to keep the enemy from destroying one's army or seizing territory once it has initiated an aggressive action. The relevant means are mainly military and must be appropriate to the offensive strategy one is countering: blitzkrieg, limited aims, or coercive diplomacy. While diplomatic and economic sanctions may be categorized as defensive reactions, they act as a deterrent strategy if the aggressive action has not yet been initiated, or would be included under coercive diplomacy once the action was under way.

A deterrent strategy is designed to convince the adversary to resist undertaking a contemplated aggressive action. It consists of a double promise based on a capacity and will to punish: the promise to increase the costs faced by the aggressor beyond what it is most likely willing to pay, and the promise to refrain from using that same capacity offensively. The requirements of a deterrent strategy are particularly difficult to meet because of the credibility problems inherent in promises made under international conditions of anarchy. Some analysts even claim that periodic use of force is necessary for deterrent strategies to have the requisite credibility.[6]

Diversionary and Cooperative Strategies

These can be either offensive or reactive. In a diversionary strategy, tactics are designed to identify an external enemy and rally domestic support behind the government. The goal is to avoid actual military confrontation, or keep it extremely limited if it should occur. Because escalation is not contemplated, this strategy is more attractive to governments of weak states than are the other offensive strategies. Ideally, a cooperative strategy would be strictly reactive, but the power aggregated in a cooperative alliance may make it tempting to undertake "preventive" operations against states identified for some reason as potential threats to the status quo.

The broad categories of resources that are best used in considering strategic balance are diplomatic, economic, and military. The relevant diplomatic resources include the ability to bring together international sentiment and law in favor of one side in a dispute. Economic resources include not only those that can be used to sanction behavior, but also those that can be used to build up national capacity as well as reward the behavior of other states. Military resources include trained personnel, armaments, and doctrines for utilizing those resources. The most favorable strategic situation a country may find itself in would combine all three factors in its favor. In the Western Hemisphere, only the United States has been able to construct such a dominant strategic position. Because the United States has effectively kept other great powers out of the region, it is favored in the strategic balance in the Americas; for Latin American states, however, strategic balance has been more fluid across time.[7]

The measures of strategic balance in Latin America are ambiguous for a number of reasons. On the diplomatic front, formal alliances among one set of Latin American nations against another, while commonplace in the nineteenth century, became rare in the twentieth. Nevertheless, the expectation that such alliances might develop in the event of an outbreak of war influences the calculations of the region's diplomats. Figures on military budgets, arms expenditures, and imports are notoriously unreliable until the 1970s, when they became merely debatable.[8] The combat readiness of people and machines forms a basis for calculating strategic military advantage, yet is not quantifiable in any scientific way. As a result, states tend to err on the high side in considering strategic balances; confidence building measures, however, give them reason to limit their military resources to a degree.

THE STRATEGIC BALANCE IN HISTORY

Highlighting the chief threats to peace in the Americas helps us to understand the strategic balances that operated historically and to speculate about how confidence building measures can help keep the balances stable in the future. In twentieth-century Latin America, interstate conflicts have largely revolved around border demarcation, migration, ideology, power projection, and resource competition.[9] Apart from the Chaco War (between Bolivia and Paraguay, 1932–35) and the Central American wars of 1906 and 1907, limited aims and coercive diplomacy were the most used strategies in conflicts in the Western Hemisphere. The use of force by both initiators and targets in intra-American disputes is guided by these strategies.

Three bilateral relationships are used here to illustrate the relevance of strategic balance over time, as well as the ways in which that balance has been, or has failed to be, modified. The brief synopses are not intended to be histories of the disputes, but rather are interpretive summaries of the aspects relevant to this discussion of strategic balances. The dyads were chosen because they show the range of possibilities for states caught in enduring disputes over territorial issues and power projection, the two factors reflected most in Latin American interstate disputes.

Argentina-Brazil

Brazil has occupied a unique position in Latin America. It is Portuguese, not Spanish, and thus is culturally different. Until late in the nineteenth century it was also a monarchy, in a hemisphere in which monarchy by definition was a suspect form of government. Brazil was also able to overcome the political fragmentation that broke up the early Spanish American states and thus physically loomed as a giant in the area. In contrast to Argentina, which stressed its links to Europe, Brazil attempted to create an American identity for itself, much as the United States had. Argentina's wealth and European culture led it to perceive itself as the natural leader among the republics created out of the Spanish American empire. It was a mantle, however, that no other Western Hemisphere state was willing to concede to the Argentines.

The Argentine-Brazilian rivalry began early, with war from 1825 to 1828 and continuous tensions leading to a war scare in 1873. One of the first fruits of this rivalry was the creation of Uruguay, guaranteed by the British, as a buffer state between the two. As with all buffer states, Uruguay became the object of the rivals' efforts to control it. The Argentines in particular utilized military threats to pressure Uruguay on issues of maritime boundaries and foreign policy.

In classic balance-of-power behavior, Argentina and Brazil did not let their rivalry get in the way of keeping out other potential rivals. They joined forces in the obliteration of Paraguay during the War of the Triple Alliance (1864–70), but the collaboration did not produce lasting friendship, especially as many Brazilians felt that Argentina used the alliance for its own benefit.[10]

Brazil and Argentina were wary of each other, but unsure of the possibility and costs of an outright military resolution of their conflict. Each also had territorial disputes with other neighbors, raising the prospect of a multifront war. Leaders in both countries studiously avoided war by utilizing international law and bilateral diplomacy to keep the level of distrust at peacefully manageable levels. Periodic arms buildups also served a deterrent function as they helped to keep alive the specter of a disastrous war if diplomacy failed. Because each perceived the threat as inevitably escalating to a war of attrition if made effective, they focused their military policies on building up total national resources.

At the turn of the twentieth century Brazil was busily settling her borders in the west and southwest. Through bilateral negotiations and arbitration Brazil was able peacefully to gain territory until it was the size of France, but became involved in the militarized Acre dispute with Bolivia in 1902–3. After losing an arbitration case, Foreign Minister Baron Rio Branco decided that the declining military capability of Brazil over the past twenty to thirty years was negatively affecting its international respect.[11] He set off to improve Brazil's standing by professionalizing the training of its military and increasing its armaments. From 1906 to 1914, the navy bought ships, armaments, and professional training from the major European suppliers. Among the ships purchased were three dreadnought battleships from the British, including the *Rio de Janeiro*, the largest built to that day. At the same time, the Baron attempted to bring Brazil into close diplomatic relations with the United States and ride its coattails to predominance in South America.

Brazil's diplomatic and military policies worried Argentina. Given Brazilian advantages in manpower and geographic depth, Argentine naval superiority was perceived as a necessary component in the bilateral strategic balance. Argentina's response to Brazil's naval program was twofold. On the diplomatic front, Argentina sought to be the interlocutor between Latin America and the great powers. This policy would, if successful, aggregate Argentina's own strategic resources with the favor of the great powers as

Table 8.1

Naval Balance: Argentina and Brazil, 1906

	Argentina	Brazil
Battleships	5	3
Armored Cruisers	4	0
Protected Cruisers	3	6
Torpedo Gunboats	5	2
Torpedo Boats	22	4
Gunboats	4	0
Destroyers	4	0

Source: D. R. O'Sullivan-Beare, Acting Counsel General, British Mission in Brazil, to Sir Earl Grey, London, November 10, 1906, Public Records Office, Foreign Office 371.13, folio 40648, pp. 291ff.

well as keep Argentina from becoming overly dependent on any one great power.[12] Argentina was also active on the military front, professionalizing its military and undertaking its own naval program, including the purchase of two dreadnoughts. Table 8.1 provides a comparison of the naval balance of the two countries during this period.

The competition between the two South American countries became tense enough that between 1908 and 1910 British diplomats in South America reported that the Río de la Plata region was experiencing a war scare. The crisis was defused after a visit by the Argentine general Roca to Brazil, during which he declared that democratic and sister nations should not fight each other. In addition, the general proposed that the two countries should increase economic relations to guarantee future congenial relations. Despite improved relations, armaments purchases continued on both sides. Brazil's new navy served a greater foreign policy purpose when it provided the country with a capacity to become a belligerent in World War I and, as a consequence, received a seat with the great powers in the Council of the League of Nations.[13]

In the late 1930s the rivalry between the two nations began to heat up again, although the two governments, now dictatorships, had been collaborating in tracking down communists.[14] This time it was the Argentine military buildup that provoked a reaction from the Brazilians. Both countries attempted to develop security relations with the United States that would increase national capabilities. But the United States, wary of Argentina's nationalism and wanting to safeguard Brazil's geographic bulge opposite Nazi-occupied Dakar, chose to fortify relations with Brazil.[15] Brazil perceived its threats differently and chose to utilize the resultant military resources to fortify its border with Argentina.[16]

From 1938 to 1960 the strategic balance increasingly favored Brazil: it consolidated its position as the dominant U.S. ally in South America; its economy boomed as Argentina's fell into a stop-go pattern of growth, thereby dramatically increasing Brazil's national capabilities relative to Argentina's; and its defense expenditures as a percentage of GNP grew significantly in the second half of the 1950s, just as Argentina's began a dramatic decline compared with the Perón years.[17]

By the 1960s the growth of Brazil's national capabilities relative to Argentina gave it a sense of security even in the context of geopolitical doctrines that emphasized interstate competition. Although Brazil was content to keep its military budget as a small proportion of the national budget, Argentina sought to balance the absolute level of expenditures of the much larger Brazilian economy. But Argentina had now lost the race with Brazil. The Argentine economy virtually collapsed under the strains induced by the domestic political battles, even under numerous authoritarian governments. In the late 1970s, the Argentine military government made the fateful error of shifting its military focus from the long-stalemated relationship with Brazil to its unstable situations with Great Britain and Chile. The Beagle Channel war scare, in which Argentina had to retreat after a great public fanfare, and the disastrous war with Britain in the Malvinas (Falkland) Islands destroyed not only Argentine military resources, but also its hopes for economic and political resources that could be used in the competition over strategic balances.

Today's "new Argentina" has transformed its traditional rivalries into partnerships, decimated its military establishment, and become the South American country most in favor of the cooperative strategy. Still, Argentine Defense Minister Oscar Camilion (a civilian) argues that the local balance of power must be maintained, that the United States should help keep the balance stable, and that Argentina will purchase what it needs in whatever markets make it available.[18]

Argentina-Chile

Argentina and Chile have historically disputed the southern Andes as well as the waterways connecting the Atlantic and Pacific. Their relationship has also been affected by the possibility that Argentina might join with Peru and Bolivia against Chile, or that Chile could ally with Brazil against Argentina. The rivals have made use of diplomatic, economic, and military resources in their efforts to influence the strategic balance. Since the War of the Pacific (1879–84), Chile has largely been the status quo power, but its reputation as a successful aggressor in the past has bedeviled its credibility even up to the present time. Argentina, until very recently, has consistently sought to make limited territorial gains and important power projection advances into countries bordering Chile's north (Peru and Bolivia). In the 1990s, Argentina abandoned power projection goals and became a status-quo power.

During the War of the Pacific, Chile worried that Argentina would come to the aid of Peru and Bolivia. Instead, Argentina chose to establish control over disputed Patagonia, which Chile was willing to concede in return for Argentine neutrality. After the war, however, the two countries found their dispute escalating toward armed confrontation. Argentina provoked an arms race by attempting to equal Chilean naval strength in 1898, and war scares continued until 1902, when British mediation successfully brokered the most famous arms control treaty in South American history. The Pactos de Mayo of 1902 resulted in both countries selling off warships they had under construction in Europe and the disarmament of some ships already in service. Of longer-lasting importance, the pacts resolved the power projection competition by assigning each country a sphere of influence—Chile in the Pacific, Argentina in the Atlantic and the Rio Plata.[19]

Diplomatic and military elements in the Pactos turned out to be confidence building measures as well, and they played a fundamental role in helping the two countries respond to Brazil's naval buildup after 1906 without damaging their own bilateral relationship. Both Argentina and Chile increased their navies and added dreadnoughts in efforts to maintain the southern naval balance, and they also collaborated diplomatically in trying to get Brazil to moderate its naval program.

Bilateral relations over the next half century were extremely pacific given the border issues that remained. Chile and Argentina traveled different routes over the period, routes that were to culminate in a new war scare that largely came about as the result of Chile's alteration of the components that constituted its understanding of the strategic balance. In brief, Argentina continued to rely heavily upon the military aspects of the balance, while Chile chose to rely more upon diplomatic alliances and economic incentives for its security.[20]

In the 1960s, however, tensions began to grow, resulting in a crisis in the Laguna del Desierto in 1965 and the Beagle Channel islands in 1967. In 1965, both countries began to increase their military budgets and personnel, and an arms race ensued in the 1970s.[21] The period of tension was punctuated by a respite in 1971 when Argentine General Lanusse's government decided to submit the dispute in the Beagle Channel to arbitration.[22] But since the 1973 right-wing coup in Chile worried the left-wing military government in Peru, Chile continued to fortify its military position.

General Lanusse had made the decision for arbitration although his advisors indicated that the islands would most likely be given to Chile. For the general, cooperative economic relations with Chile, rather than territorial competition or military balances, were the road to security and prosperity. But the general ignored certain geopolitical realities which became clearer after the arbitral award became known.

As predicted, the arbitration awarded the islands to Chile. By now, however, a new military government in Argentina feared that possession of the islands would allow Chile to project itself into the Atlantic, thereby upsetting the bioceanic principle that was embodied in the Pactos de Mayo and that had underpinned peaceful coexistence between the two countries.[23] Argentina attempted to negotiate a resolution with Chile that would provide for sovereignty over the islands without rights to maritime projection. Chile's military government, however, refused to give up any of the advantages that it had won in arbitration.

Argentina adopted a coercive strategy in the face of Chilean intransigence. Splits within the Argentine military government indicated that they could not decide if they would be content with a Chilean decision to accept maritime limitations or if they would insist on getting the islands themselves. It did not matter; Chile was not negotiating the issue. When military threats failed to push Chile to negotiate, the Argentines sought to implement a limited aims strategy by seizing the islands and presenting Chile with a fait accompli.

Chile's reliance on diplomacy and economic statecraft now failed to generate a stable relationship with Argentina. Because of the massive violations of human rights by both governments, neither could appeal to the international community for support in a conflict. This situation was more dangerous for Chile because it had specifically reoriented its strategic policy to depend upon the resources of the inter-American community (specifically the United States), while Argentina continued its long-standing policy of self-reliance. With a war scare on its Peruvian border and increasing tensions on the Argentine front, the strategic balance had shifted decidedly against Chile, leaving it in an extremely vulnerable position.

The Chileans moved quickly on two fronts to remedy the strategic imbalance. In the face of Argentinian coercive tactics, Chile made attempts at bilateral cooperation. Chile would not discuss any sovereignty issues related to the Beagle Channel islands, but offered to discuss a variety of territorial and economic questions. Chile also would not give in to Argentine military threats. Instead the Pinochet regime attempted to deter Argentina from undertaking military action by proclaiming its intent to fight if necessary.

Chilean deterrence efforts lacked credibility, largely because its strategic policy over the previous thirty years had undermined the reputation it had gained in the nineteenth-century wars. Deterrence, therefore, failed until the last moment. The Argentine government advanced its forces to seize the islands but discovered that the Chilean navy was ready and waiting. At this point, the Chilean government also seemed to have some change of heart concerning the wording of an agreement to ask for papal mediation. War was thus avoided and mediation begun, although militarized confrontations continued until after Argentina was defeated by the British in the Malvinas (Falklands) War.

After 1984, Argentina and Chile were able to diplomatically resolve all outstanding border issues except the Laguna del Desierto. This dispute was submitted to arbitration, and in 1994 the area was awarded to Argentina. This time Chile objected, and domestic politics pushed President Frei's government to request that the arbiters reexamine the reasoning behind their decision. Argentina's government claimed nothing was wrong with the process. Although appeal is allowed on technical grounds, the Chilean response to the arbitral decision is potentially damaging to a cooperative strategy based on confidence building. It should not be assumed that the Chilean government would reject a reconfirmed arbitral decision. But if the arbiters were to significantly alter their original decision, it will most likely lead not only Argentina but other nations that may be considering this path to confidence building to question the impartiality of such panels.

Ecuador-Peru

These two countries have disputed the Amazonian headwaters since independence. Both countries have tried diplomatic as well as military means to resolve the issue, but it remains alive to this day. In the numerous military confrontations that occurred, Ecuador lost approximately 40 percent of the territory it claimed upon separation from Gran Colombia in 1830. Peru successfully utilized blitzkrieg, limited aims, and deterrent strategies to develop its favorable position up to 1995, at which point its deterrent strategy appears to have failed. Ecuador failed miserably in its attempts to utilize defensive, coercive diplomacy, and limited aims strategies until 1995, when it successfully implemented a strategy that combined limited aims and deterrent tactics.

In the 1890s, after decades of jockeying for a definitive resolution with military threats and bilateral diplomacy, Ecuador and Peru agreed to arbitrate their border. In 1910, while the King of Spain was preparing to deliver his decision, word leaked out that it would support almost completely the Peruvian position. Riots broke out across Ecuador and the government found itself compelled to denounce the entire arbitration. A war scare ensued, during which Ecuador armed itself, partly with the aid of Chile, which had its own dispute with Peru over Tacna and Arica. The United States and the British acted as mediators and the dispute subsided into a series of periodic, small-scale armed skirmishes.

The strategic policies of the two countries were basically set in this period. Peru, now confident of its legal position, would utilize the demand for arbitration as its first line of defense on the border issue. But it also maintained a significant military advantage in case Ecuador attempted a limited gains strategy to provoke an incident and draw in international mediators. This was precisely the Ecuadorian approach to strategic balance: provoke border incidents that would convince other actors (the United States, the U.N., the Pope, etc.) to intervene to find a "just," rather than a juridical, solution to the problem.

A crisis situation began to build in the late 1930s. Ecuador believed that it had gotten the United States to deter Peruvian use of its military advantage. Both sides began to establish outposts in the disputed territory and major skirmishes occurred in 1939. In 1941, Peru decided to resolve the issue once and for all, and implemented a blitzkrieg strategy against Ecuador, using paratroops and tanks to penetrate overextended Ecuadorian defenses. Peru's rapid victory rendered Ecuador's attempts at inter-American diplomacy extremely difficult: no American states were willing to pay the costs for coercive diplomacy against the victorious Peruvians, especially in the face of U.S. pressure for hemispheric unity during World War II. The end result was a peace treaty (the Protocol of Rio de Janeiro) that legitimized Peruvian battlefield conquests.

When the formula for delimiting the territorial boundary proved unfeasible in one mountainous section, Ecuador seized the opportunity to reconfigure its strategy on the border issue. First it pressed for a negotiated border that would provide access to the Marañón River, and from there to the Amazon. When Peru refused to negotiate away the fruits of its victory, Ecuador attempted to get the international guarantors of the protocol (Argentina, Brazil, Chile, and the United States) to pressure Peru. Although Ecuador could make a good case diplomatically, Peru's intransigence was sufficient to dissuade the guarantors from taking any effective action.

By 1960, Ecuador's renewed emphasis on the diplomatic components of its policy to redress the strategic balance had made little progress. Ecuadorian strategists attempted to increase diplomatic pressure on Peru by proclaiming the entire protocol null because it was the result of an aggressive act. But rather than the guarantors being goaded into pressuring Peru to acquiesce in one small section to save the entire treaty, they turned against Ecuador for questioning the legality of the protocol itself. Now isolated in a deteriorating strategic situation, Ecuador began to prepare itself to raise unilaterally the cost of the dispute to Peru.

Ecuador began to occupy positions along the disputed border (a limited aims strategy) to force Peru to negotiate a resolution. But in 1981 Peru responded with coercive diplomacy—a concentrated attack on Ecuadorian positions with paratroops, attack helicopters, and fighter-bombers. Peru also threatened to escalate the conflict and invade Ecuador if it did not pull back from the east side of the Cordillera del Condor. Ecuador retreated quickly in the face of a strategic balance that fully favored Peru.

Peruvian President Fujimori tried to move beyond the dispute with a cooperative strategy that would make the border issue irrelevant. Fujimori's plan was to create an economic development region that would benefit Ecuador even though it would not have a sovereign outlet to the Amazon. Ecuador refused to accept the offer and unsuccessfully attempted to get papal arbitration of the border dispute.

At the same time Ecuador reevaluated its strategy. Drawing in international mediators who could force Peru to make concessions in the name of inter-American harmony required that Ecuador be able to provoke an incident and hold out against Peruvian military retaliation until other international actors could mobilize a response. This had failed in 1941 and 1981, and Ecuador had paid dearly for miscalculating the overall strategic balance; a new strategy had to pay attention to the relevant military balance.

During the mid-1980s Ecuador began both to retrain forces specifically for jungle warfare and to develop lines of communication into the disputed territory. Arms purchases were increased and designed specifically to counter Peruvian military tactics in the jungle; plastic mines and light surface-to-air missiles were purchased from the People's Republic of China. In addition, Ecuadorian military analysts believed that Peru's armed forces were being weakened after years of fighting the drug and guerrilla wars (corruption and human rights violations experienced in those battles were believed to sap the soldiers' morale); by 1995, the Ecuadorian military was ready to redress the strategic balance.

Peru had responded to increased activity in the region by attempting first to deter further activity and then fell back on coercive diplomacy when Ecuador refused to be deterred in late 1994. But the Peruvians got a double surprise in January 1995. Surface-to-air missiles shot from the dense jungle neutralized Peru's advantage in helicopter gunships; mines wreaked havoc on the advancing infantry. Before the Peruvians could respond by escalating the conflict out of the region to a location where they could make effective their advantage in overall military capacity, Ecuador unveiled its diplomatic strategy: it recognized the legitimacy of the Rio Protocol. By doing so, Peru was faced with beginning a war to resolve a border delimitation issue rather than to make effective an internationally recognized treaty. This diplomatic coup effectively restrained President Fujimori even as he faced domestic opposition from the military and rival politicians.

As a result of Ecuador's recognition of the importance of relating strategic resources to specific threats, the Ecuador-Peru border dispute is currently at a stalemate. Although Ecuador and Peru have been negotiating as part of the MOMED peacekeeping process since armed conflict ended in 1996, Ecuador does not appear willing to accept a resolution that does not give it some sovereign access to the Amazon. Ironically, Ecuador's recent military success, which brought Peru to the negotiating table, may also make it impossible for either Ecuador or Peru to make the concessions necessary to produce an agreement that could make Fujimori's cooperative strategy effective.

Generalizations

While this chapter has focused on these three pairs of disputants and examined them across time, the basic argument that governments pay attention to some notion of military balance applies to other Latin American countries and the present time. Perhaps most important for contemporary discussions, the historical preoccupation with strategic balances, including their military components, is not limited to military governments.

Common opinion erroneously attributes increased arms expenditures to the assumption of power by the military. The left-leaning Peruvian military took power in 1968, but did not embark on a major arms push (including the purchases of the only Mirage-2000s in Latin America) for five years. Arms proliferation did speed up in 1973 after rightist military coups in neighboring Bolivia and Chile and later in Argentina.[24] Before concluding that the heightened perception of threat lies in the military nature of the two parties, we should examine another democratic dyad, lest we view the Peruvian-Ecuadorian relationship as somehow idiosyncratic.

The long-standing Colombia-Venezuela relationship is one of the most conflictive in contemporary Latin America. Tensions reached the point that, in March 1995, a leading Venezuelan historian felt it necessary to appeal in the press for calm, lest war break out. The two countries dispute thirty-four points along their border, and illegal immigration, transborder guerrilla activity, and smuggling heighten Venezuelan concerns about Colombian intentions. In 1987, the appearance of the Colombian navy vessel *Caldas* in Venezuelan-claimed waters provoked a major interstate dispute that kept military forces on alert for two weeks.[25] After the crisis, Colombia dramatically increased the size of its armed forces, partly due to increased guerrilla activity, but also stimulated by congressional concerns that, during the crisis, Venezuela's superior military standing put Colombia at a disadvantage. In short, a decision was made to redress the military balance, despite the fact that both countries were democracies and in the process of increasing their economic ties.

Another example is the Chilean-Peruvian dyad. Although Chile does not currently perceive an immediate threat from Peru, it is upgrading its air force (with the purchase of Mirages), which will be renovated to be, as the air force commander-in-chief said, on a par with the Peruvian air fleet.[26]

CONCLUSION AND POLICY RECOMMENDATIONS

The conceptualization of "strategic balance" in terms of the full range of resources that can be brought to bear on an adversary not only makes intuitive sense, but the history of Latin American security conflicts demonstrates its real-world utility. Separating the concept of strategic balance from the straightjacket of military balance in this way opens up important possibilities for thinking about ways to keep the strategic balance stable and enhance confidence building measures. Of course, as contemporary Argentina demonstrates, new thinking about cooperative strategies does not imply ignoring the military balance.

This quick analysis of three South American dyads produces some intriguing suggestions about the impact of strategic balances on interstate conflict. At different times, military buildups have had a stabilizing effect (e.g., Chile's response to Argentina in 1978) and also been destabilizing (Brazil's military buildup in 1906–10). The inappropriate design of defensive and deterrent strategies has had disastrous consequences (for Ecuador in 1941 and for Peru in 1995). Cooperative strategies have helped decrease tensions (between Chile and Argentina after 1984), but also proved to be irrelevant (Peru and Ecuador between 1991 and 1994). Diplomatic strategies have been irrelevant (Chile and Argentina from 1977 to 1978), have backfired (Ecuador in 1960), or have proven useful (Ecuador in 1995). In short, strategies themselves do not seem to be determinative of how states relate to each other.

This historical analysis of the strategic balances that have operated in the region has fundamental implications for any attempt to develop inter-American confidence building measures and peaceful resolution of conflict. In a context in which so many issues that touch the core interests of states remain outstanding, a blanket approach for specific confidence building measures is unlikely to prove fruitful. Just as the discussion of strategic balances had to be made relevant to the specific threats confronting a nation, so must the remedies.

NOTES

1. Since abolishing its army, Costa Rica has appealed three times for international military support against Nicaraguan aggression. The United States sent its air force to communicate such support against Somoza twice (1940s and 1950s); Venezuela had its F-16s overfly Costa Rica in the 1980s.

2. Victor-Yves Ghebali, *Confidence Building Measures within the CSCE Process*, United Nations Institute for Disarmament Research, Research Paper No. 3. (New York: United Nations, 1989).

3. For a discussion of credibility issues, see Thomas Schelling, *The Strategy of Conflict* (Cambridge, Mass.: Harvard University Press, 1960).

4. Robert Jervis, "Cooperation under the Security Dilemma," *World Politics* 30, no. 2 (January 1978): 167–214; Jack S. Levy, "The Offense/Defense Balance of Military Technology: A Theoretical and Historical Analysis," *International Studies Quarterly* 28, no. 2 (June 1984): 219–38.

5. For a discussion see Alexander George, David K. Hall, and William E. Simons, *The Limits of Coercive Diplomacy* (Boston: Little, Brown, 1971).

6. Elli Leiberman, "What Makes Deterrence Work?" *Strategic Studies* 4, no. 4 (Summer 1995): 851–910.

7. Even in the one case where some argue that it failed—Cuba after Castro consolidated power—the U.S. ability to isolate a regime in the Americas effectively condemned it to a slow death. The United States has paid very little to achieve Castro's ultimate failure.

8. Joseph E. Loftus, *Latin American Defense Expenditures, 1938–1965,* RM-5310-PR/ISA (Santa Monica, Calif.: RAND, 1968).

9. Michael A. Morris and Victor Millan, eds., *Controlling Latin American Conflicts* (Boulder, Colo.: Westview Press, 1983), 2–5.

10. Amado Luiz Cervo and Clodoaldo Bueno, *Historia da Politica Exterior do Brasil* (São Paulo: Editora Atica, 1992).

11. D. R. O'Sullivan-Beare to Sir Earl Grey, November 10, 1906, Haggard to Grey, September 30, 1906, Barclay to Grey, October 5, 1906, all in Public Records Office.

12. Cable traffic between the British Minister in Buenos Aires and London at this time contains many Argentine admonitions for Her Majesty's Government to pressure Brazil to moderate its naval program.

13. The importance of this international recognition to Brazil can be ascertained by its actions in the League of Nations in 1927. That year Germany, the enemy in World War I, was admitted to the League and given a permanent seat on the Council in recognition of its great power position. Brazil demanded that the seat which it had held by election since the founding of the League be converted into a permanent seat as well. When the Council refused, Brazil resigned indignantly.

14. Stanley E. Hilton, *Hitler's Secret War in South America* (Baton Rouge: Louisiana State University Press, 1993).

15. While it is true that Argentina's military government and Nazi sympathies made the United States reluctant to have close ties with that country, it must not be forgotten that Brazil was governed at the time by a dictatorship with fascist sympathies as well.

16. David R. Mares, "Middle Powers under Regional Hegemony: To Challenge or Acquiesce in Hegemonic Enforcement," *International Studies Quarterly* 32 (December 1988): 453–71.

17. Loftus, *Defense Expenditures.* These figures are not entirely reliable, but they are the best we have and confirm impressionistic conclusions.

18. Argentine-American Forum, October 31–November 2, 1993. In fact, Argentina has significantly increased its radar capabilities in the most recent purchases, and even threatened to buy radar equipment from Israel if the United States continued to respect British desires for a weakened Argentine air force. See the discussions concerning the recent purchases from the United States of Skyhawk A4s with top-down radar. Though old, the Skyhawks had been responsible for destroying

some of the British ships during the Malvinas (Falklands) War. Adrian J. English, *Battle for the Falklands (2) Naval Forces* (London: Osprey, 1982), 27–29.

19. The classic history of this period is Robert N. Burr, *By Reason or by Force: Chile and the Balancing of Power in South America, 1830–1905* (Berkeley: University of California Press, 1965).

20. Emilio Meneses, "Ayuda Económica, Política Exterior y Política de Defensa en Chile, 1943–1973," *Estudios Públicos* 35 (Winter 1989): 39–69.

21. Data from "Correlates of War Project, 1816–1980," Inter-University Consortium for Political Information, University of Michigan, cited in Emilio Meneses, "La Percepción de Amenazas en Chile," MS inédito, s.f., p. 8.; see also his chapter in V. A. Rigoberto Cruz Johnson and Augusto Varas Fernandez, eds., *Percepciones de Amenazas y Políticas de Defensa en América Latina* (Santiago: FLACSO, 1993).

22. Thomas Princen, "Beagle Channel Negotiations," Pew Case Studies in International Affairs Case 401, Parts A, B, and C (Washington, D.C.: Institute for the Study of Diplomacy, Georgetown University, 1988).

23. The bioceanic principle recognized Chile as a Pacific power and Argentina as an Atlantic one. Latin American maritime policy allows a country to claim exclusive rights 200 miles into the ocean from its land base. If Chile retained these islands it could legitimately project itself into the Atlantic. This situation also had implications for Argentine claims to Antarctica, since unobstructed continental projection southward forms the basis for South American claims.

24. Daniel M. Masterson, *Militarism and Politics in Latin America* (New York: Greenwood Press, 1991).

25. For a review of actions and the accusations traded by important politicians and policymakers in both countries during the crisis, see Leandro Area and Elke Nieschulz de Stockhausen, *El Golfo de Venezuela: Documentación y Cronología,* vol. 2: 1981–1989 (Caracas: Universidad Central de Venezuela, 1991), 64–87.

26. For a discussion of the Chilean Mirages see *America Vuela* 25 (1995): 22–27. On Peruvian threat perceptions, see Ronald Bruce St. John, *Foreign Policy of Peru* (Boulder, Colo.: Lynne Rienner, 1992), 203–5; Masterson, *Militarism and Politics in Latin America,* 265. The Soviet Union provided Peru with 115 military advisors in the army and air force and trained 200 commissioned and noncommissioned officers, citing Pentagon sources (CLADDE-RIAL, 1988, 348). Military expenditures can be found in ACDA, "World Military Expenditures and Arms Transfers," various issues.

CHAPTER NINE

A LATIN AMERICAN VIEW OF THE INTER-AMERICAN DEFENSE BOARD AND STRATEGIC EQUILIBRIUM IN LATIN AMERICA

VICENTE CASALES

To a large extent modern political relations in Latin America have been determined by the geography and history of the hemisphere. America is made up of two vast areas, North and South, linked by the narrow isthmus of Central America. North America (the United States and Canada) was colonized primarily by the Anglo-Saxons of Great Britain (although in Canada a large minority of French origin remains), while Latin America (South and Central America and Mexico) was colonized by Spain and Portugal.

North America today is highly developed economically. The advanced technology available to its agricultural sector, for instance, makes its small workforce highly productive. North America also enjoys an enormous industrial potential thanks to an abundance of natural resources, a large internal market, a high concentration of capital, and advanced technology (a major element of any nation's power base today). North Americans enjoy the highest standard of living in the world.

In contrast, Latin America is divided into many countries and remains, to a large extent, economically underdeveloped. Because of certain natural resource deficits and other conditions created by history, Latin America today has a restricted range of crops, low agricultural and industrial productivity, inadequate technological development, an insufficient national capital base, and intense population growth—all of which thwart the region's economic growth. The low standard of living in this region is made still worse by a semifeudal social structure and great disparities in wealth—both of which have led to significant periods of political turbulence in modern times.

The development of Latin America would only be possible in a peaceful political climate, with the cooperation of every country at every level, and the support (primarily economic and technological) of the developed world.

Any steps taken to foster confidence in order to maintain peace and security throughout the hemisphere must coincide with the principles outlined in the U.N. charter. (One such principle, for instance, is the importance of outside monitoring—not only in the area of military capacity but also in the five major recognized areas of legitimate government power, including science and technology.)

During the Cold War, much of Latin America lived with constant attacks on their democratic institutions. These attacks weakened governments internally and frequently led to conflicts among neighbors. But with the end of the East-West dispute, the rule of ideology also ended. Latin Americans are increasingly seeking to address jointly their social and economic problems (such as drug trafficking, corruption, poverty, and trade imbalances) at the national, regional, and international levels, agreeing on the need to cooperate in their search, for the well-being and security of their people.

THE INTERNATIONAL STAGE

Many predicted that the end of the Cold War and the collapse of communism would bring about a more secure, harmonious, and cooperative world. But in the real "new world order," political and economic disputes have only become more intense and regionalized. Paradoxically the advent of détente between East and West has not made the world's citizens more secure. The so called new order is not fully defined: the world is in a state of high political, economic, and military turmoil. Potential conflicts once under Soviet control have now been unleashed, and new states have emerged from the remains of the Soviet empire, from the Czech Republic to Slovakia and the Chechnya region. To the dismay of the international community, change is often accompanied by bloody ethnic and nationalist conflicts—such as those in former Bosnia-Herzegovina.

During the Cold War years, the East-West confrontation was largely guided by the contest between the United States and the Soviet Union. Throughout four decades these two great powers stockpiled ever larger nuclear arsenals, and the press of a button could have obliterated humankind.

Currently only the United States has the overpowering economic and military capacity needed to impose its will on the rest of the world. With just one hegemonic global power, we have shifted from having a low probability of a single, highly destructive global confrontation to having a high probability of having many smaller, less destructive confrontations. Although the number of conflicts has increased, they have largely been contained within regional limits and are not (like the Cold War that preceded it) potentially apocalyptic, and pose no significant threat to world peace.

The "new world order" has also affected international commerce. Once split into a bipolar world, it is now evolving into a worldwide network of regional economic trading blocs. Recognizing that no state can survive alone in this new economic order, the world's nations have joined together to form economic coalitions.

One such coalition—NAFTA, which unites the United States, Canada, and Mexico into a single commercial entity—surprised the South American countries because it increased the power of the North-North economic megabloc. In part to balance the new coalition, therefore, South America formed MERCOSUR, initially joined by Brazil, Argentina, Uruguay, Paraguay, and now including Chile.

But the formation of new economic megablocs (such as one in Southeast Asia headed by Japan or one in the Middle East led by Islamic leaders and including the former Islamic republics of the Soviet Union) is potentially destabilizing and therefore worrisome. For if new regional economic powers with conflicting economic interests emerge and the world is not able to establish an open system of trade, the probability of open conflict among the industrialized nations—principally the United States, Germany, and Japan—is greatly increased.

Japan and Germany recovered their seats as permanent members of the U.N. Security Council. It is not enough to be a member of the Group of Seven (G-7) without the political power given by the right to veto decisions within the most important political organization in the world. The 108 members of the nonaligned movement voiced their concern about the admission of these two countries as permanent members of the Security Council at a meeting held in Indonesia in 1992.

Replacing the now-defunct rivalry between East and West, the G-7 will try to contain the Third World in a classic North-South conflict. The industrialized countries of the North fear the effect of the South's burgeoning populations, underdeveloped economies, and indiscriminate exploitation of natural resources. Conditions of poverty, ethnic discrimination, extreme nationalism, religious radicalism, drug trafficking, unchecked migration, and a degraded natural environment threaten world peace far more than political differences.

In part because of this dynamic, many developing countries mistrust the increasing involvement of the U.N. (through its Security Council) in regional disputes. To many, the increased presence of U.N. troops and peacekeeping forces interferes with the sovereignty of the nations and the principles of noninterference.

Politically the end of the Cold War has meant the end of many authoritarian regimes. Developing world governments are actively seeking new ways to meet the demands of their people and to become integrated into the international political and economic scene. Under these circumstances, international organizations exert more influence on their member states' political attitudes. Nationalism is on the rise. The ideal of individual enterprise has superseded that of working for the community, the government, or even the state. The influence of ethnic and religious affiliations has increased, which has sometimes led to open conflict.

Another major area of contention between North and South is the transfer of technology. The industrialized world has established mechanisms to control developing countries' access to advanced technology, whether related to military applications in particular or overall economic development in general.

Finally, military establishments throughout Latin America are now dedicating their efforts to more peaceful ends (in some cases, under the management of international groups), including the furthering of their countries' social development. Military spending worldwide has also decreased substantially since the end of the Cold War, although this situation could be reversed in the coming years. The world is reducing its stores of long-range, mass-destruction nuclear arms and preferring instead to invest in nonnuclear, high-technology weapons.

REFLECTIONS ON LATIN AMERICA

The terms "Latin America" and "Latin American" are discriminatory rhetorical terms created by the Europeans. They fail, moreover, to reflect the profound geopolitical differences that separate the countries of Hispanic origin of Central America and the Caribbean from those of South America—despite the fact that the region's geostrategic peculiarities accentuate those differences. Some American countries participate in regional economic and military alliances and some do not. Some have modest armed forces; others have powerful military machines designed to deal with political insurgents or drug-related terrorism. We must remember that the region includes more than twenty individual nations, each with its own divisions, suggesting that "Latin America" is more of a geographic continuum than a unified community of thought or geopolitical reality.

Mexico, for instance, which borders on the most powerful nation of the modern world and is now a member of NAFTA, always had—and always will have—a perspective different from that of other Latin American countries. Because the countries of Central America and the Caribbean will come under the direct economic influence of NAFTA, moreover, they will receive special investments from the United States and Canada in the energy and health sectors to help reduce the development gap. Otherwise, these countries will remain as focal points of tension and potential threats to peace on the North American continent.

Despite real differences among nations in terms of territory, population density, ethnic mix, productivity, and level of development, it is possible to address South America as a whole. This region is defined by underdeveloped economies and an inadequate distribution of resources. Each country has a large segment of its population that is marginalized economically and by social inequality. Despite their distinct national characteristics and cultures, all suffer the results of economic underdevelopment.

Yet Latin America also has many strengths. It boasts, for instance, one of the world's most extensive areas of uninhabited arable land, the world's largest reserve of biodiversity, and the world's largest freshwater reserve (while some other world regions have already depleted this resource).

Despite these natural endowments, however, if Latin America today is to wield power internationally, it will have to deal with a number of pressing issues.

Poverty

To help the many Latin Americans living in poverty, governments of the region must seek to improve the implementation of social programs and to adopt macroeconomic polices—despite the difficulties associated with meeting the requirements imposed by outside financial institutions—that promote economic integration and development. Such moves would go far toward improving living conditions among the poor, reducing their numbers, and stemming migration to developed countries.

Regional Integration

To achieve a significant impact internationally, Latin American countries need to act in concert politically and to join together into regional economic blocs. Regional goals must supersede national or international goals, and nations will sometimes be obliged to set aside issues of national sovereignty to achieve a common good. Acting as a region will also change the mission of the national armed forces in Latin America and require countries to redirect—and significantly reduce—their levels of defense spending.

Intraregional Problems

In the "new world order," Latin America's new democracies will have to deal with an increasing number of regional disputes and border questions. Many will face the possibility of sabotage by drug dealers. Most will have to take measures to reduce their countries' excessive dependency on external savings and introduce sound resource management practices to preserve the environment.

Foreign Relations

Because powerful nations from outside the region are so heavily involved in the affairs of Latin America, its countries need to define the major indigenous interests of the region as a whole. Countries need to set aside inter regional disputes and become integrated into a working unit—an achievement that would, ironically, enhance each member state's ability to meet its national goals. Individual states therefore need to make every effort within the region to allay mutual mistrust and to avoid making unilateral deals with external powers. Latin America has the dual problem of having to forge new and more functional relationships with those powers from outside the region while overcoming national images left over from the Cold War. Establishing harmonious dealings with the rest of the world is an essential part of keeping the peace needed for Latin American countries to pursue their national objectives.

Armed Forces

The national armed forces in Latin America must be properly prepared to carry out their constitutionally defined roles and to back up political positions taken by the government. (In any country, the degree to which soldiers enforce nonmilitary sovereign decisions reflects their strategic influence within—and therefore the health of—the political system.) Recent consensus by G-7 political leaders, however, that military spending in the developing world should be drastically reduced is worrisome. Some have suggested that the developing world's armed forces be reduced, reshaped, and reassigned to a mission similar to that of a National Guard or police force.

Security

A regional outlook requires that Latin American countries adopt only such security measures as are prudent, continental in scope, and in accordance with the Inter-American Defense System. Although in the new world order the relevance and credibility of the Inter-American Reciprocal Assistance Treaty is likely to diminish, the accord still has legal status. As of now no general consensus exists in favor of a system to ensure the security of Latin America as a whole.

Technology

Latin America needs to develop its own technology to become a major economic force in the world. Having an indigenous technology base creates jobs and gives a region the power to resist outside interference. It is well known that Latin America imports most of its technology and capital goods while exporting chiefly raw materials and manufactured goods. This dependence on primary goods is especially acute in times of recession—and in the past decade as a result of the debt crisis and general state of economic stagnation. Consequently, the relative poverty of the region presents great difficulty in obtaining the capacity for state-of-the-art technology necessary for rapid industrial development.

Capital

As of now South America has very weak capital markets and must continue to depend on foreign investment to support its development.

NATIONAL SOVEREIGNTY WITHIN
THE NEW WORLD ORDER

The development of a new world order has had important implications for the sovereignty, identity, and security of states. Sovereignty, for instance, can no longer be considered an absolute, because groups of countries that share common interests now drive the policy decisions that any state can adopt. Thinking globally, however, may make it difficult for governments to deal with matters of more local concern.

Another great concern to many nations is the recovery of territories that have been taken over by other countries in the past. Should such situations become exacerbated in Latin America as they have in the former Yugoslavia and other areas of the world, they could seriously undermine peace in the region.

National identity is further threatened by the accelerated development of technology and the globalization of communications, both of which allow the world to observe political, cultural, economic, and military developments as they occur. The instantaneous reaction—and interaction—of the world can substantially affect the cultural, ideological, and sociological identity of a nation.

A NEW ROLE FOR THE ARMED FORCES

As for national security, Latin Americans question the motives behind the industrialized world's insistence that developing countries be demilitarized and disarmed and that they cut their defense spending. Whether well- or ill-intentioned, such demands intrude upon the laws and circumstances particular to sovereign nations.

In both North and South America, each country's laws clearly lay out the mission of their armed forces with regard to the defense of country and constitution. A tradition of conquest in some of these countries has led them to include territorial expansion as one of their national objectives.

In Latin America today, it can be expected that the role of national armed forces will evolve along with the political and strategic stature of the state. Each country will of course have to deal with such endemic problems as containing inflation in its military expenses, having only limited resources with which to acquire and replace equipment, and increasing its forces' efficiency in the implementation of programs and projects. Public support for the military, moreover, declines in the absence of serious conflicts, being overshadowed by more pressing social demands. During long periods of peace, countries tend to underestimate their need for security, both internal and external. Yet while such concerns are common to all countries, no two nations share the same historical reality, mission, and constitutional constraints, and therefore none have the same military needs.

Latin Americans ought to note that they—the most disarmed large region in the world—have the fewest international conflicts. On the whole, South American armed forces carry out their peacetime assignments well. Many of these assignments are too costly to be undertaken by the private sector and cannot be done by government agencies because they are prohibited from doing so by law.

Developing countries often use the engineering and logistical skills of their military to help manage natural disasters and construct and repair roads, railways, bridges, and communications—particularly in areas of difficult access where the cost to private entrepreneurs would be prohibitive. They may use their marines to perform life-saving activities at sea, prepare nautical maps and signals, and perform other duties of a coast guard. The military can even deliver medical and dental care to citizens in the interior of the country. Many of the tasks presently handled by the armed forces would be difficult to hand over to private operators or to other government entities, yet all such projects impose heavy financial burdens on the government.

A PROPOSED STRATEGY FOR LATIN AMERICA

Latin America as a whole is economically maladjusted—both internally and externally—and this has led to vast inequities in the distribution of wealth. As a result, every Latin American country harbors festering pockets of poverty. Since governments in North America have shown no real desire or ability to curb the activity of large drug buyers, moreover, a number of Latin American countries also suffer from the violence and economic distortion brought about by large-scale drug trafficking.

Bearing these chronic regional problems in mind, I propose the following strategy, by area, for the nations of Latin America.

Political

The democratic institutions within each country need to be strengthened; borders need to be accepted as presently defined; all steps necessary must be taken to maintain peace within the Americas; bilateral and subregional agreements (such as one guaranteeing Bolivia access to the Pacific Ocean) to settle present disputes and promote cooperation within the region must be sought; the OAS and its subsidiary organizations (including the Inter-American Defense Board) must be strengthened—both as a forum for the discussion of problems within the Americas and as an agency for resisting the imposition of Northern solutions on Latin America—as Latin America's principal mechanism for averting North-South conflicts; and increased access to advanced technology must be negotiated.

Financial

The rest of the countries in the region should be admitted to MERCOSUR; traditional multilateral trade relations must be maintained while new relations with emerging markets in Asia and Africa are actively sought; optimal conditions for the free play of market forces should be created by reducing government interference in the economy and eliminating state-run enterprises and markets; new technology should be funneled to less-developed areas in order to equalize the potential for development throughout the region; education ought to be heavily invested in; more-equitable policies for public resource distribution should be instituted; national restrictions on regional waterways must be reduced in order to lower users' transportation costs and increase regional trade; and family planning measures should be instituted to help control population growth.

Military

Present national force levels should be maintained as a mutual deterrent to conflict in the region; mutual trust within the region ought to be increased through military exchange programs and close relations among the military establishments of neighboring countries; regional militaries should be trained through exchange programs, collective operations, and close relations with the U.S. military establishment; the Inter-American Defense College and its subsidiary organizations must be strengthened in order to maintain peace and security in the region; and close relationships between the military and universities should be established, and military skills and personnel ought to be used for development projects and in times of natural disaster in order to keep the peacetime military mission in line with civilian needs.

Social

Policies to help integrate indigenous communities economically while maintaining their traditional culture should be introduced, as well as policies that ban all forms of ethnic and religious discrimination; the press and mass communications must be kept free and privately owned; broad-based political parties should be strengthened and the political influence of pressure groups should be reduced; and leaders both inside and outside the government should be encouraged to participate in international conferences promoted by nongovernmental organizations.

THE CASE FOR REGIONAL COOPERATION

No one looking at Latin America's relations with the rest of the world can ignore the role played by the giant to the north. A realistic evaluation must factor U.S. dominance into any objective assessment of Latin American strategies and actions. For its part, Latin America today has begun to learn to live with the asymmetry of power in the hemisphere and to accept how that asymmetry affects its relations with the rest of the world.

Issues within the United States that particularly affect Latin America include, first, the split between the U.S. belief in unlimited abundance, full employment, peace, and social well-being and its role as "policeman of the world," on which its international preeminence is actually based. Second is the lack of equilibrium—subtle yet undeniable—between the U.S. military supremacy and the worrisome economic outlook of a country deeply in debt and competitively challenged in the areas of technology and management.

In analyzing U.S. and Latin American relations, it is essential to look beyond the obvious asymmetry of power to consider the diverse, profound problems (drug trafficking, terrorism, insurgencies, internal migrations, unemployment, extreme defense of the rights of minorities) that threaten interhemispheric and mutual stability.

In fact, solutions to many of the conflicts between Latin America and its mighty neighbor to the north are now being negotiated naturally as a consequence of their being joint owners of the same geopolitical space. In sum, since both the United States and Latin America are here to stay, both need to seek the best possible terms of partnership for cohabitation.

I believe the asymmetry of power in the hemisphere—plus the multitude of indigenous threats in the region—points to collaborative regional associations as Latin America's most effective policymaking tool. Alliances whose policies depend on the formation of broad coalitions of the countries in a subregion can guarantee security for the entire area by helping to prevent local conflicts and resolve bilateral disputes. They can also promote the development of democratic institutions within their member countries and encourage national economic behavior that furthers the interests of the region. Acting regionally, countries can anticipate conflict, act jointly against common threats, and resolve disputes among neighbors. By averting any need for interference by the great powers or international organizations, moreover, weaker countries enhance their ability to determine their own fate.

Finally, regional economic cooperation opens up new markets in neighboring countries and new areas for economic development. Joining forces is the best strategy for enabling developing countries to survive and thrive in a competitive world.

THE ROLE OF THE INTER-AMERICAN DEFENSE BOARD

The OAS's Inter-American Defense Board, which is the oldest military forum in the world, is without doubt the natural forum for regional dialogue in the Americas. As such it is central to shaping the military regional agreements of mutual cooperation that are needed to build trust and ensure the security of the region. Also a key to the making and enforcement of Latin American regional policy, the Inter-American Defense Board could facilitate the military integration of the region.

All initiatives designed to foster mutual confidence among the American states must be in accord with the charters of the U.N. and the OAS and the various agreements they have helped to achieve. Cooperative agreements should also extend to cover military issues and all major areas of state power.

Cooperative military agreements, moreover, must take into account the security requirements (determined by the civilian authorities) of each member country if they are to be considered valid throughout the region. To be effective, they must address the potential threats identified by each country. Finally, regional agreements must take into account prevailing conditions throughout the area affected and be targeted to deal with the salient type of threat at hand.

The most outstanding examples of successful regional cooperative agreements in the Americas to date are those signed by Brazil and Argentina to ban the use of nuclear weapons, to establish a peace zone, and to enter into the South Atlantic Cooperative Military Alliance. Agreements such as these build mutual confidence within the region, reduce the possibility of military action between neighboring states, and inhibit the use of force to settle regional disputes.

But building mutual confidence is a slow process. Only success in one phase justifies following on to the next step, and a series of measures is required before all participating states can reach their regional objectives. The first steps in building a climate of trust are of necessity delicate and complex. States must risk taking part in cooperatively designed and operated military and economic initiatives. For this reason it is particularly important that such measures—incorporated in treaties and agreements—be insulated from sudden change in the participating nations' goals and from shocks imposed from outside the region.

In order to increase military cooperation among the countries of Latin America, the Inter-American Defense Board should seek to implement the following recommendations, by area.

Information Exchange

The board should act as a conduit for reaching Latin American members of the U.S. Congress on questions related to security; encourage the free and open exchange of technological information among the region's armed forces; encourage the exchange of information related to the control of conventional, chemical, biological, and nuclear weapons; create incentives for inter-regional exchanges among military schools at all levels; encourage military personnel to receive university-level training in public administration and business; maintain a center at the Inter-American Defense College where military and civilians can exchange ideas regarding matters of security and defense; and promote the study of issues of regional disarmament and security.

Regional Cooperation

The board should create opportunities for intraregional military cooperation within the context of an international organization; devise plans for the military to provide humanitarian support (such as removing mines and providing aid in times of natural disaster); provide a forum for the discussion of military activities (such as maneuvers and exercises) that could cause anxiety among neighboring states; establish mediation procedures to better relations within the region and reduce the possibility for misunderstandings and conflict; and provide a mechanism so that national military establishments can be represented and exchange information at specialized military conferences.

Peacekeeping

The board should establish mechanisms for the control of modern warfare within the context of existing agreements; monitor peacekeeping measures; provide and coordinate the actions of international teams of military observers; and work with the OAS to devise strategies to combat drug trafficking, control the sale of arms, provide humanitarian support, and identify and deal with other issues concerning the region's military forces.

It is important for regional relations that the OAS continue to endorse the actions and accomplishments of the Inter-American Defense Board and thereby to enhance the Board's standing among the region's civilian authorities. A strong Defense Board capable of bringing about an integrated regional military is vital to the establishment of lasting peace within the region.

CONCLUSIONS

In this last decade of the twentieth century, international relations no longer reflect the simple bipolarity of the Cold War years. Rather, modern nations must compete for political and economic power on a world stage where the interests of the industrialized nations are frequently in conflict with those of developing countries. Developing nations are therefore learning to drop old rivalries and come together into blocs to increase their bargaining power.

Latin America's effectiveness within the context of this new world order will therefore depend on its ability to abandon old differences among neighbors, reduce internal conflict, promote democracy, and achieve wide international integration. It is therefore imperative for the region's future to strengthen the OAS—the only political forum where issues related to hemispheric security can be usefully discussed. It is also necessary to strengthen the ability of the OAS's Inter-American Defense Board to put Latin America's military capacity to good use in times of peace.

CHAPTER TEN

CONFIDENCE BUILDING IN THE AMERICAS: A CONCLUSION

JOSEPH S. TULCHIN AND RALPH H. ESPACH

In the aftermath of the Cold War, strategic relations in the Western Hemisphere have been characterized by wide-ranging confusion and episodes of profound lack of confidence between states. It is as if the Cold War, for all of its anxiety and threat, provided the nations of the Americas with a structure within which to understand their relations with other states in the hemisphere. During the Cold War the United States provided the definition of threat and influenced threat perception for most Latin American countries. Today, however, the United States is as befuddled as any of its neighbors regarding the definition of threats to its own national security and the selection of means to address them. In addition to leaving the region without a clear working model for hemispheric security relations, the end of the Cold War has brought significant revision to the security agenda of the Americas by adding transnational, non-state-sponsored threats such as drug trafficking, international crime, and migration and by giving greater salience to a number of older, nineteenth-century boundaries disputes. As a result, interstate relations continue to be marked by distrust and suspicions, which inhibit cooperation, and latent tensions over past conflicts threaten to boil over into violence—as they did on the Peruvian-Ecuadorian border—and to destabilize the region as a whole.

Current pressures toward globalization, however, suggest that confidence among nations should increase. The post–Cold War era has seen a convergence among the nations of Latin America regarding the value of democratic governance and open, market-based economies. The commitment shared across the hemisphere—with the exception of Cuba—to the ideals of democracy and civilian rule has allowed for a level of international cooperation and exchange unprecedented in regional history. At the subregional level, cooperative and integrationist projects such as the Rio Group, MERCOSUR, the Andean Pact, and the Caribbean Community have proliferated as nations have sought economic growth and political consolidation through partnership with their neighbors. At the hemispheric level, this trend has led to the ambitious Free Trade Area of the Americas initiative launched at the Miami Summit in 1994, arguably the most significant pan-American project in history.

Greater integration in commercial and political affairs has not, however, translated automatically into improved cooperation in matters of security. Closer, more dense interstate relations tend to improve stability, but they also create more frequent episodes of conflict. The resurgence of old nationalist threats, along with the introduction of new ones based on the new technologies and globalization of the post–Cold War era, is a significant theme of this volume. In the new regional security agenda, both traditional areas of conflict—such as those over border demarcation and military buildup—and newly evolving threats—such as international drug trafficking and criminal networks—endanger regional security, and the composition of threats varies widely among subregions. This variety of threats and the changing nature of the international environment within which they must be addressed necessitate new mechanisms of conflict resolution.

The largest incident to date in the post–Cold War era of armed conflict among American neighbors, the flare-up between Peru and Ecuador in 1996, suggests that as economic integration intensifies, the permeation of borders will tend to exacerbate archaic nationalist tensions. To maintain regional stability, it is imperative that these disputes be addressed and negotiated, if necessary, through a transparent, legalistic process supported by the hemispheric community. It is significant, therefore, that the Peru-Ecuador conflict was successfully mediated (although not completely resolved) by the group of guarantor nations named in the original peace treaty of 1942. The legal resolution of other disputes regarding border demarcation and control, such as those between Colombia and Venezuela, Chile and Argentina, and Honduras and El Salvador, must be a foremost priority of the hemispheric community. As happened in the Peru-Ecuador case, cooperative international initiatives that address these particular cases can strengthen significantly the framework of regional stability. A central message of this volume is that confidence building measures at the subregional level that are operational in nature and aimed at addressing specific concerns can serve as essential building blocks toward a more effective, cooperative hemispheric security environment. In fact, hemispheric cooperation may be impossible without first preparing confidence at the subregional level.

Cooperation among Latin American states on security matters is complicated by tension in many countries between their civilian governments and the military. Until the 1980s, many countries were held under military dictatorship or under the control of autocrats with strong ties to the military. Today, the painful divisiveness and antagonisms of that period still present serious obstacles to civilian governments, especially in their relations with the armed forces, which in many cases continue to be dominated by an older generation of officers jealous of their institution's autonomy. Whereas agreement prevails among political leaders as to the merits of increased political and economic openness, much of the region's top military brass, trained under the tensions and threats of the past, are more skeptical of cooperative initiatives. These attitudinal and cultural differences between the political and military communities of many Latin American nations complicate the formulation of internationalist policies. Supporters of increased cooperation and integration must be sensitive to these institutional obstacles when creating timetables and standards, in order to avoid the possibility of inciting nationalist backlashes. Confidence building measures can be useful tools for bridging these institutional gaps. Colonel Cope's description of changes in the U. S. strategic attitude toward Latin America suggests that the predominant recent political environment of openness and exchange has begun to show effect even within traditionally conservative regional military institutions. In this regard, the declaration by Admiral Casales that the national security agenda must be defined by civilian authorities has resounding significance. As many of the authors emphasize, in order to facilitate these institutional transitions, confidence building measures and other cooperative initiatives must be designed not only to build confidence between the security institutions of different countries, but also to strengthen the understanding and leadership of civilian governments in the area of security.

The various subregional and institutional perspectives presented in this volume make clear that the new regional security agenda of the post–Cold War era demands new approaches at the national, subregional, and hemispheric levels. If threats arise not merely from traditional military sources but also from economic, political, social, and environmental problems, then cooperative activities of many forms must be encouraged in order to widen the space for effective joint action. Progress in economic integration, arbitration of legal disputes, technological cooperation and information sharing, cultural exchange, and informal organizational networks all contribute, therefore, to increased stability in regional relations. Donadio and Tibiletti emphasize that, contrary to other subregional experiences, in the case of the Southern Cone the success those countries have had in building closer economic ties has facilitated the improvement of relations in other areas, including security. Joint military exercises—an important, historically proven confidence building measure—were held for the first time among Brazil, Argentina, and Uruguay in the fall of 1997, and such joint exercises between Argentina and Chile have been instrumental in easing the way to settling the last border dispute between the two countries. Rojas Aravena and Mares also emphasize the multifaceted nature of modern international relations, and argue that long-term regional stability will depend on broader social, cultural, political, and economic exchange and understanding.

The broadening of the regional security agenda to include economic, social, and environmental concerns, and the increasing diversity of the actors it involves, from state- or local-level governments to multinational corporations, nongovernment organizations, and lending institutions, complicate the creation of cooperative initiatives. The concept of security becomes increasingly ambiguous, and the institutions charged with its preservation find it difficult to define their goals and operations. This is especially true when trying to address security at the hemispheric level. Comparing the histories and institutional capacities of different subregions, from the relatively developed Southern Cone to the lingering tensions over border demarcation and other issues that mar Andean relations to the unique vulnerability of the Caribbean Basin to transnational threats, it is clear that progress is best pursued in the short term by focusing first on subregional problems and issues. Confidence building measures that build upon already existing linkages and institutional bonds among neighbors—such as those in the Andean subregion described by Bustamante—are more likely to be successful than are broad, regionwide attempts with less institutional precedent. Confidence building measures at the bilateral or subregional level can be designed to work within the specific institutional and political conditions of the nations involved, and can be more sensitive to subregional asymmetries. As such, they can be expected to vary from region to region and from issue to issue. While by itself each of these localized initiatives may seem of little importance, their implementation lays the groundwork for wider, more comprehensive regional cooperation.

Another way of overcoming the confusion caused by the manifold threats and agents of the new regional security agenda is by focusing on action at the operational level. In their day-to-day operations, military and police throughout the hemisphere are limited in their effectiveness by their incapacity to coordinate and to share information and resources with their colleagues across borders or on the open seas. For this reason, confidence building measures at the operational level, aimed at specific objectives and confined to individual institutions or functionally related groups, can be particularly helpful in establishing institutional networks upon which future cooperative projects can be built. In the short term, small-scale initiatives are also advantageous in that they require fewer resources—an important consideration in a period of fiscal downsizing and budgetary constraints—and are less controversial politically.

Within the current climate of general confusion regarding regional security affairs, progress is less served by high-level political gestures than by the establishment of specific, transparent actions among institutions at the operational level. Our conclusions point to the need for self-conscious, deliberate effort on the part of the governments and security institutions of the region to augment the rich economic and political relations in formation since the end of the Cold War, with a renewed emphasis on building mutual confidence in security relations. Confidence building measures are a proven instrument for the enhancement of these relations, and their implementation at the subregional and operational levels serves as a concrete step forward toward greater stability and security for the hemisphere as a whole.

THE ADVANCEMENT OF CONFIDENCE IN THE WESTERN HEMISPHERE

JOHN HOLUM

This publication brings together the hard work of analysts from throughout the region in order to encourage dialogue and the exchange of ideas on hemispheric security. Many of the writers and guests also attended a special seminar on measures for the promotion of confidence and security in Latin America, held in Mexico City on August 28, 1995. I am pleased that the United States Arms Control and Disarmament Agency (ACDA) has been able to support this valuable publication. Efforts of this kind help promote regional dialogue, which strengthens confidence and security in the Americas. The cooperation among the ACDA, the Canadian Foundation for the Americas, the Latin American Faculty of Social Sciences (FLACSO), and the Woodrow Wilson Center has been most rewarding. Such intellectual creativity and exchanges are essential to support measures that foster confidence and security (MFCS [or confidence building measures]) in the Americas.

Throughout history, humankind has tried to eliminate distrust and foster confidence, frequently through symbolic gestures that demonstrate peaceful intentions. It is possible that the very first of these gestures was a handshake, something normal between human beings as a demonstration of friendship and respect. Today, we count on more formal arrangements, to such an extent that at the end of the 1990s, MFCS stand out as undervalued promoters of arms control. As for the United States, the valuable experience that we have gained in the negotiation and implementation of MFCS has contributed to the conclusion in the last few years of important and complex agreements on arms reduction. The MFCS work continuously to reduce or eliminate the causes of distrust, fear, tensions, and hostilities. The MFCS increase candor and clarity regarding military activity and strength, and thus allow for the behavior of other nations to be more predictable and to demonstrate clearly the absence of hostile intentions. The measures fostering confidence have merit as the first step in the arms-control process or as auxiliary measures in the area of arms reductions. In their role as the latter, they are able to contribute to improving the negotiation process by assigning responsibilities to all nations, including those that are not carrying out any reductions; they also could serve as additional measures when no reductions are necessary.

The most far-reaching and unique experience as far as MFCS are concerned has taken place in Europe. The measures negotiated on that continent are a reflection of the particular features of European security, especially the magnitude and type of forces in its territory and the long political division of the continent into two large opposing blocs. The MFCS, which began in an international environment of tension and distrust, are being implemented in a new environment of cooperation among allies, friends, and former adversaries.

It is impossible to transplant the European process of the MFCS to other regions. The experiences of the MFCS in every region of the world will be different, as each initiates the process with its own cultural, historical, political, economic, and military security backgrounds. But it is also true that other regions can benefit from the experiences of the Organization for Security and Cooperation in Europe. Generally, the European experience has made it possible to take advantage of the great benefits that the MFCS offer in the economic, political, and regional-security arenas.

Debates over the MFCS have become generalized throughout the world: in Europe, Africa, Southern Asia, the Middle East, and the Far East. Some of these regions have peace; others have histories marked by conflict and distrust. Every region is searching for a way for peace to take hold and greater security to exist through democracy, economic integration, disarmament, arms control, and, particularly, measures to foster mutual confidence.

At the Summit of the Americas, held in Miami, Florida, in December 1995, our leaders agreed to promote measures to pave the way toward a regional conference on MFCS. I hope that by working together on the continent they will be able to set the basis for a region that is even more open, candid, and stable.

The Organization of American States and its member countries have been at the diplomatic forefront as far as MFSC are concerned, which should be a matter of pride for the continent. Since 1991, the General Assembly of the OAS has adopted several resolutions that seek the implementation of MFCS. In fact, the Latin American countries have a long tradition of bilateral MFCS, but under different names. Today, as well as in the past, MFCS have been implemented between many Latin American countries, including Argentina and Chile, Brazil and Argentina, Chile and Peru, Ecuador and Peru, and Venezuela and Colombia, and between the five Central American nations. The Central American Treaty for Democratic Security, signed on December 15, 1995, in San Pedro Sula, Honduras, by the presidents of Costa Rica, Honduras, El Salvador, Guatemala, Nicaragua, and Panama, stands out as a positive instance of a peaceful resolution of conflict and the strengthening of confidence in the post–Cold War period. I hope the Central American agreement will serve as an example to stimulate other regional or subregional agreements to create clear and mutual confidence in other parts of the world.

The meeting of OAS's government experts held in Buenos Aires in 1994 began with an extensive dialogue on MFCS at the regional level. The conference was useful in that it helped to further the dialogue and the establishment of a common language between countries and subregions with different concerns and security challenges.

The meeting on MFCS held by Deputy Defense Ministers in Santiago in November 1996 was a historic event for the region, as it marked the way for a new stage of inter-American cooperative efforts aimed at creating greater confidence. The conference and its final declaration indicate the creation of a hemispheric consensus on the value of arms control, and the MFCS in particular, as a component of a national security strategy. The conference agreed on an agenda of MFCS for the hemisphere for future action. This hemispheric meeting in Santiago reinforced the basic principle that the joint participation of civilian and military officers constitutes an important factor for the development and implementation of MFCS.

At the time of this writing, many of the eleven MFCS adopted in the declaration by the members of the OAS are being implemented at the bilateral and regional levels. This book is an essential part of this historic process: it promises to help the Americas sail forward.

ADDRESS TO THE FIRST REGIONAL CONFERENCE ON CONFIDENCE BUILDING MEASURES AND SECURITY

PABLO CABRERA GAETE

Nothing is more modern than peace. This is one of the most significant statements made in the context of the Regional Conference on Measures for Fostering Confidence and Security held in Santiago in November 1995. This conference reappraised the contemporary nature of peace efforts. The different delegations, speaking from their own national experiences and their particular geographical contexts, emphasized that without peace and security it would not be possible to manage global issues adequately. Without peace, our nations will not be able to lean towards economic growth and development. The absence of peace prevents the creation and development of democracy. Peace and democracy are synonyms that reinforce stability and security at the local, regional, and planetary levels.

As a generation of Latin American diplomats, we have witnessed the extraordinary international changes brought on by the end of the Cold War. No region was able to escape or to isolate itself from the dramatic changes produced by this era. Therefore, we understand that towards the end of the 1980s a new era began in which the regional agenda for political discussion changed considerably. The foreign policy outlines changed hand in hand with the international agenda that arose at the end of the Cold War. Thus the issues of peace and international security became a priority with respect to other issues on the agenda. Subsequently, global issues such as the environment or those related to development have gained more weight. In spite of this, there are still some important issues regarding international security that we have not yet managed to solve totally. Thus the development and fostering of confidence building measures have a very important role to play in completing this process of change and transition from an era of bipolar tensions to a new one of more international complementation and cooperation.

It was in this context that at the beginning of the 1990s, given the return of democracy to Chile as well as the rest of Latin America, Chile launched the idea to hold a Regional Conference on Measures for Fostering Confidence and Security, in the framework of the Geneva Conference of Disarmament. The experience and the spirit of Helsinki that had guided the process of détente, dialogue, and cooperation in Europe became a necessary reference in the growing and sustained process in the promotion of confidence and security that took place in Vienna and ended after the end of the Cold War with the establishment of a comprehensive international security system for the European countries. If Europe, a continent that endured two devastating world wars and political, diplomatic, and military tensions of great significance during more than four decades, managed to overcome the wounds and traumas of the past and recover its confidence, it should prove easier for the Latin American and Caribbean regions to do so. The idea to advance this process of confidence building was introduced by Argentina, a country that presented it as an initiative at the OAS, with the goal that the countries of the Americas would engage in an open and clear debate on the issues and the sources of distrust and insecurity on our continent.

This marked the beginning of a process of dialogue, of the exchange of information, of evaluations and of new initiatives in the framework of the OAS. Several consultations between countries took place, the existing information was organized, and the intellectual debate was encouraged.

During 1994, a meeting of experts was convened in Buenos Aires. During this gathering, the different national realities, the advances and deficiencies in questions of conceptualization, were verified; a registry was developed including the measures that would be appropriate for the region with the aim of advancing the creation of confidence, and at the same time, there was an opportunity to initiate a wide discussion regarding the new dimensions of international security and how this affected or influenced security on the American continent. This discussion on the concept of security is not finished yet; on the contrary, it needs to be explored in more depth and be more systematized.

In this context, the Peace and Security in the Americas program invited some government representatives, among whom I had the honor to be included, to contribute and participate in a debate on measures for mutual confidence and their relationship with the so-called strategic balance and the verification measures for international agreements related to international defense and security. The texts, analyzed and discussed at the Matias Romero Institute in Mexico City and provided in this book, make an important intellectual contribution by recounting and conceptualizing the measures for mutual confidence in the region.

In this scholarly debate as well as in other seminars and conferences, we were able to verify and indicate how an increasingly more common approach to the international agenda was emerging. In analyzing the profound changes found at the beginning of the 1990s, a growing connection between different events is evident, which enables the consolidation of a process of compromise with international peace and security of a dimension we could not have imagined only a few years ago. In fact, the Mendoza Compromise allowed our region to join in the control and proscription of chemical and bacteriological weapons, with strength, decision, and imagination. This initial step allowed our nations to join the Chemical Weapons Convention, whose international treaty may be qualified as one of the most democratic and less discriminatory signed by different nations for the benefit of the international community. For the smaller and developing nations, it not only reduces the danger of the use of weapons of mass destruction, it also—in a parallel fashion—allows these nations access to the technologies and management of issues of a global nature. The Tlatelolco Treaty stands out in this chain of events because its improvements allowed the nations that had not fully adopted it to finally participate in an international system for the prohibition of nuclear weapons on the Latin American and Caribbean continent. Indeed, it allowed countries such as Chile to join the Non-Proliferation Treaty. But the chain of events has not stopped. It is moving toward a definitive ban on nuclear tests that will reinforce the com mitment of every nation toward international peace and security.

In this frame of reference, Chile hosted the first Regional Conference on Measures for Fostering Confidence and Security in November 1995. This was the result of a process that had begun, as we already mentioned, several years before and has been given renewed dynamism by the general framework of the conference. The conference sought to respond to specific needs and to suggest a way to deal with issues related to peace and development in the American region within the Latin American institutional framework. It is important to emphasize that every country was in attendance and that the concept of measures for confidence was extensively discussed. The issue of security was raised in a broad sense, but at the same time a practical and realistic plan of action was contemplated, as stated in the Declaration of Santiago. The conference allowed many objectives to be achieved. It allowed different countries to develop their vision and, at the same time, provide an evaluation of the possibilities for regional peace, stability, and security. The conference also allowed participants to listen directly and learn about the perception of vulnerability that various changes and situations generate in the different subregional contexts. Moreover, during the discussions, new ways were visualized to express continental solidarity in the search of solutions, which, prompted by the peace and the principles that rule inter-American relations, would allow the continent to face the challenges of the twenty-first century more adequately.

The conference also proved that it is impossible to expect immediate advances, particularly in sensitive areas such as security and defense. This means that we must recognize the potential to generate a gradual but constant process that will allow the establishment of long-term goals through programs that encourage action in the different areas and fields of association in the Americas. Of special importance are those global issues such as education for peace, dialogue, and understanding, along with the implementation of standard practices based on international law for the solution to controversies. This gradual progress allows a significant advancement of the core issues, generating a process of confidence and stability in the long term. This process is reinforced daily by the greater commercial exchange and by the economic integration occurring in the Americas.

This book brings together many experiences and suggested ideas. Today, we have the Declaration of Santiago on measures for mutual confidence and security as an action guide for bilateral and subregional relations. The gradual and systematic approach of each one of the initiatives proposed in the global context of the declaration will enable the consolidation of stability never known before in the Americas.

Efforts of reflection and systematization on this subject must be encouraged. It helps establish a better understanding among the different players who seek change aimed at implementing a process of modernizing the Americas and at reaching the main objective: peace. We repeat: nothing is more modern than peace.

REVITALIZATION OF THE
INTER-AMERICAN SYSTEM
AND SECURITY IN THE
WESTERN HEMISPHERE

RICARDO MARIO RODRÍGUEZ

The inter-American system (IAS) might be described as an expanding universe. It is in the process not only of adapting to new circumstances, but also of enlarging its sphere of influence. The IAS is also being expanded, or revitalized, by the appearance of new actors. The Inter-American Development Bank, in addition to being concerned with financial programs dedicated to the economic growth and physical infrastructure of the countries, now supports social programs and the strengthening of the basic institutions of state apparatuses—for example parliaments and administrative justice systems. The Pan-American Health Organization concentrates on prevention and is entering new fields, like the war against AIDS. The Inter-American Confederation of Women seeks answers to the new emphasis on the struggle for respecting women's rights. We could add a new actor, or group of actors, to this list and to its influence on the institutions of the IAS—the nongovernmental organizations that are of increasing importance in this hemisphere. In addition, we note the major efforts of the Organization of American States in lessening its judicial emphasis to make room for hemispheric dialogue and to become a principal actor in the continental scenario.

This rapid evolution of the IAS shows a strong tendency toward a high level of economic integration and political dialogue. The North American Free Trade Agreement, the Common Market of the South, the Group of

Three (G3), the Caribbean Common Market, and the efforts to revitalize the Andean Pact all require re-outlining the system's institutional procedures.

The tendency toward integration has an impact on other fields as well. One of the consequences in security matters is the growth of mutual confidence. Trade, the transfer of capital, and the creation of binational enterprises require the development of mutual confidence. Now, exploring the possibilities for peace in the hemisphere is not only a political and diplomatic quest, as it was in the past, but an economic demand resulting from the advance toward integration. Together with economic integration, there is a parallel tendency in politics toward dialogue and high-level consultation. The summits of Central American Presidents, the presidential meetings of the Rio Group, the summits of Iberian-American Presidents, the installation of the Association of States of the Prime Ministers, and frequent regional meetings of heads of state demonstrate a solid movement in this direction. In addition, frequent meetings of the Ministers of Foreign Affairs and the increase in interparliamentary contacts also point to increased integrative trends.

The IAS is characterized today by the homogeneity of political systems in the hemisphere. For the first time in the history of the OAS, all members have democratic governments. Even though these democracies are at different levels of consolidation and maturity, the uniformity of political systems facilitates dialogue. Until only a few years ago, authoritarian governments impeded dialogue on issues like human rights, nonintervention, and the legitimacy or illegitimacy of dictators. As for the OAS itself, the appointment of César Gaviria as Secretary General is significant. The OAS now stresses topics such as defending democracy and the struggle against poverty and is seeking to insert itself in the search for concrete solutions to regional problems.

In 1992, the General Assembly of the OAS raised the level of the Working Groups on Hemispheric Security by transforming them into the Special Commission on Hemispheric Security. The effort was initiated by highlighting the legal-institutional bond between the OAS and the Inter-American Defense Board. Since 1992, the Special Commission on Hemispheric Security has been working to develop measures for military confidence, sponsoring the Reunion of Government Experts on Confidence Building Measures and Security Mechanisms in the Region (held in Buenos Aires in 1994).

The General Assemblies of 1992 and 1993 approved a resolution entitled "Cooperation for Hemispheric Security and Development: Regional Contributions to Global Security." This resolution focuses on many aspects of security, such as the illicit use of drugs, arms control, proliferation of weapons of mass destruction, and the antipoverty campaign.

The General Assembly of 1992 initiated a dialogue regarding the registration of conventional arms and defense spending, warning all countries to regularly submit information to the U.N. Conventional Arms Registry. The General Assembly of 1994 added issues concerning the use of antipersonnel mines.

In 1995, the Regional Conference for the Development of Confidence Building Measures and Security, which took place in Santiago, Chile, significantly contributed to the expansion of dialogue on mutual confidence and the adoption of confidence building measures in the rest of the hemisphere, which are being applied with success in some countries.

The succession of César Gaviria as Secretary General of the OAS also influences the treatment of the issue of security. As indicated above, Gaviria's term is not only characterized by his desire to promote dialogue concerning the treatment of hemispheric problems, but also by his commitment to contribute to their solution. In this sense, Gaviria has outlined the direct intervention of the OAS in the hemisphere using four strategic principles: trade, protecting the environment, defense of democracy, and protection and defense of human rights.

The circumstances of the hemispheric dialogue on security have changed as well. First, the dialogue is now being facilitated by the establishment of democracies; that is to say, the dialogue is now between countries that share the same conceptual framework and language. Second, the dialogue does not have a derisive tone. The goal is not to devise a strategy in the face of a common enemy, as it might have been when the Inter-American Reciprocal Assistance Treaty was in force and when communism and the Soviet Union still prevailed. It is possible now to find areas of cooperation and consensus in the field of security, which allows for dialogue on security to continue, though less charged and confrontational and more progressive than it was a few years ago.

Since the 1991 General Assembly of the OAS, resolutions have been limited to the relative problems of "pacification" in Central America and to the warning signs of clandestine arms trafficking. Yet already, in 1991, in the General Assembly at Santiago, a working group was created to study and formulate recommendations on various aspects of cooperation on hemispheric security. This is important because it creates a request for formal discussion on the topic of security. A resolution was also approved, entitled "Cooperation for Hemispheric Security: Limitation on the Proliferation of Instruments of War and Weapons of Mass Destruction."

The Inter-American Convention for facilitating cooperation in cases of disaster, adopted in 1991, formalizes practical coordination between armies, since the institution of the armed forces has the greatest capacity for lending support in matters of transportation, communications, and supplies in cases of disaster.

In April 1995, the Secretary General presented a document entitled "A New Vision of the OAS." On security matters, Gaviria proposes to restructure, at least for the moment, the definition of the juridical-institutional bond between the OAS and the Inter-American Defense Board. The extremely antagonistic positions that were directed toward the OAS concerning the definition of OAS-Board relations range from the unconfirmed (yet implicit) desire to convert the board into a major state entity to those who advocated eliminating the board. Progress seems impossible, with dismal possibilities for consensus.

The 1995 General Assembly of the OAS resolved to offer a more formal and permanent framework for discussions on hemispheric security, creating a Commission on Hemispheric Security. There is not only a Special Commission, of a transitory and less formal nature, but also a Permanent Commission. This indicates a hemispheric will to advance security dialogue and also represents a consensus on a difficult issue that could not have been reached a few years ago. Hemispheric security strategy centers on cooperation between states, with the ultimate end being the exploration of confidence and peace. Advances in this field will provide the basis for a new international regime for hemispheric security, characterized by respect for sovereignty, economic integration, and transparency and cooperation in security matters.

My country, Venezuela, actively participated in the Special Commission on Hemispheric Security and supported the creation of a Permanent Commission for Hemispheric Security. The Venezuelan government firmly endorses exploring mutual confidence measures and is also open to considering new initiatives with a regional focus on limitations to military spending and cooperation on security issues. Perhaps we are getting closer to one of the fundamental proposals of the OAS: "A limitation of conventional weapons that allows for the dedication of a great number of resources to the economic and social development of the Member States."

Editors and Contributors

Fernando Bustamante is the academic coordinator of the Latin American Faculty of Social Sciences in Quito, Ecuador.

Pablo Cabrera Gaete, a Chilean ambassador, served as the president and coordinator of the First Conference on Confidence-Building Measures and Security.

Vicente Casales is an admiral of the Brazilian navy and serves on the Executive Council of the Inter-American Defense Board in Washington, D.C.

John A. Cope is a retired colonel of the United States army and director of the Latin American Program at the National Defense University (USA) in Washington, D.C.

Marcela Donadio is the editor of the Argentine journal *SER en el 2000*, in Buenos Aires, Argentina.

Ralph H. Espach is a program associate at the Latin American Program of the Woodrow Wilson International Center for Scholars in Washington, D.C.

Ivelaw L. Griffith is a professor of Political Science at the Florida International University in Miami, Florida, and a member of the Peace and Security in the Americas research network.

Thomaz Guedes da Costa is the planning advisor to the president of Brazil at the National Council for Scientific and Technological Development. Guedes de Costa also works as a researcher at the Center for Strategic Studies in Brasília and is a member of the Peace and Security in the Americas research network.

John Holum was appointed by the president of the United States to serve as the executive director of the United States Arms Control and Disarmament Agency in Washington, D.C.

David R. Mares is a professor of political science at the University of California, San Diego.

Miguel Navarro Meza is an associate professor at the Institute of International Studies at the University of Chile, in Santiago, and a member of the Peace and Security in the Americas research network.

Ricardo Mario Rodríguez, a Venezuelan ambassador, was the president of the Commission on Hemispheric Security at the Organization of American States in Washington, D.C., at the time of the First Conference on Confidence-Building Measures and Security.

Francisco Rojas Aravena is the director of International and Military Relations at the Latin American Faculty for the Social Sciences (FLACSO) in Santiago, Chile, and one of the co-coordinators of the Peace and Security in the Americas project.

Luis Tibiletti is director of the journal *SER en el 2000*, in Buenos Aires, Argentina.

Joseph S. Tulchin is the director of the Latin American Program of the Woodrow Wilson International Center for Scholars in Washington, D.C., and one of the co-coordinators of the Peace and Security in the Americas project.

INDEX

ABC countries, strategic regional balance, 25. *see also* Southern Cone
Africa, 51
airplanes: 45n, 52, 154, 156n; aviation control, 53
Alliance for Progress, 64
Amazon Basin, 57–58
"Americanist" or continental approach, 29, 31, 62–63
Andean Pact, 186
Andean subregion, security problems, 11–14
Angola, 54
anticommunism, 63–65, 77, 100, 187; Caribbean, 77; Southern Cone, 100
Antigua-Barbuda, 80
antiterrorism, 93
appendixes, significance discussed, 6
Argentina: alignment with U.S., 101, 109–10; armed forces role, 116n; arms race, 34, 36–37, 53, 145–46; battleships, 34, 145; Brazil relations, 52, 100–01, 144–47; British presence, 28; center for strategic studies proposal, 112; concept of security, 92; confidence building initiative, 182; conflicts with Chile, 27, 31, 42, 105, 147–50; costs of war, 105; economic development, 107; globalism, 68, 71; Great Britain conflict, 52; joint military exercises, 175; military reform, 103; military supremacy, 34–35; nineteenth-century conflict with Chile, 31; nineteenth-century conflicts, 30; Pactos de Mayo (1902), 24; Peru-Ecuador conflict (at Alto Cénepa), 73; radar control, 103, 156n–157n; stature, 116n; strategic balance, 25; U.S. military training, 70; weapons treaties, 128
armed conflicts, nineteenth-century, 29
armed forces: arms agreements, 129; autonomy and civil-military relations, 126; budget restrictions, 103; civilian control, 21, 174; developing world reduction, 164, 165; end of Cold War, 102; modernization, 108; new role, 165–66; nineteenth-century view, 32; peacetime skills, 166; reciprocal calculability, 21; regime transition, 102–03
arms control: Brazil, 52–53, 58–59; deterrence role of armed forces, 18; major agreements, 183; measures that foster confidence and security (MFCS), 177–78; Pactos de Mayo (1902), 148
arms race: of 1970s and 1980s, 36–37, 41, 52–53; Argentina, 39, 53; Brazil-Argentina, 145; Chile, 39, 41;

arms race: (*continued*)
  Chile-Argentina, 110–11; farcical aspects,
    45*n*; military regimes and, 154; Pactos de
    Mayo, 32–34; Southern Cone, 33; strategic
    balance evolution, 32; types of, 33;
    Venezuela, 52; War of the Pacific, 33, 34
arms reduction: confidence building
    measures, 177–78; Conventional Arms
    Reduction Pact (Europe), 43; Pactos de
    Mayo, 33–34; relatively low levels, 21;
    strategic parity, 43; United States, 177–78
arms sales, 60–61, 64
arms trafficking, clandestine, 187
Association of Southeast Asian Nations
    (ASEAN), 78
asymmetric strategies/power, 54–55, 168–69
authoritarian rule, 14, 19, 161, 186
aviation control system (SINDACTA), 53

Bahamas, 82, 83, 84
balance, concept of, 93
balance of power: Brazil view, 52; Chile, 30,
    37–41; concept of, 99; historical context,
    44*n*; history of concept, 94–97;
    integration and security, 93; neoliberal
    institutions, 96–97; nineteenth-century,
    30, 38, 44*n*–45*n*; realist view, 94; Southern
    Cone, 41, 100; U.S. view, 72
"balances of terror," 10
Balmaceda, José, 37, 46*n*
battleships, 33, 34, 37, 45*n*–46*n*, 148
Beagle Channel conflict, 105, 147, 149, 150
Belize, 79–80, 81, 83, 84
bilateral agreements, 167
bioceanic principle, 149
biological weapons, 109
blitzkrieg strategy, 141–42, 151
Bogotá Pact for the Peaceful Solution of
    Controversies, 129
Bolivia, Acre dispute with Brazil, 24, 30,
    111, 145
border disputes: Andean region, 12;
    Argentina-Brazil, 100, 144–47; Brazil-
    Bolivia, 145; Brazil on, 58; Chile-
    Argentina, 31, 38, 39, 100, 105, 175;
    Chile-Bolivia, 38, 39; Chile-Peru, 151;
    collective agenda, 3; colonial legacy, 128;
    conflict avoidance measures, 140; greater
    relative importance, 21; growing irrele-
    vance, 11–12; as priority, 173;

undermining regional security, 2; U.S.
    arms transfers, 60; Venezuela-Guyana, 81.
    see also Peru-Ecuador conflict (at Alto
    Cénepa); territorial disputes; Venezuela-
    Colombia disputes
Brazil, 47–59; Argentina and, 35, 101,
    144–47; arms races, 36; battleships, 34;
    constitution of 1988, 48, 49, 50; drug
    trafficking, 82, 86; foreign policy, 50, 56;
    as global actor, 58; hemispheric security,
    55–57; interests linking to U.S., 56–57;
    joint military exercises, 175; nineteenth-
    century, 30; Peru-Ecuador conflict (at
    Alto Cénepa), 73; prospects for regional
    security system, 4; regional potential, 106;
    Secretary for Strategic Matters, 112;
    sensitive technology, 110; stature, 116*n*;
    strategic balance, 25; U.S. military
    training, 70; weapons treaties, 128
Bush administration, 64–65

Caldera, Rafael, 81
Camilion, Oscar, 147
Canada, 69, 79
Canadian Foundation for the Americas, 177
capital markets, 164
Cardoso, Fernando Henrique, 49–50
Caribbean, 76–89; anticommunism, 64–65;
    economic factors, 75; NAFTA impact,
    162; new strategic environment, 5;
    strategic geography, 81–82; strategic
    placement for drugs, 82–83; strategic
    significance, 78; U.S. policy/interventions,
    62, 69, 77
Caribbean Basin Initiative, 65, 79
Caribbean Common Market (CARICOM),
    186
Catholic Church, 97
caudillos, 30
Central America: Belize, 79–80; NAFTA
    impact, 162; "pacification," 187; spillover
    conflicts, 13; U.S. anticommunism,
    64–65; U.S. military training, 70–71; wars
    of 1906 and 1907, 144
Central American Treaty for Democratic
    Security (1995), 179
Chaco War (1932–35), 144
chemical weapons, 58, 109, 183
Chile: Argentine military superiority, 35;
    arms control, 183; arms from Great

Britain, 101; arms race, 34; balance of power, 30, 37–41; battleships, 34; Bolivia relations, 38; British presence, 28; cooperative security, 111; crisis of 1978 with Argentina, 42; direct opposition with Argentina, 27; early warning systems, 110; joint military exercises, 175; naval arms race, 36–37; nineteenth-century, 30, 31, 32; Pactos de Mayo (1902), 24; Peru-Ecuador conflict (at Alto Cénepa), 73; Peru relations, 38, 42, 154; pivotal role, 25; prospects for regional security system, 4; regional conference initiative, 182; regional strategic parity, 24; stature, 116*n*–117*n*; strategic balance, 24; U.S. military training, 70; weapons treaties, 128

China, People's Republic of, 153

civilian regimes, 12, 21

Civil War in Chile (1891), 39–40

Clausewitz, Carl von (1780–1831), 9, 10, 17

Clinton administration, 61, 65, 68

cocaine, 82, 83, 84, 85, 86, 87, 89

coercive diplomatic strategy, 142, 144, 151, 152, 155

coherence, 134–35

Cold War: antidemocratic nature, 159; Caribbean security emphasis, 69, 77; conventional tactics in Vietnam, 141; Cuba threat seen, 64, 77; Euro-Atlantic system, 14–16; European compared to Andean subregion, 4; hemispheric allocations, 35–36; logic of deterrence, 10; military administration, 64; Southern Cone, 25, 100; strained relations, 63–64; threat perception, 172; as transnational conflict, 13; U.S. policy to Brazil, 64

Cold War, end of: Andean subregion, 11; armed conflict in peripheral regions, 42; armed forces, 102; Brazil, 47–48, 50, 51; Caribbean, 77–78, 124; Central America, 124; collapse of hemispheric security system, 42; decline in aid, 127–28; economic power relationships, 78; embargo on Cuba, 72; European system, 182; global issues, 42, 181–82; Latin America, 124–25; megabloc phenomenon, 78–79; multipolarity, 77; new opportunities for American neighbors, 5; new proposals questioned, 54, 56; new roles for armed forces, 5–6; new trends noted, 65;

postcommunist conflicts, 159; principal hemispheric tendencies, 122–25; regional partnership, 63; rule of ideology, 159; security agenda of Americas, 172; significance, 1; South America, 125; U.N. importance, 56; U.S. security agenda, 2, 124

collective security, 51, 57. *see also* cooperative security

Colombia: drugs, 82, 86; nineteenth-century, 30; U.S. military training, 70; U.S. oil links, 69

Colombia-Venezuela disputes. *see* Venezuela-Colombia disputes

colonial inheritance, territorial issues, 128

Commission on Hemispheric Security, 6

Common Market of the South (MERCOSUR): Brazil objectives, 58; as confidence building measure, 109; economic integration, 1, 185; as economic megabloc, 160; need to expand, 167

communications: in confidence building measures, 133; decoding signals and motives, 10; in global era, 125; immediacy of, 165

competence, 135

competition model, 24, 28–29

complex interdependence, 96

confidence, concept of, 9

confidence building measures (CBMs), 130–37; as basis of enhanced relations, 6; blanket approach questioned, 5; Brazil view, 47; characteristics of, 133–35; concept and basic assumptions, 10; context for cooperation, 139; conventional military, 21; current initiatives, 43; defined, 130–31; early European, 14–15; efficiency in resource use, 103; existing linkages and institutional bonds, 175; flexibility, 132; hard measures, 108, 109, 113; logic of cooperation, 108–13; MERCOSUR as, 109–10; military-civilian antagonisms, 174; nonproliferation, 109; objectives, 131; operational level, 176; Peace and Security in the Americas (PS&A) program, 3; political forces, 112; soft measures, 109; strategic balance, 43, 140; ten areas to develop, 135–36; transparency, 122; validity in Europe, 16; varied initiatives, 175–76